Daphne Fulton

Sam Houston State University

Introduction to
Health Promotions &
Health Professions

Kendall Hunt
ublishing company

Table of Contents

Preface v

Introduction vii

Prologue ix

Section I 1

  1. Health Defined, Health Dimensions, and
Health Determinants 3

  2. Health Behavior and Health Promotion 21

  3. A Historical Context for Health Promotion 35

  4. Settings for Health Education and
Health Promotion Practice 53

  5. An Overview of Changing Health Behaviors 65

Section II **101**

  6. Health Professions 103

  7. Health Professions with Patient Contact 109

  8. Allied Health Professions 159

  9. Health Professions without Patient Contact 209

  10. Trends in Health Professions 223

Preface

This book was written to condense all the class, Introduction to Health Promotion and Health Professions, into one book so students would not have to purchase many books instead of just one. I want to thank the faculty of Sam Houston State University for helping me get this together and for their encouragement. I also want to thank my family who had to give up some of my time to get all of this completed. I especially want to thank my mother for her encouragement even after health challenges and a terrible car accident.

Introduction

Welcome to Health Promotion and Health Professions. This book was written with the student in mind to help you learn and understand what health promotion is, how it can help you as a health professional, and explores some of the different types of healthcare professions. The first part of the book talks all about health and the different dimensions of health and how they influence your health and perception of it. It also discusses why people do the things they do, health-wise. We call that health behaviors. Over the years, scholars have sought to understand why people choose certain lifestyle behaviors and why they do not live healthy lifestyles. I hope that after reading these chapters, you will have a better understanding of why some people choose certain actions over others. We will also discuss the history of health and how that influences much of our outlooks and cultural practices today.

The second half of the book talks about health professions and includes professionalism and different vocations a person interested in health may choose. You will learn how many jobs are available in the USA, how many jobs are projected to be available, how to become that profession, and what their duties and responsibilities are. All of the information for this book is taken directly from the U.S. Bureau of Labor Statistics, The Texas Department of State Health Services, The Texas Medical Bureau, The Texas Board of Nursing, The Texas Department of Licensing and Regulation, the U.S. Centers for Disease Control and Prevention, and professional organizations. Because of time constraints, there are many more healthcare occupations that were not included in this book but will be included in the future editions as will interviews and personal stories from people who work in those fields.

I hope this book helps you in preparing for your career in the healthcare field.

Prologue

As students of public health or community health, you are most likely planning for a career in the health care field. Many of you may hope to make major contributions to making populations at home or abroad healthier with improved opportunities to live healthier and happier lives. Have you considered how you will accomplish this goal?

There is much discussion currently about health. Many people are searching for the answers to their personal health challenges and problems. Many who are healthy are seeking ways to prolong their present health or to enhance it. Researchers are dedicated to discovering the answers to the many health problems that nations and the world face daily through medicine, lifestyle changes, social changes, and environmental changes. Governmental agencies produce guidelines on what the experts consider optimum healthy lifestyle behaviors and environmental concerns. With all of this activity to make individuals and populations healthier, do health care providers really know what health is and how to help individuals, communities and nations become healthier? Do we know health and healthy behaviors or unhealthy behaviors when we see them? Let us visit with the Helpum family and observe them and their health.

The Helpum Family: A Picture of Health?

Grandma Helpum is so excited today, because her son and his family have travelled a long way and are visiting her today. Every two years, all of the Helpum family members try to come together at her home to reminisce and enjoy each other's' company. She misses her family. Everyone has moved so far away. She feels lonely a lot of the time. But not today!

This year she notices some real changes in her family members. Her daughter-in-law, Cheryl, is always beautifully dressed, but today she does not look very healthy and rested. She has not been sleeping well. She has been working overtime so that she and Carl Helpum, Grandma Helpum's son, can pay for the youngest child's college education and avoid adding to their growing debt. Carl and Cheryl thought that they planned well in advance to meet their children's educational needs, but college education is becoming extremely expensive. Their youngest daughter, Trish, seems to be troubled. She is 18 years old and just completing her first semester in college. She is concerned that she may be pregnant, but cannot possibly figure out who the father might be. She feels badly about this, because she knew better than to have sex without some sort of contraception after stopping the pill. She was gaining too much weight taking those pills. Trish thinks, "maybe I am not pregnant, maybe I am just getting fat." She wonders what this will do to her parents if she is pregnant; they work so hard to give her a great education and everything that she wants. Well, at least she is not having problems like her brother, Michael, who is supposed to be building his career in the banking industry. However, he seems to be spending a lot of money on his fancy car and seems high all of the time. He always has an entourage of young women following him, most of whom he does not know. Carl Helpum is suspicious about what his son might be doing. He intends to have a long talk with him, but Carl cannot seem to find the time to talk to Michael, because Carl is always busy; always working to stay ahead of the younger men and women in his organization who are frequently trying to take his position. He finds himself smoking more and drinking alcohol more than ever before.

Here comes Grandma Helpum with her camera. "Let's take pictures! I want all of my friends to see my beautiful and healthy family!"

Application Challenge

Activity A

You, the reader, are invited to look more closely at Grandma Helpum's photograph of her family. What do you see? The Helpums are a fictional family, but do they provide a snapshot of the typical American way of living—and dying? Please answer the following questions.

1. What would you say about the health status of each family member?
   - Grandma Helpum

   - Carl Helpum

   - Cheryl Helpum

   - Trish Helpum

   - Michael Helpum

2. Do each of the Helpums appear to be seeking a healthier lifestyle? What would you recommend as you attempt to assist each of them in planning and achieving healthier lifestyles?

Activity B

As you observed the Helpums, perhaps you used your own definitions and standards for health, illness and disease in assessing this family.

Define health, illness, and disease from your own perspective.

1. As you proceed through this course, return to your definition and compare it to the definitions that you will encounter in this textbook.

2. How close are your definitions to the definitions of a) those who you serve, b) those with whom you work, and c) those who administer programs and policies in your public health agency, in your community, and in your state?

Section I

Chapter 1

Health Defined, Health Dimensions, and Health Determinants

© Aleksandr Bryliaev, 2013. Used under license from Shutterstock, Inc.

Health Defined

Health professionals and those preparing to be health professionals in health education and health promotion seek to understand health and to improve it for the populations and individuals that they serve. There can be no successful efforts to improve health without a clear understanding of what health is. In their efforts, health professionals will realize that people may ascribe definitions for health, illness, and disease that are not the same across populations and cultures.

For many generations, health was defined as the absence of illness and disease. Unlike the definition for health, the definitions for illness and disease may seem fairly straightforward. Illness is defined as the visible presentation of symptoms which make one feel distressed. Illness can be observed objectively by the health professional. However, for the lay person illness may mean being sick and in need of help from someone who can provide relief. The person providing relief may be a physician, folk healer, or other practitioner identified formally or informally, depending on the cultural and social orientation of the sick person.

Disease is defined as the underlying defect or malfunction within the organism. Disease may occur without illness. For an example, diabetes mellitus when it is controlled may not result in illness from diabetes. However, the individual still has diabetes. The causes of diseases and illnesses are often explored and determined as host, agent, and environmental factors. There may be differences between the practitioner and the population in determining what these factors really are. The sociocultural aspects of illness and disease present other explanations, besides carcinogens, bacteria, viruses, etc., for determining the causes or agents for illness and disease, such as "soul loss," "evil eye," demonic or spirit possession, spells, even another person for the populations that are served by health professionals.

Health is even more difficult to define than illness and disease. Examine the following definitions for health.

- Health is a state of complete physical, mental, and social well-being and not merely the absence of disease or infirmity *(World Health Organization, 1947)*.

- Health is the condition of the organism, which measures the degree to which its aggregate powers are able to function *(Oberteuffer, 1965)*.

- Health is the quality of life involving dynamic interaction and interdependence among the individual's physical well-being, his mental and emotional reactions, and the social complex in which he exists *(School Health Education Study, 1967)*.

- An integrated method of functioning which is oriented toward maximizing the potential of which the individual is capable. It requires that the individual maintain a continuum of balance and purposeful direction with the environment where he is functioning *(Dunn, 1967)*.

- Health is a state of being—a quality of life. It is something that defies definition in any precise, measurable sense. It is affected by a host of physical, mental, social, and spiritual factors which no single profession or academic discipline can effectively monitor and study *(Greene and Simons-Morton, 1990)*.

Examining these definitions, illustrates that health can be so many things, because it truly does affect so many aspects of life and is in turn affected by a great many factors. These are not likely to be the ways that the lay constituency would define health. One important factor that is observed by many health practitioners and lay persons is that health is not static, it is dynamic. The individual is always required to adapt to various factors that can impact his or her health positively or negatively. One moment an individual may be healthy, but in another instance may become ill. Health and illness cannot coexist. However, those who suffer from a disease, but who are effectively managing the disease may actually experience a high level of health.

Perhaps the following definition can best serve as a general definition that works for the professional and the populations that are served by the professionals.

> *Health is the combination of the physical, psychological, social, and spiritual dimensions of life that can be balanced in a way that produces satisfaction and joy in life.*

The definition implies that humans are not one dimensional, but multidimensional. They are not static, but dynamic, constantly impacting or being impacted by their environments. The concept of balance in these dimensions of health implies that one can compensate for the lower level of health in one dimension by improving the levels of other dimensions of health. The definition implies that the balance of these dimensions will result in satisfaction that brings a sense of fulfillment and joy that is evoked by well-being and success as the individual lives a full and healthy life. The joy that is produced is more than momentary happiness; joy is both the result of and the perpetuation of hope, faith, and love (Nobles, 2010). Healthy people are joyful people who can weather the storms and the sunshine of life's circumstances and conditions. Health, then, if viewed holistically, will impact every aspect of one's life and also be impacted by many factors in life, within the physical, social, cultural, and political environments that surround every individual. Health is not an end in itself, but the means to an end or the life goals of the individual or population.

So what exactly are these dimensions of health and what do they involve?

Dimensions of Health

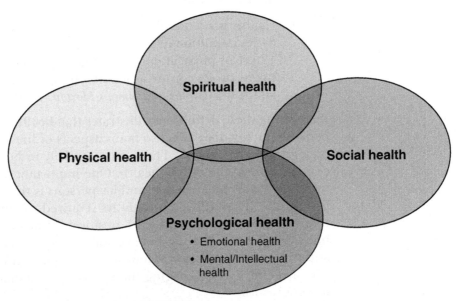

Figure 1.1 Dimensions of Health

© Kendall Hunt Publishing Company

The origin of the word "health" is derived from the Old English word "*hale*," meaning wholeness, being whole, sound or well, strong, uninjured, of good omen—cognate with holy and implies involvement of the entire individual. Clearly this means more than the physical dimension. The nature and number of dimensions which comprise health have been debated, but health researchers and professionals are in agreement that there are varying dimensions of health and that these dimensions function in an integrated, coordinated way, never in isolation, to produce health in the individual (Dolfman, 1973). For the purposes of this text, the author presents four primary dimensions of health that can be balanced to produce joy and satisfaction:

- Physical Health
- Psychological Health (Emotional Health, Mental/Intellectual Health)
- Social Health
- Spiritual Health

Physical Health

Physical health is defined as the absence of disease and disability. It implies that the individual is functioning adequately from the perspective of physical and physiological abilities. Physical health relates to the biological integrity of the individual, incorporating the following:

- body size and shape
- sensory acuity
- susceptibility to disease
- body functioning and recuperative ability

Psychological Health

Psychological health is the appropriate intellectual, mental, and emotional practices and dimensions of the individual. Generally, psychological health reflects the following:

- values and belief systems as well as the level of self-esteem, and self-confidence
- coping skills and mechanisms
- hardiness

Within psychological health, the emotional health aspect is generally defined as the ability to feel and express the full range of human emotions, giving and receiving love, achieving a sense of fulfillment and purpose in life, and developing psychological hardiness. Mental or intellectual health encompasses the intellectual processes of reasoning, analysis, evaluation, curiosity, humor, alertness, logic, learning, and memory.

Social Health

Social health refers to the ability to perform and fulfill the expectations of our roles in society, "effectively, comfortably, with pleasure, without harming other people" (Butler, 2001). An individual's social health includes, but is not limited to the following:

- interactions and connections with others
- the ability to adapt to various social situations
- the daily behaviors and actions
- the ability to communicate effectively
- the ability to show respect
- a sense of belonging within a larger social context
- having responsibilities that often affect others and involve meeting their needs
- needs for love, intimacy, companionship, safety, and cooperation

Spiritual Health

Spiritual health has been defined by Hawks (1994) as "a high level of faith, hope, and commitment in relation to a well-defined worldview or belief system that provides a sense of meaning and purpose to existence, and that offers an ethical path to personal fulfillment which includes connectedness with self, others, and a higher power or larger reality." Banks (1980) and Butler (2001) find that the spiritual dimension of health has a unifying force within the individual that integrates all of the other dimensions of health, affecting the total health and well-being. Spiritual health may or may not be reflected in religious practices. Spiritual health is the core that makes the following possible:

- the ability to discover, articulate, and act on one's basic purpose in life,

- learning how to give and receive love, joy, and peace,

- contributing to the improvement of the spiritual health of others,

- pursuing a fulfilling and meaningful life,

- transcending the self with a sense of selflessness, or empathy, for others and establishing a commitment to a power beyond the natural and rational,

- having the power to pursue successes in life through a defined set of moral principles and ethics.

Some research indicates that the spiritual component may actually provide the unifying context for all other components of health.

Other Health-Related Definitions

Wellness

While the terms "health" and "wellness" are often used interchangeably, they are not synonyms (Penhollow, 2012). Wellness is a concept that describes the process of adopting behaviors that determine one's quality of life. Anspaugh et. al., (1997) pronounced that wellness means engaging in attitudes and behaviors that enhance the quality of life and maximize personal potential. The dimensions of wellness are very similar to those in the description of health, but may also include the dimensions of environmental, and occupational wellness. Often health professionals refer to the wellness scale that indicates the quality of life as a range from optimal wellness to premature death. The individual can choose to exercise control over a variety of life factors that will influence the level or ranking of wellness. The more positive life factors present in a person's life at any given time, the greater is the likelihood of optimal health and wellness. If one approaches wellness as a continuum with the midpoint as no signs or symptoms of disease, as in Figure 1.2, one's choices in behaviors can move the individual toward illness or premature death or the individual may choose behaviors that move him/her toward wellness and optimal health.

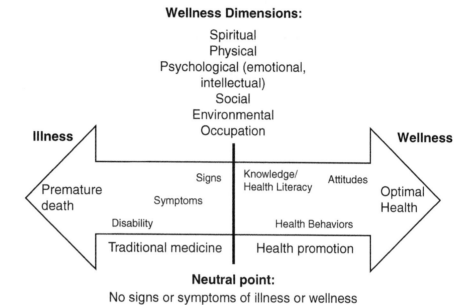

Figure 1.2 A Continuum for Wellness

© Kendall Hunt Publishing Company

Personal Health

Personal health is the actions and decisions made by the individual that affect his or her own health. It is important to note that some of the decisions and actions may be impacted by factors outside of the person's control.

Community Health and Population Health

People interact with each other in many ways for many reasons. These interactions with common bonds are generally referred to as community. Community is defined as a unified body of people with common interests living in a particular area; an interacting population of various kinds of individuals in a common location; or, a "body of persons with a common history, ethnic heritage, political interests, or social and economic characteristics (Merriam-Webster Dictionary, 2013). Community health refers to the health status, issues, activities, and events of a community. This includes the organized responsibilities of public health, school health, transportation safety, other tax-supported functions, with voluntary and private actions, to promote and protect the health of local populations identified as communities. Sometimes the term population health is used. Population health refers to the health status and the conditions influencing the health of a category of people (for example, women, adolescents, prisoners) whether or not the people included in the category define themselves as a community.

Determinants of Health

An examination of the health of individuals and communities will lead to determining how certain health, illness, and disease conditions come into existence. Throughout history, societies have sought answers to the questions about how to achieve greater health and avoid injury, disease, illness, and premature death. There are various models and theories on disease and disease interventions to reduce the transmission of diseases and to promote health. The following have helped health professionals to arrive at the most current understandings about what factors determine health and enable health care providers to help individuals and communities reach greater health and quality of their lives.

Communicable disease is a disease that requires a pathogen to spread the disease. The communicable disease model describes the spread of disease requiring the elements of an agent, host, and environment. Figure 1.3 illustrates the traditional epidemiologic triad model for the transmission of infectious disease resulting from the interaction among the host, the agent, and the environment. Figure 1.4 shows the transmission occurring as the agent moves from the host or reservoir through a portal of exit by a mode of transmission and then enters through a portal of entry to infect a new host. This disease process is referred to as the chain of infection and will continue until the chain is broken.

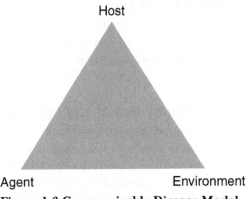

Figure 1.3 Communicable Disease Model

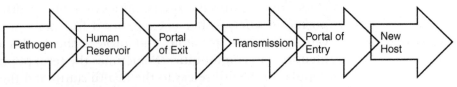

Figure 1.4 Chain of Infection Model

© Kendall Hunt Publishing Company

These models do help the health professionals working in health education and health promotion explain and intervene in reducing the spread of communicable or infectious disease. In more recent years, there is greater knowledge and experience related to diseases that are communicable and those that are the result of lifestyle choices. Canada in the 1970's implemented a national plan to insure health care for all Canadians. Canadian health professionals began to examine the health field rather than the health care system to broaden their assessment of the many matters that impact and affect the health of their people. The Lalonde Report, *A New Perspective on the Health of Canadians* (1974), introduced the concept of the "health field" which at that time consisted of four categories of elements that could influence death and disease for humans: human biology or heredity, environment, lifestyle or behavior, and inadequacies of the health care services. Shortly after the Lalonde Report the United States government officially entered health promotion with the publication of *Healthy People: The Surgeon General's Report on Health Promotion and Disease Prevention* (1979). No longer was the focus totally on the treatment of disease, but the emphasis moved to the prevention of illness and health promotion.

For many years, the Health Field Concept provided a framework that is used by many health professionals to identify causes of morbidity and mortality, by examining the contributions of heredity, environment, health care services, and behavior to a variety of health conditions and problems. In the most recent years, the Health Field Concept has yielded to the use of the term "determinants of health," as a way to assess and explain the many factors that determine the health of populations. According to McGinnis, et. al., (2001), the impacts of these determinants on premature mortality are distributed as ". . . genetic predispositions, about 30%, social circumstances, 15%, environmental exposures, 5%, behavioral patterns, 40%; and shortfalls in medical care about 10%." It is important to note that while these determinants are listed individually, they do interact and interconnect having impacts on each other and reflecting the total health of the individual, the family, and the community.

According to the 2011 Joint Committee on Health Education and Health Promotion Terminology (2012), determinants of health are "the range of personal, social, economic, and environmental factors that influence health status." The categories of determinants affecting individual and community levels of health are:

- Genetic Factors/ Heredity (Micro/Internal Environment)
- Physical Environment
- Social Environment
- Health Care
- Personal Health Behavior And Lifestyle Choices

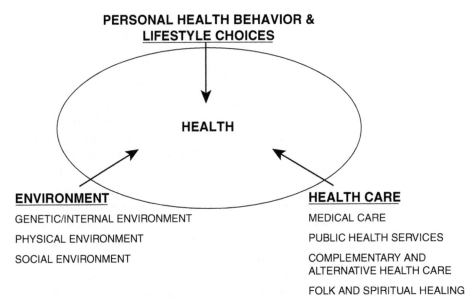

Figure 1.5 Categories of the Determinants of Health

© Kendall Hunt Publishing Company

Genetic Factors/Heredity

Generally, it is believed that there are a number of factors affecting our health over which we have little control. However, it may be difficult to separate the influences of heredity from those of culture and social circumstances for individuals and groups of people. The genetic factors determining the health of individuals and populations include the following:

- Genetic traits affecting optimal functioning

- Sex

- Body size and composition

The Physical Environment

The physical environment has great importance and influence on the health of individuals and communities. Increasingly, individuals, communities, and health professionals understand how pollution and contamination of the water, air, and food supply are linked to greater incidence and prevalence of a variety of diseases and allergic reactions. Some of the determinants of health in the physical environment are:

- Air

- Water

- Soil

- Animal life
- Plant life
- Natural disasters

The Social Environment

Social scientists and social epidemiologists examine the relationships of health problems and social factors. They try to determine the influence on health and their associations with health. Research has documented the importance of social variables in predicting and describing health and health problems. John Ratcliffe (1980) believed that society's social structure greatly affects the lives and the health of all people.

In many communities, socially designed systems have become more important than the physical environment to individual survival, because they control the distribution of and access to those very factors that determine mortality and morbidity levels. To be sure, the physical environment still exacts a great toll through incidents such as hurricanes, tornadoes, earthquakes, tidal waves, floods, etc. Nevertheless, the socioeconomic systems created by and for people constitute, to all intents and purposes, the human individual's "natural" environment (Ratcliffe, 1980). Some of the following factors can determine the health and quality of life for individuals and populations.

- Culture
- Socioeconomic factors
  - Social class
  - Personal income
  - Economy
  - Residence
- Politics
- Race and ethnicity
- Education
- Gender
- Religion
- Resources
- Community & societal organization
- Population density
- Crowding
- The pace of modern civilization

- Stressful life events
- War
- The health care environment

Health Care

Access to quality medical care and public health services can help individuals and populations experience better health. However, health care professionals must always be conscious that diverse populations may also participate in complementary and alternative health care, as well as folk healing and spiritual healing experiences. The determinants of health care will include the following:

- Medical care
- Public health services
- Complementary and alternative health care
- Folk and spiritual healing

Personal Health Behaviors and Lifestyle Choices

Most advances in optimal health and wellness in the United States have not resulted from advances in medical care, but from many of the environmental improvements and public health advances. Evidence demonstrates that the most important factors in improving health in modern societies have been improved nutrition, well-nourished babies, children, and adolescents, and relative affluence. The individual can make lifestyle changes that affect health positively or negatively, in spite of the social environment. It is in this category of determinants that health educators focus great effort. Behavior changes have great impact on health and the quality of one's life. The leading causes of death in the United States are cancers and cardiovascular diseases, which are strongly linked to lifestyle and behaviors. The following factors are supported by much research and have greatly impacted on improved health.

- Nutritional and dietary behaviors and status
- Physical activity and exercise patterns
- Adequate sleep
- Maintaining appropriate weight
- Avoidance of inappropriate use of alcohol and illegal drugs
- No tobacco use

- Prevention of unintentional injuries
- Appropriate management of stress
- Use of preventive health services

Just as there are behaviors that support optimal health there are also behaviors that cause health problems (Kolbe, 1993).

- Drug and alcohol abuse
- Risky behaviors that result in unintentional and intentional injuries
- Sexual behaviors that result in unwanted pregnancy and sexually transmitted diseases, including HIV infection
- Tobacco use
- Excessive consumption of fat and calories
- Insufficient physical activity

Risk Factors

The Health Field Concept and the Determinants of Health provide those who research and practice health education and health promotion with a framework to study and intervene with health. Such a framework helps health professionals to target factors that generate or influence the health and quality of life for the individuals, groups, and communities served. The study of determinants of health assists health professionals to target risks that are associated with disease or poor health outcomes. Risk factors are defined by the World Health the Organization as ". . . any attribute, characteristic or exposure of an individual that increases the likelihood of developing a disease or injury. Some examples of the more important risk factors are underweight, morbid obesity, unsafe sex, high blood pressure, tobacco and alcohol consumption, and unsafe water, sanitation and hygiene (2013)." A risk factor increases the probability of developing disease, disability, injury, or premature death, but does not guarantee that those with the risk factor will suffer poor health outcomes. Risk factors may be categorized as modifiable risk factors (changeable or controllable) or nonmodifiable risk factors (nonchangeable or noncontrollable). Modifiable risk factors may include smoking behaviors, sedentary lifestyle, poor nutritional habits, and poor dental care. Nonmodifiable risk factors are inherited genetic factors, race, age, sex: things that cannot be changed by the individual. Professionals involved in health education and health promotion have major responsibility for helping clients identify and control risk factors that are modifiable (Cottrell et. al., 2012).

Application Opportunity

Now that you have studied the definitions for health, its dimensions, and its determinants, return to your definition for health that you wrote in the prologue.

    1. Is your definition, written in the prologue, the same as the definition(s) you studied in chapter 1?

    2. What are the similarities?

    3. What are the differences?

    4. Which definition would serve you best as a health professional? Why?

References

Anspaugh, D. J., and G. Ezell. 1995. *Teaching Today's Health,* 4th ed. Boston: Allyn & Bacon.

Butler, J. Thomas. 2001. *Principles of Health Education & Health Promotion,* 3rd ed. Belmont, CA: Wadsworth/Thomason Learning.

Cottrell, R. R., J. T. Girvan, and J. F. McKenzie. 2012. *Principles and Foundations of Health Promotion and Education.* Boston: Benjamin Cummings.

Dolfman, M. L. 1973. "The Concept of Health: An Historic and Analytic Examination." *Journal of School Health* 43 (8): 491–7.

Dunn, H. 1967. *High Level Wellness.* Arlington, VA: R. W. Beatty.

Hawks, S. 1994. "Spiritual Health: Definition and Theory." *Wellness Perspectives: Research, Theory and Practice* 10 (4): 3–13.

Joint Committee on Health Education and Promotion Terminology. 2012. "Report of the 2011 Joint Committee on Health Education and Promotion Terminology." *American Journal of Health Education* 43 (2).

Kolbe, L. J. 1993. "Developing a Plan of Action to Institutionalize Comprehensive School Health Education Programs in the United States." *Journal of School Health* 63 (1): 12–13.

Laframboise, H. L. 1973. "Health Policy: Breaking It Down into Manageable Segments." *Journal of the Canadian Medical Association, 108* (February 3). 388–393.

Lalonde, M. 1974. *A New Perspective on the Health of Canadians: A Working Document.* Ottawa, Canada: Ministry of National Health and Welfare.

McGinnis, J. M., and W. H. Foege. 1993. "Actual Causes of Death in the United States." *Journal of the American Medical Association* 2 (18): 2207–12.

McGinnis, J. M., W. H. Williams-Russo, and J. R. Knickman. 2002. "The Case for More Active Policy Attention to Health Promotion." *Health Affairs* 21 (2): 78–93.

Nobles, Sherman. 2010. "Joy is Not Happiness?" *Theologia.* Retrieved May 18, 2013, from http://theologica.ning.com/profiles/blogs/joy-is-not-happiness.

Oberteuffer, D. 1960. *School Health Education: A Textbook for Teachers, Nurses, and Other Professional Personnel.* New York: Harper and Brothers.

Penhollow, T. M. 2012. *Points to Health: Theory and Practice of Health Education and Health Behavior.* Dubuque, IA: Kendall Hunt Publishing Company.

Simons-Morton, B. G., W. H. Greene, and N. Gottlieb. 1995. *Introduction to Health Education and Health Promotion.* Long Grove, IL: Waveland Press, Inc.

Sliepcevich, E. M. 1967. "Health Education: A Conceptual Approach to Curriculum Design." In E. M. Sliepcevich. *School Health Education Study.* St Paul: 3M Education Press.

World Health Organization. 1947. Preamble to the Constitution of the World Health Organization as adopted by the International Health Conference, New York, 19–22 June 1946; signed on 22 July 1946 by the representatives of 61 States (Official Records of the World Health Organization, no. 2, p. 100) and entered into force on 7 April 1948.

World Health Organization. 2013. http://www.who.int/topics/risk _factors/en/. Retrieved May 25, 2013.

Chapter 2

Health Behavior and Health Promotion

Health Behavior

While heredity, environment, and medical care have profound influences on the health and quality of life that every individual experiences, health behavior, or lifestyle is the greatest determinant that impacts morbidity and premature death. Poor health behaviors account for as much as 40% of the morbidity and premature death in the United States' population (McGinnis et. al., 2002). Lifestyle reflects practices and behavioral patterns in the individual and population that are influenced by one's cultural heritage, social relationships, social and economic circumstances, geography, and personality. While all of these factors do influence behaviors, the individual makes many decisions on his or her own, which, in turn, impact the person's health and the quality of life. Individuals can make the decision to adopt behaviors that are health enhancing or disease producing. The individual can choose to improve the level of physical activity, avoid the use of tobacco, improve the intakes of fruits and vegetables, or avoid risky sexual behavior. The foundational basis for health education and health promotion is that individuals can voluntarily make personal choices to experience the best health outcomes. It is incumbent on the health education specialists to know the factors that influence the behaviors and lifestyle choices of the individuals and target populations that they serve. Such knowledge and experience will assist the health education specialist in facilitating changed health behaviors in the target population and in individuals.

David Gochman (1982, 1997) defines health behavior as "those personal attributes such as beliefs, expectations, motive, values, perceptions and other cognitive elements; personality characteristics, including affective and emotional states and traits; and behavioral patterns, actions and habits that relate to health maintenance, health restoration, and health improvement." This definition underscores three foci for health education specialists in helping to enhance health behaviors in individuals, groups and communities: health maintenance, health restoration, and the improvement of health.

The greatest challenge to specialists in health education and health promotion is to help individuals make the best choices for health. People will make poor choices if they do not relate health to their personal life goals, if they do not value health, if they like risk-taking, and if they are unaware of the risks for sickness or death connected to their behaviors. People will make poor choices if they lack the knowledge and the skills necessary to change their behaviors to support optimal health.

There are three categories of factors that influence all of the health choices that people make. They are predisposing factors, enabling factors, and reinforcing factors.

Predisposing factors are the antecedents of a behavior; they are the things that the individual brings to the point of making a decision or choice. These factors include demographic variables such as age, sex, gender, education, race, ethnicity, and socioeconomic conditions.

Predisposing factors also consist of life experiences, values, beliefs, cultural perspectives, attitudes, and knowledge. The knowledge and attitudes may be accurate or erroneous. The health education specialists must determine what the person brings to the decision making process. This is an important key to the health education and health promotion process.

The second category of factors that influence all behaviors is enabling factors. Enabling factors are also present before the behavior occurs. Enabling factors are the person's arsenal of skills and abilities that they bring to their decisions related to behavior. Enabling factors will include the availability of health resources, affordable health care and services, or the easy availability of those things that may negatively affect health choices as well.

Reinforcing factors are the third category of factors which occur after the behavior. These are the things that can encourage the repetition of a new behavior or the extinguishing of the behavior. Reinforcing factors may include support of family and friends, feedback, and reward from instructors or employers. Often the good feelings that one experiences from improving health by a positive behavior change may help the individual to repeat the behavior, allowing the behavior to become a positive health habit.

Health Education

According to the Joint Committee on Health Education and Health Promotion Terminology (2012), health education is "Any combination of planned learning experiences using evidence based practices and/or sound theories that provide the opportunity to acquire knowledge, attitudes, and skills needed to adopt and maintain healthy behaviors." Health education is also described as a planned process that combines various educational experiences to facilitate voluntary adaptations or establishment of behaviors that are conducive to health (Green and Kreuter, 1999). The practice of health education focuses on a goal of helping people (individuals, families, groups, and communities) choose a pattern of behaviors which moves them toward optimal health rather than the reverse and to give them the ability to avoid many of the imbalances, diseases, and accidents of life (Oberteuffer et. al., 1972). Even though the field of health education has many practitioners, this goal generally describes the mission of the field and its professionals.

The fundamental principle of health education is that individuals, families, and communities can be taught to assume responsibility for their own health and, to some extent, for the health of others. The facilitation of voluntary individual and community behavior change without violating individual freedoms guaranteed by the United States Constitution is the challenge for health education professionals.

In order to bring about the voluntary changes in these persons for behaviors that support health, there is the process of health education.

Butler (2001) describes the process of health education as going beyond the memorization of information, but must also include the following:

1. The process begins with a planned intervention based on a health issue, with stated goals, objectives, activities, and evaluation criteria.

2. The intervention occurs in a specified setting and at a specified time.

3. The components of a health education intervention or program are the sequential introduction of health concepts at appropriate learning levels at each stage of the learning process and resulting in changed behaviors to support optimal health.

4. The planned intervention comprehensively helps the learner to realize how various aspects of health are interrelated and how all health behavior affects the quality of life.

5. The learner interacts with a qualified and competent educator.

In most cases the health education process improves the health knowledge base, but more importantly, there will be enriched attitudes to support behavior change, enhanced skill development, values awareness that can advance decision-making in the individual, family, and community, leading to improved health and quality of life. Positive outcomes will depend on how effectively the health education specialist plans the process.

Common misconceptions about health education are that anyone can teach health, that anyone can write an effective health education curriculum, and that health education is hygiene class. It is important to note that improving the quality of life and health status of individuals, groups, and communities are very complex and not changed in short periods of time. In examining the process for health education, the health educators must be competent in program planning, implementation, program evaluation, and in quality service delivery. Health education interventions require the health education specialist to be professionally prepared to perform various roles depending on the nature and needs of the learners. Most health education interventions will center on teaching, training counseling and consulting (Simons-Morton et. al., 1995).

Teaching

The health education specialist employs a variety of strategies, methods, and activities to help individuals, groups, and communities establish and change patterns of behavior to improve health. The health education specialist's success is dependent on what to teach and how to teach it. Conveying information alone is not sufficient to effect behavior change, because knowledge does not necessarily change attitudes or behavior.

Training

The health education specialist teaches other health professionals and volunteers how to accomplish health education goals and objectives and how to employ health education methods.

Counseling

In counseling, the health education specialist is involved in an interpersonal process of guidance that helps people learn how to achieve personal growth, improve interpersonal growth and relationships, resolve problems, make decisions, and change behavior for optimal health.

Consulting

The health education specialist employs the process by which his/her knowledge and experience are used to help another professional or organization make better decisions or cope with problems more effectively to address a group or population's health status.

The discipline and practice of health education are supported by contributions from a vast body of research in the health sciences and the social sciences that can help to reduce the risks for poor health through behavior change. The primary contributors are public health, behavioral sciences, and education. Public health contributes health statistics for epidemiologic data as the health education specialist assesses the health status of target populations. Public health also contributes to the understanding of health issues in the environment, personal lifestyles, medical care, population dynamics, biomedical science, and epidemiology. Behavioral sciences are the integration of knowledge from psychology, sociology, and cultural anthropology, providing a foundation for understanding human health behaviors. The behavioral sciences contribute greatly to defining the determinants of behavior that are key to healthful behavior change, which is the desired outcome for health education practice. Education is the study of teaching and learning which is central to health education. Education provides the health education specialist with learning theory, educational psychology, human development, curriculum development, and pedagogy. Measurement and testing are also contributions from education (Butler, 2001).

Health education has transitioned from its earliest appearance as a profession. Health education specialists are now central to the health promotion efforts that many local, state and national organizations are engaged in as these agencies seek to address the many health challenges facing the nation and the world. Sometimes the terms of health education and health promotion are used interchangeably; however, health education has the longest history regarding its extensive mission within society and health care (Penhollow, 2012).

Health Promotion

The Joint Committee on Health Education and Promotion Terminology (2012) defines health promotion as "any planned combination of educational, political, environmental, regulatory, or organizational mechanisms that support actions and conditions of living conducive to the health of individuals, groups and communities." O'Donnell (2009) defines health promotion as both art and science combined to help people ". . . discover the synergies between their core passions and optimal health, enhancing their motivation to strive for optimal health, and supporting them in changing their lifestyle to move toward a state of optimal health." He additionally emphasized the important and dynamic balance among physical, emotional, social, spiritual, and intellectual health. The role of health education in health promotion can be observed in lifestyle changes that are facilitated through selected combinations of learning experiences and strategies. Health promotion efforts also seek to enhance awareness, encourage commitment to action, and build needed skills. According to O'Donnell (2009), health promotion's most important contribution is "through the creation of opportunities that open access to environments that make positive health practices the easiest choice."

Health promotion is a broad field encompassing educational, social, economic, and political efforts to improve the health of a population, emerging as an unifying concept bringing a number of separate fields under one umbrella. Health promotion enables people to take control and responsibility for their health, requires close cooperation of heterogeneous sectors, and combines diverse methods or approaches, while encouraging effective and concrete public participation. Many of the strategies in health promotion come from an ecological perspective that seeks to empower individuals, groups, communities in developing behaviors and lifestyles that enhance health.

Health promotion is made up of three important areas of practice, each of which has a vital role in achieving health for the individual and the community: health education, health protection, and disease prevention. These are commonly referred to as the triad of health promotion. The professionals in these areas of practice work together providing the best opportunities for individuals, groups, and communities to make choices for optimal health.

Health Education

Health education is at the core of total health promotion programming. Health education professionals provide knowledge, skill development, and support that help clients understand their options and voluntarily choose health behaviors for optimal health and high quality of life. While other professions are involved in the work of health promotion, health education is the primary profession devoted to health promotion and whose practitioners are trained in a range of health promotion processes (Simons-Morton, Greens, & Gottlieb, 1995). Health education is a planned process which usually combines educational experiences to facilitate voluntary adaptations or establishment of behavior conducive to health. Health education specialists educate individuals about their own health as well as educate the media, elected officials, and community leaders.

Disease Prevention

Disease prevention is a major emphasis for health promotion. Disease prevention, according to the Joint Committee (2012), "is the process of reducing risks and alleviating disease to promote, preserve, and restore health and minimize suffering and distress." Prevention consists of three levels of prevention. Each has specific implications for the health education specialist or health promoter. Each requires different objectives, methods, and interventions (programs).

Primary prevention emphasizes interventions to avert disease, illness, injury, or deterioration of health before these occur. Primary prevention may include vaccinations and immunizations for children and adults. Vaccinations will cause the production of antibodies which will prevent future cases of a disease so that people will not get sick.

Another example of primary prevention is early pregnancy interventions that teach pregnant women to adopt healthy behaviors that support healthy pregnancies, deliveries, and healthy newborns. There are legislative actions that are considered primary prevention, such as water fluoridation, seat belt laws, laws requiring child restraint seats in vehicles, laws requiring immunizations before attending school, and laws requiring food handlers to be periodically tested for infectious diseases. All of these actions are designed to prevent diseases, disabilities, and injuries. It is at the primary prevention level that health education specialists and health promoters can have their greatest impact on the health of a population. Primary prevention is the most cost-effective form of disease prevention.

Secondary prevention identifies diseases at their earliest stages and applies appropriate measures to limit the consequences and severity of the disease. The efforts in secondary prevention center on early detection and treatment of diseases. The focus is curative and this has been the primary focus for medicine. Secondary prevention directs resources to identify diseases at the earliest stage possible so that the damage from the disease can be limited. Examples of secondary prevention are mammograms, Pap tests, testicular exams, regular blood pressure measurements, measurements for blood cholesterol and blood glucose, and vision examinations. The health education specialist or patient educator in many of these situations plays an important role in getting clients to schedule tests for early detection of diseases and for providing the knowledge and skills for clients to reduce or avoid the destructive disease progress and improve their health.

Tertiary prevention helps people who already have diseases and disabilities. Tertiary prevention prescribes specific interventions to limit the effects of disabilities and diseases and may also prevent the recurrence of disease. The level of tertiary prevention will depend on the medical care that is available to the individual or community. Some of the critical components of tertiary care are rehabilitation services, physical therapy, and occupational therapy that may not be available to individuals because of costs or lack of health insurance, or because such services are not available in some communities. This level of tertiary prevention will depend heavily on surgery, medications, and counseling. Tertiary prevention and the care required at this level is the most expensive, when compared to secondary or primary prevention. It is the least cost-effective in preventing illness and disease.

Health Protection

Health protection includes ". . . the legal or fiscal controls, other regulations and policies, and voluntary codes of practice, aimed at the enhancement of positive health and the prevention of ill health" (Downie et. al., 1996). Health education specialists and promoters must overcome many barriers to health protection. The mission of health protection is to provide legislative, political, and social constructs that reduce the likelihood of people behaving in unsafe ways or to remove environmental hazards that impact health outcomes. Rules that forbid smoking in the workplace, laws that tax tobacco products, and regulations forbidding smoking in schools and other public places are all examples of health protections that have reduced smoking among some populations and reduced the likelihood that these populations will develop certain cancers or cardiovascular diseases. Many efforts to establish and enforce health protection have met with great opposition because it violates one of the tenets of health education and health promotion: individuals have the constitutional right to voluntarily choose to change behaviors that promote health. This opposition to certain efforts for health protection is found among lobbying organizations, political groups, and industries, with just as many groups and organizations supporting these efforts.

The Triad of Health Promotion

Tannahill (1985) noted that these three areas that make up health promotion generate seven domains. As the health professionals in disease prevention, health education, and health protection relate to, intersect, and interact with each other, the following seven domains arise in health promotion.

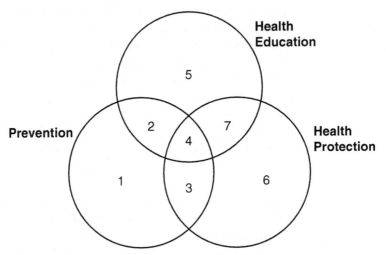

Figure 2.1 The seven domains produced by triad of health promotion

Tannahill, A. (1985). "What is health promotion?" *Health Education Journal*, 44, 167–8.

1. Prevention:
   This domain includes the primary, secondary, and tertiary prevention measures and programs.

2. Lifestyle:
   This domain results from the interaction of disease prevention and health education. It is comprised of educational efforts to influence lifestyle to prevent health problems and to encourage participation in preventive services.

3. Preventive Policies:
   This domain results from the interaction of disease prevention and health protection. This domain represents preventive health protection. Examples of the work in this domain would be water purification, water fluoridation, restaurant inspections, etc. The domain would be considered to be policy commitments to preventive efforts under domain 1.

4. Policy Maker Education:
   The interactions among disease prevention, health education, and health protection gives rise to professionals and services that are involved in preparing and stimulating the social environment, legislators, and policy makers to support preventive health protection actions and measures.

5. Health Education:
   This domain involves all aspects of health education that influences health behaviors for positive health outcomes.

6. Health Protection:
   This domain supports the implementation of policies and the commitment of funds for health protection efforts.

7. Policy Support:
   This domain is an interaction of health education and health protection. It involves a policy commitment to positive health and raising awareness and securing support for positive health protection measures among the public and policy makers.

Primary Themes in Health Promotion

Health promotion seeks improved health and quality of life for the individual, but also for groups and the general population. In observing the many health promotion interventions and strategies, it becomes obvious that there are specific themes in health promotion efforts. Some of these themes are listed below (Butler, 2001).

- Empowerment:
  Empowerment is a multilevel construct that involves people assuming control over their lives in the context of their social and political environment.

- Ecological Perspective:
  The ecological perspective views health as a product of the interdependence of the individual and subsystems of the ecosystem such as family, culture, and physical and social environment.

- Community Organization:
  Community organization is a multi-phased process by which community groups are helped to produce change and develop their community for improved health and quality of life.

- Individual Behavior:
  Although we emphasize social and economic factors, we must not forget the crucial role of individual behavior in one's health.

- Official Recognition:
  Many official United States, Canadian, and international pronouncements have recognized the importance of health promotion and have laid a groundwork for its continued growth.

Application Opportunity

Activity A

As you read about health behavior, health education, and health promotion, what in these fields or areas appeal to you and relates to your future preparation for a career in the health care field? Why?

Activity B

Examine the themes of health promotion. As a future health professional, which of the primary themes in health promotion speaks to your passion about helping people improve the quality of their lives? Why?

Activity C

As you read this chapter and answered the questions in Activities A and B, you may have realized that to perform as a health professional in health education and health promotion, your personal life's philosophy is important and foundational. Write below your philosophical foundation that you would bring to health education and health promotion.

References

Butler, J. T. 2001. *Principles of Health Education and Health Promotion,* 3rd ed. Belmont, CA: Wadsworth/Thomson Learning.

Downie, R. S., C. Tannahill, and A. Tannahill. 1996. *Health Promotion: Models and Values,* 2nd ed. Oxford, England: Oxford University Press.

Doyle, E., and S. Ward. 2005. *The Process of Community Health Education and Promotion.* Long Grove, IL: Waveland Press, Inc.

Gochman, D. S. 1982. "Labels, Systems, and Motives: Some Perspectives on Future Research." *Health Education Quarterly* 9: 167–74.

Gochman, D. S. 1997. "Health Behavior Research: Definitions and Diversity." In D. S. Gochman (Ed.), *Handbook of Health Behavior Research: Vol.1. Personal and Social Determinants.* New York: Plenum Press.

Green, L. W., and M. W. Kreuter. 1999. *Health Promotion Planning: An Educational and Ecological Approach,* 3rd ed. Mountain View, CA: Mayfield.

Joint Committee on Health Education and Promotion Terminology. 2012. "Report of the 2011 Joint Committee on Health Education and Promotion Terminology." *American Journal of Health Education* 43 (2).

McGinnis, J. M., P. Williams-Russo, and J. R. Knickman. 2002. "The case for more active policy attention to health promotion." *Health Affairs* 21 (2): 78–93.

Oberteuffer, D., O. A. Harrelson, and M. B. Pollock. 1972. *School Health Education,* 5th ed. New York: Harper & Row.

O'Donnell Michael P. 2009. "Definition of Health Promotion 2.0: Embracing Passion, Enhancing Motivation, Recognizing Dynamic Balance, and Creating Opportunities." *American Journal of Health Promotion: September/October 2009* 24 (1): iv.

Penhollow, T. M. 2012. *Points to Health: Theory and Practice of Health Education and Health Behavior.* Dubuque, IA: Kendall Hunt Publishing Company.

Simons-Morton, B. G., W. H. Greens, and N. H. Gottlieb. 1995. *Introduction to Health Education and Health Promotion,* 2nd ed. Prospects Heights, IL: Waveland.

Tannahill, A. 1985. What is Health Promotion? *Health Education Journal* 44: 167–8.

Chapter 3

A Historical Context for Health Promotion

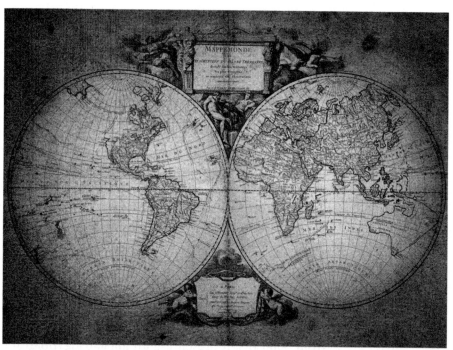

© Triff, 2013. Used under license from Shutterstock, Inc.

This chapter presents a brief overview of history as it leads to the development of the health education profession. It is not meant to be an exhaustive account but allows the reader to examine some of the events and developments that have led to the field and practice of health education and health promotion. Health education and promotion share the same historical roots as many other health professions that lead in protecting the health of populations. This history started with the beginning of civilization. Historical and archaeological evidence reveals a preoccupation by people with their survival. Acquiring behaviors and developing rules and regulations that protect people's health have been major factors in the development of civilizations throughout the world. Humans have investigated and determined, to the best of their abilities and resources, how to be safe and healthy, avoiding injuries, sickness, and premature death. Historically, health information has been passed from person to person in a variety of ways, starting with word-of-mouth, the oral traditions, traditional customs, and spiritual and religious beliefs and practices.

Early Civilizations

Ancient writings and records reflect varied approaches for medicine and public health. Much of what earlier cultures and societies learned and accomplished resulted from trial and error, scientific exploration and research, and through spiritual and religious beliefs and practices. In fact, in earlier societies, there were strong associations among sciences and religion and spiritual beliefs in supporting health for the individual and the communities. In many early cultures, priests or spiritual leaders served as physicians (Ferngren, 2009).

This history of health care similarly is reflected in many civilizations and cultures throughout the world. There are many documented efforts for the protection of the population's health. Early efforts at public health are identified by existing evidence of bathrooms and drain systems in the Indus Valley dating back at least 4,000 years. The ancient kingdoms of Africa such as Egypt and Mali and those of China were noted for their advanced knowledge in medicine and surgeries in many archaeological finds.

Smith Papyri documents Africa's early contribution to health care. The Smith Papyri is the oldest written documents related to health care dating from 3000 BC, representing an ancient Egyptian medical textbook on surgery (U.S. National Library of Medicine, 2010). It begins with clinical cases of head injuries and works systematically down the body, describing, in detail, the examination, diagnosis, treatment, and prognosis in each case. It reveals the ancient Egyptians' knowledge of the relation of the pulse to the heart and of the workings of the stomach, bowels, and larger blood vessels. Historically, the first physician of notable reputation was Imhotep, who existed at least 1,000 years before the Greek Hippocrates. Monuments to Imhotep's wisdom, medical expertise and power still stand in Egypt today.

A major document for health laws in the Babylonian Empire is in the Code of Hammurabi, which dates back to about 1772 BC. The sixth

Babylonian king, Hammurabi, enacted the code, which exists on a human-sized stone *stele* with various clay tablets. The Code consists of 282 laws, some of which deal with punishments and also contains directives and rules for health practices and physicians, including the first known fee schedule for health services (Butler, 2001).

Judeo-Christian history contributes many formal directions for health and the quality of life in the tenets of Judaism and Christianity that illustrated the close relationship of spiritual beliefs and practices with health practices and regulations. Throughout the Pentateuch of the Old Testament, especially the Book of Leviticus, the Hebrews are directed by God on how to live holy and healthy lives through spiritual practices, sanitation, care of the sick, childbirth, dietary directives, and burial practices. The early Christian church during the Roman Empire made important innovations with patient care for the sick with the establishment of hospital and nursing care (Guenter, 1999; Ferngren, 2009).

The ancient Greeks placed great emphasis on prevention rather than treatment of disease. They actually compartmentalized the aspects of physical, mental, and spiritual health, but maintained the importance of balancing these aspects of health. Greeks believed in the perfect balance of mind, body, and spirit, actualized through the study and practice of philosophy, athletics, and theology. Greek mythology played a significant role in the history of health in Greek culture. In the classic, *The Iliad*, a Thesalian chief named Asclepius received instruction in use of drugs and was later endowed as the god of medicine. He had two daughters Hygeia and Panacea. Hygeia was given the ability to prevent disease. Panacea was given the ability to treat disease. The words *hygiene* and *panacea* traced back to these mythical daughters of Asclepius. Throughout Greece, temples were erected to worship the mythical god Asclepius. The caduceus, the symbol of the staff and serpent of the physician, was an important symbol of these temples. Hippocrates was a famous and authentic Greek physician who practiced medicine in the Asclepian tradition. Hippocrates was known for his approach to medicine that included observing and recording associations between certain diseases and factors such as geography, climate, diet, and living conditions. He was able to distinguish endemic diseases and epidemic diseases. The Hippocratic Oath still serves as the basis for medical ethics in the western world today. Hippocrates is also considered to be the first epidemiologist and the father of modern medicine.

The Roman Empire conquered the Greeks and many other kingdoms, but did not destroy their cultures; they expanded them. The Romans brought the ancient world great engineers, builders, and administrators. The Romans built an extensive and efficient aqueduct system. They developed an extensive system of underground sewers and public and private baths. These great innovations made sanitary and healthful environments possible. Roman civilization developed a system of private medical practice. They expanded the study of anatomy and surgery that began with the Greeks (Rosen, 1958).

The Pre-Modern Era

With the fall of the Roman Empire, many of the advances in western medicine and public health were lost. Without the power of Rome and the invasions of barbarian hordes, great fear existed among Rome's former subjects. This was the period of the Middle Ages which are also referred to as the Dark Ages. Fear drove many people into walled cities for protection. Rosen (1958) describes how people lived with their animals within these cities and how, as the populations grew in these confined areas, sanitation and health broke down. The norms for cleanliness disappeared, replaced by often filthy conditions by the common people and aristocracies. The Roman advances in community health were lost during this period. Superstition and misinterpretation of Christian beliefs led to the destruction of many of the written science and medical advances from the Greeks and Romans. Some few documents were saved by the Christian Church.

It is not surprising that the Middle Ages gave rise to many deadly epidemics. One of the most deadly of all diseases was the Black Death or bubonic plague. It is estimated that the bubonic plague may have claimed more than 30 million lives. Europe may have lost a quarter to one-third of its populations. The cause of the disease was unknown at that time, so great fear and superstition existed around the disease. Often, the first to respond to the people suffering from this disease were the religious leaders and the doctors. This meant that the mortality rate among these practitioners was very high and often left communities with no spiritual or medical leadership (Cottrell, 2012).

Great numbers of lives were lost as those of the Middle Ages grappled with epidemics of the bubonic plague, leprosy, smallpox, diphtheria, measles, influenza, tuberculosis, anthrax, and finally, syphilis (McKenzie et. al., 2008). While there was no agreement about the causes of these diseases, it eventually became clear that contagion might be involved. Education about how to handle the diseases and avoid contracting the diseases became important. While there were no professional health educators at this time, there were professionals that took on this task of educating the public about disease prevention: priests, pastors, medical doctors, and community leaders. They attempted to teach anyone who would listen about how to protect their health, even though the information was limited.

The Middle Ages lasted until about 1500 AD, with the advent of the Renaissance (1500–1700 AD). The disease conditions of the Middles Ages continued, but science began to emerge as a legitimate means of inquiry. Eventually there were many advancements to begin some improvement in the health and quality of life in populations of this time period. It was again deemed appropriate to study the human body. The search for knowledge was renewed. This led to great exploration for new lands and new trade routes. However, in Europe, some problems still persisted. Problems such as the inappropriate disposal of human waste and lack of bathing were prevalent among the poor, the growing middle class, and the aristocracies of the time. While perfume is an ancient tradition, during the Renaissance, "cloaking scents" were used to cover the bad odors left in clothing (Hansen, 1980).

As many of the superstitions of the Middle Ages were being replaced by observations of cause and effect, there were numerous advances in health care during this period. Through his orderly study of the human body, John Hunter became known as the father of modern surgery. The invention of the microscope by Antoine van Leeuwenhoek enabled mankind to see life forms too small to be seen by the naked eye. However, this new science was not associated with discovery of disease. John Graunt expanded the fields of biostatistics and epidemiology with his studies and publications on mortality (Goerke and Stebbins, 1968, p.61). Cipolla (1976) found that many Italian cities had established boards of health to fight the communicable diseases, but by the middle of the sixteenth century their control and jurisdiction expanded to include the food trade, wine, water, the sewage systems, the hospital practices, burials, cemeteries, as well as the professional practices of physicians, surgeons, and pharmacies. These boards of health even had jurisdiction over beggars and prostitutes.

The New World

Explorers had come to North America from all over the world for many centuries. When Europeans arrived in North America, they found generally healthy populations of American Indians. Among American Indian nations, health information and healing practices were passed from generation to generation by traditional practices and word-of-mouth. They were not prepared for the life threatening challenges that would come from Europe. Arrival of Europeans to North America brought new diseases and epidemics to the American Indians as well as to the colonists who had settled in the New World for a new life. The new life was fraught with many hardships, dangers, and challenges. Diseases and epidemics would destroy whole settlements of colonists and whole communities of American Indians. Perhaps smallpox was one of the deadliest diseases impacting these people. There was little experience or expertise to deal with the overwhelming challenges to life. Community health action in the colonies was usually ineffective, and taken only in crises. The practice of medicine was primitive.

In the Massachusetts colony, there was legislation passed in 1701 to provide isolation and quarantine practices for those who suffered from smallpox. As various cultures and nations fought the spread of disease and major epidemics, it became apparent to some leaders that such disease and health challenges with the accompanying unsanitary conditions in many areas could be alleviated with organized community efforts and improving the educational levels of the people. Many of the colonies in the New World followed the community health actions in Europe by establishing several local boards of health in the late 1790s due to yellow fever epidemics. In 1746, the Massachusetts Bay colonies passed laws for the prevention of pollution in the Boston Harbor.

Harvard College became the first institution of higher education in the colonies, founded in 1636, before compulsory schooling for children was installed. Harvard offered the first required hygiene course in American higher education. In early America, only boys went to school. In 1642, Massachusetts became the first colony to establish a law requiring all children to read and write. Benjamin Franklin advocated health and physical exercise and in 1751 he realized the founding of the first Academy in Philadelphia, the first secondary education in America that also supported these principles. In 1821 the American high school was established.

A Case History of Smallpox in the Ancient and New World

Smallpox is a vicious disease that ravaged all civilizations from antiquities until the 20th century. The smallpox scars on the mummified features of Pharaoh Ramses V testify to the long relationship with this disease, a disease unique to humans and one that has killed millions (Behbehani, 1983). Descriptions of smallpox appear in the earliest Egyptian, Indian, and Chinese writings. Smallpox spread through contact with living sufferers or the bodies of the dead; it was especially cruel on previously unexposed populations—at least one-third of all Aztecs died after Spanish colonizers brought smallpox to the New World in 1518.

Survivors of smallpox carried its legacies for life. Many people were left blind and virtually all survivors were disfigured by scars from the disease. By the 1500s, the disease had reached most of the world and the smallpox scarred faces were familiar sights. The wealthier survivors in Elizabethan society used shaped beauty patches to camouflage the damage or coated their faces with white lead powder. The ghostly pale face of Queen Elizabeth I was as much a sign of her brush with smallpox as it was a fashion statement. Eventually, many survivors of the dreaded disease realized that they had gained an advantage over those who had not experienced smallpox. Their bouts with smallpox yielded lifelong immunity from any further infection from smallpox.

All over the world people were discovering that immunity was not inherited, because an outbreak in one generation in a city did not protect future generations in that city from smallpox. However, in many countries, investigations of the smallpox led to the idea that immunity could be induced through inoculation. The idea of preventing smallpox epidemics by inducing immunity was first exploited in China, where a form of inoculation existed as early as the tenth century. Immunity was gained by provoking a mild form of the disease in healthy people, for example by blowing powdered smallpox scabs up their noses. Other world cultures used varying forms of inoculation to protect its citizens. The form of inoculation for smallpox in Africa became an important weapon against the disease in the New World. By the early 1700s, smallpox inoculation, known as *variolation*, had spread from parts of Africa, India, and the Ottoman Empire. Lady Mary Wortley Montagu, a well-known writer and wife of a wealthy English aristocrat, moved to the Ottoman Empire when her husband was assigned to be ambassador to the Ottoman Empire. While there, Lady Mary Wortley Montagu encountered this smallpox variolation process in 1717. She witnessed local peasant women performing inoculations or variolations at seasonal 'smallpox parties'. Upon returning to Britain, she had her own children inoculated during an outbreak in 1721.

Even with Lady Montagu's campaigning on behalf of inoculation, the British were reluctant to adopt this practice to thwart the devastation of smallpox. In 1721, at the urging of Montagu and the Princess of Wales, several prisoners and abandoned children were inoculated by having smallpox inserted under the skin. Several months later, the children and prisoners who were deliberately exposed to smallpox did not develop the smallpox disease. When none contracted the disease, the procedure was deemed safe and members of the royal family were inoculated. The procedure then became fashionable in Europe.

While the slave trade in the New World was horrific, evil, and inhumane, it was the African slaves who introduced variolation into America. In Massachusetts, Cotton Mather learned about the practice from his slave, Onesimus, who had received the treatment as a child in Africa. Onesimus was immune from smallpox and so were many other slaves as Mather discovered as he investigated this fully (Herbert, 1975). Mather publicized the technique and the procedure was first tried during the smallpox epidemic in Boston in 1721. Inspired by Onesimus's knowledge, Mather campaigned for inoculation in the face of the growing epidemic, a call that met with some success and much hostility. However, the actions of Lady Montagu, the knowledge of Onesimus, and the persistence of Cotton Mather ultimately hastened this knowledge transfer to the Western world. Edward Jenner, an English country doctor, later adapted the practice, and developed a safer, more effective technique he called vaccination. He noted that local people who caught cowpox gained immunity from the far more dangerous smallpox. Jenner's relentless promotion and devoted research of vaccination changed the way medicine was practiced. Late in the 19th century, it was realized that vaccination did not confer lifelong immunity and that subsequent revaccination was necessary.

The mortality from smallpox had declined, but there were still epidemics, showing that the disease was still not under control. In the 1950s a number of control measures were implemented, and smallpox was eradicated in many areas in Europe and North America. In 1967, a global campaign began under the direction of the World Health Organization and finally succeeded in the eradication of smallpox in 1977. On May 8, 1980, the World Health Assembly announced that the world was free of smallpox and recommended that all countries cease vaccination (Riedel, 2005).

Pre-Industrial Era (1800–1850)

The United States was swept by a series of epidemics and physicians were poorly trained. Medical problems were addressed by poorly prepared physicians with unsanitary conditions. There were many political and social problems that led to changes in education. States gradually made education mandatory and health education principles and policies were starting to form. William Alcott, the father of school health education in the United States, wrote an important book on the healthful construction of schoolhouses, and he was the first to write a health book for children. Horace Mann was the first secretary of the first board of education in the United States. Horace Mann was also one of the most influential educators of his day. He made powerful recommendations for physiology and hygiene in the curriculum of the elementary school, resulting in the mandatory addition of these subjects to the curriculum of all public schools in 1850 in Massachusetts.

As communities became more industrialized in England, health and living conditions plummeted especially with the working poor. Edwin Chadwick published the *Report on the Inquiry into the Sanitary Condition of the Labouring Population in Great Britain* in 1842. The report described the wretched conditions of Great Britain's working class in both their homes and in the workplaces. With much opposition, Chadwick proposed that political unrest and poverty were not the most critical contributors to the poor health, but the filth and the immorality of the poor were the primary and direct causes of poor personal and community health, family discord, and alcohol abuse among this population (Rosen, 1993; Hamlin 1995). Chadwick's work led to the 1848 Public Health Act and the establishment of the General Board of Health in England. This organization authorized local boards of health to oversee the water supply, sewage, and to conduct surveys and investigations of sanitary conditions in given districts.

Chadwick's work had far reaching implications for public health practice that impacted not only England, but also impacted public health foundations in the United States. In the United States, Lemuel Shattuck published the *Report of the Sanitary Commission of Massachusetts* in 1850. This report publicized and supported community health promotion and it served as a guide in the health field for a century. The report made fifty recommendations that were established in public health practice. Shattuck's report helped society address health problems in a more disciplined way and endorsed an ambitious program of health education in schools.

The Modern Era: 1850–Present

Report on the Inquiry into Sanitary Condition of the Labouring Population of Great Britain (Edwin Chadwick, 1842) and *Report of the Sanitary Commission of Massachusetts* (Lemuel Shattuck, 1850) ushered in the modern era of health.

Society began to attack health problems in a disciplined way, even though there were some false assumptions. The modern era of health has been divided into five phases that reflect the foci and beliefs about community health during these periods, but not always with accurate science and evidence. Each of these phases were marked by various major advances in the health of populations, medical and public health innovations, educational programming, and the importance of health education and health promotion in personal and public health improvements. These phases include the following:

- Miasma Phase (1850–1880)

- Bacteriology Phase (1880–1910)

- Health Resources Phase (1910–1960)

- Social Engineering Phase (1960–1975)

- Health Promotion Phase (1970s–Present)

The Miasma Phase (1850–1880)

Miasma refers to toxic vapors or fumes. During the miasma phase, people thought that disease was caused by toxic vapors. The effect of quarantine and isolation led to the mistaken assumption that confining the unhealthy air that carried disease was beneficial in preventing the disease. It was believed that the use of herbs and incense to perfume the air and the body would "fill the nose and crowd out the miasma.

Local and state powers were directed to the fight against infectious diseases. The American Public Health Association was founded in 1872. Florence Nightingale actively defined laws for nursing and developed the concept of nursing as a profession. The Women's Christian Temperance Movement, very strong scientific temperance movement, preached the evils of alcohol and other drugs, forced passage of many laws requiring instruction on the effects of drugs and hygiene education in 38 states between 1880 and 1890. The American Medical Association (AMA) was founded on May 7, 1847.

Bacteriology Phase (1880–1910)

The bacteriology phase was ushered in by the work of such scientists as Louis Pasteur and Robert Koch, presenting evidence that microorganisms cause infectious diseases. This information was not readily accepted, so the nineteenth century ended with major epidemics and the primary tools used in the attacks on these diseases were still isolation and quarantine.

The physical education movement began in this period, pioneered by Catherine Esther Beecher and Thomas Denison Wood. Their work laid some of the foundation for health education. During this era of medical inspection, physicians and health workers examined school children and teachers to identify those whose health problems made them dangerous to others in efforts to reduce the incidences of communicable diseases. The Modern Health Crusade of the National Tuberculosis Association was a multiphasic program to encourage healthy behaviors in school children. School children were encouraged to practice several health chores daily and various levels of achievement were rewarded and recognized. The campaign for "open-air classrooms" provided open-air schools and classrooms, usually in hospital settings, that provided fresh air and an opportunity to integrate health education into the overall education plan for children with tuberculosis.

Health Resources Phase (1910–1960)

With the growing recognition of the importance of health education in preventing and addressing diseases came much social reform that improved health in United States. Upton Sinclair's book "The Jungle" in 1906 revealed the deplorable working conditions of immigrants working in the meat packing industry and the contamination of food. This led to the passage of the Pure Food and Drug Act of 1906 and the passage of workman's compensation laws. During the health resources phase, large financial investments were made in hospitals, health staffing, and biomedical research.

Until 1910, health education, hygiene education, and physical education were considered synonymous (Anderson, 1972). Then the American Physical Education Association recognized the difference between hygiene education and health education, professionally separating the two. Most degree programs offered training in physical education and hygiene. However, the Health Department of the Georgia Normal and Industrial College became the first institution to offer a curriculum and an undergraduate degree in health education in 1921. This was followed by the Teachers College of Columbia University and the Harvard University-Massachusetts Institute of Technology combined program awarding degrees in health education. The *Cardinal Principles of Secondary Education*, published by the National Education Association (NEA) in 1918, marked a turning point in United States secondary education and legitimized school health education. In 1918, the Child Health Organization was founded in response to concerns about childhood malnutrition and is often considered the beginning of the health education movement. Health education curriculum changed during the 1920s due, in part, to the Report of the Joint Committee on Health Problems in Education published by the NEA and the AMA, *A Survey of 86 Cities*, showing that health education across the country was not consistent. Health education became the focus of several commercial companies and industries that produced high quality curricula and audiovisual materials to be utilized in health education efforts. The American School Health Association was founded in 1927. A number of research studies conducted during this period provided a science base for health education.

The Great Depression struck during this phase and impacted every aspect of the American society, even in education and health care. The Depression resulted in program cuts and educational reconstruction, but it was followed by a period of tremendous medical advances and federal investments in the health care system. A series of important conferences, including a series of White House Conferences on Child Health and Protection focused attention on the health of children and the roles of the schools and communities in protecting it.

Social Engineering Phase (1960–1975)

During this phase, there was recognition that not everyone in American society benefited from the educational, technological, and health advances realized at this time. The social engineering phase began in the 1960s, emphasizing and assuring equal access to educational and health services to all citizens regardless of race, ethnicity, and socioeconomic status. Programs such as "New Frontier" and "War on Poverty," were administered to address social wrongs. However, the most significant services to be established by legislation were Medicare and Medicaid in 1965. These programs were amendments to the Social Security Act of 1935 and addressed the needs of two groups who were not likely to have health insurance and health coverage: the elderly and the poor. These programs by law did not allow for discrimination in the provision of health care and quality of services. The School Health Education Study, completed in the mid-1960s, was the first attempt to define what children and youth in the United States knew about health. The results would be used to scientifically develop a health education curriculum following basic principles used for all other educational curricula. During the 1970s, health education moved away from the emphasis on acquisition of facts to more emphasis on the affective domain and later to health behavior choices. The federal government's priority became the cost containment of health care. The Coalition of National Health Education Organizations was established in 1972.

Health Promotion Phase (1970s–Present)

As cost containment for growing health care costs became the priority of the federal government, the focus on changing health behavior also grew as a priority in health education. There was growing understanding that helping individuals establish or make more responsible health behavior choices would lead to greater prevention of costly health problems. The health promotion phase has focused on innovative programming to change behaviors that pose health risks and to encourage behaviors that are beneficial to health. The Society for Public Health Education (SOPHE) published the first genuine code of ethics for health educators in 1976 and American Association for Health Education (AAHE) adopted the AAHE Code of Ethics in 1993. There was a call for all health education organizations to develop a profession-wide code of ethics. After much commitment and work, in February 2011, delegates of the Ethics Task Force of the Coalition of National Health Education Organizations (CNHEO) approved the most recent Code of Ethics for the Health Education Profession.

The Lalonde Report, *A New Perspective on the Health of Canadians* introduced the "health field" concept that identified four elements to which death and disease could be attributed: human biology (heredity), environment, lifestyle (behavior), and inadequacies in health care provision. The Lalonde report directly influenced the health promotion movement in the United States. The US government published several documents recognizing the importance of lifestyle in promoting health and well-being (US Public Health Service, 1979). The US government through the leadership of the US Surgeon General embarked upon the challenge to set a national agenda that communicated a common vision for improving health and achieving health equity. The series of publications include *Healthy People: The Surgeon General's Report on Health Promotion and Disease Prevention* (1979), *Promoting Health/Preventing Disease: Objectives for the Nation* (1980), *Healthy People 2000* (1990), *Healthy People 2010* (2000), and the more recent *Healthy People 2020* (2010). These all have called attention to the roles of individuals, their communities, and their governments in supporting health. Each publication provided measurable health objectives for the nation to meet overarching national goals within a given ten-year timeframe.

Table 3.1 Healthy People 2020; Vision, Mission, and Goals

Vision: A society in which all people live long, healthy lives.
Mission: Healthy People 2020 strives to: • identify nationwide health improvement priorities • increase public awareness and understanding of the determinants of health, disease, disability, and the opportunities for progress • provide measurable objectives and goals that are applicable at the national, state, and local levels • engage multiple sectors to take actions to strengthen policies and improve practices that are driven by the best available evidence and knowledge. • identify critical research, evaluation, and data collection needs.
Overarching Goals: • Attain high-quality, longer lives free of preventable disease, disability, injury, and premature death; • Achieve health equity, eliminate disparities, and improve the health of all groups; • Create social and physical environments that promote good health for all; • Promote quality of life, healthy development, and healthy behaviors across all life stages.

Source: Centers for Disease Control and Prevention, Healthy People 2020.

There have been and continue to be several international conferences that support and nurture the health promotion movement in a global context as well. The HIV+/AIDS epidemics beginning in the 1970's and continuing currently, major natural disasters and international terrorism continue to emphasize the need to work through health education and health promotion to assess health needs, encourage positive behavior changes, plan effective programs for disease prevention, health protection, and to evaluate these efforts to improve methods, strategies and outcomes.

The decades of the 1990s and 2000s have focused on the ecological perspective, taking into account the social, political, and economic forces impacting and affecting health. Butler (2001) suggests that this era, 1990s through the present, may be known in the future as the beginning of the phase of social ecology.

In March 23, 2010, amid much controversy, the Affordable Care Act became national law. The intention of the law is to expand health care coverage to 31 million uninsured Americans. The law will also focus on prevention and prevention services through community and wellness programs, worksite wellness programs and strong support for school-based health centers. Time will tell if these goals will be realized for the American people.

Professional Credentialing

The potential for making our society healthier with the practices of responsible health behaviors has seldom been greater for health education specialists and those working in health promotion. With the evolution of health education as a profession, there has been debate over the qualifications necessary for successful health education and health promotion practice. The process of identifying the competencies of professional health educators began in 1948 with the National Conference on Undergraduate Professional Preparation in Health Education, Physical Education and Recreation. In 1962, the American Association for Health, Physical Education and Recreation identified seven areas upon which principles and standards for health education were centered and for which professional competencies were identified.

As a result of the First Bethesda Conference in 1978, the National Task Force on the Preparation and Practice of Health Education was given the responsibility of developing a credentialing system for health education. This resulted in the Role Delineation Project which identified the responsibilities, tasks, and competencies of practicing health educators. Next, the Role Delineation Project established the concept of a generic health educator, regardless of title, audience or setting, and the required competencies and skills of such a professional. The competencies and skills for entry-level health educators were defined in *A Guide for the Development of Competency-Based Curricula for Entry-Level Health Educators* in 1981. This became a resource document that was revised and retitled *A Competency*

Based Curriculum Framework for the Professional Preparation of Entry-Level Health Educators.

In 1988, the National Commission on Health Education Credentialing, Inc. (NCHEC) was established to promote and sustain a body of credentialed health education professionals. NCHEC monitors and awards the Certified Health Education Specialist credential, certifying health education specialists, promoting professional development and enhancing professional preparation and practice (National Commission for Health Education Credentialing, 2012).

Summary

This brief historical account of health, public health, and health promotion takes the reader through many different periods of time and stages of health conditions in the world and in the United States. We have seen the plight of humans as they dealt with disease and epidemics in the past when primarily all health efforts were focused on preventing or avoiding disease and early death to the current times when there is greater emphasis on promoting health and improving the quality of life for all citizens. It has been interesting to follow the transitions from Lemuel Shattuck's era in Boston, when tuberculosis was raging and the average age of death decreased from 27.85 years in 1820–1825 to 21.43 years in 1840–1845. In New York, over the same time periods the average age of death decreased from 26.15 years to 19.69 (Butler, 2001). By the 1900s, life expectancy in the United States was 49.24 years, and by the 1990s, life expectancy had risen to 76.1. In 2007, US life expectancy reached 77.9 years (CDC/NCHS, n.d.). Many of the factors that contributed to this improved health status and increasing life span in the United States are due to many health and medical advances, an explosion of new knowledge and practices that protect and promote health, the conquering of many life-threatening communicable diseases, improved and safer food sources, and populations making better health choices. However, the successes that have improved the health of the American people may mask health challenges that are still causing disabilities and premature death for high risk populations. Still, poor socioeconomic conditions, discrimination, and health inequities in this country are impacting the health of significant numbers of people in the United States. Many of the current challenges are related to health and lifestyle choices and behaviors. More than 40 percent of the primary causes of death are directly impacted by health behaviors and lifestyle choices. The primary causes of death are lifestyle diseases. The work before those in health education and health promotion is great in this country and in the world.

Application Opportunity

Activity A

Visit the National Library of Medicine and explore the history of medicine and health exhibits.

Go to http://www.nlm.nih.gov/hmd/explore-history.html

Choose two exhibits to visit. Report your findings here.

Activity B

Take the time to visit and study the website for Healthy People 2020.gov. You will be able to gather much information about the goals and objectives for the nation and how these are developed. Many of you who will work in public health or community health agencies may use these goals and objectives in program planning and evaluation.

1. Examine the topics that are listed and choose three topics that interest you and list them below.

2. For each of the topics that you listed, state one goal and one objective that you would want to address

References

Anderson, C. I. 1972. *School Health Policies*. St. Louis: C.V. Mosby.

Behbehani, Abbas M. 1983. "The Smallpox Story: Life and Death of an Old Disease." *Microbiological Reviews* 47 (4): 455–509.

Butler, J. T. 2001. *Principles of Health Education and Health Promotion*. Belmont, CA: Wadsworth/Thomson Learning.

Centers for Disease Control and Prevention, Healthy People. 2020. Retrieved at: http://www.cdc.gov/nchs/ppt/nchs2012/SS-25_WRIGHT.pdf.

Chadwick, E. 1842/1965. *Report on the Inquiry into Sanitary Condition of the Labouring Population of Great Britain*. Edinburgh, Scotland: Edinburgh University Press.

Cottrell, R. R., J. T. Girvan, and J. F. McKenzie. 2012. *Principles and Foundations of Health Promotion and Education*. Boston: Benjamin Cummings.

Ferngren, G. B. 2009. *Medicine and health care in Early Christianity*. Baltimore: The Johns Hopkins University Press.

Guenter, B. R. 1999. *Mending Bodies, Saving Souls: A History of Hospitals*. Oxford, England: Oxford University Press.

Herbert, E. 1975. "Smallpox Inoculation in Africa." *The Journal of African History* 16 (4): 539–59.

McClellan, J. E., and H. Dorn. 2006. *Science and Technology in World History: An Introduction*. Baltimore, MD: Johns Hopkins University.

Riedel, S. 2005. "Edward Jenner and the History of Smallpox and Vaccination." *Baylor University Medical Center Proceedings 2005* 18 (1): 21–25.

Rosen, G. 1958. *A History of Public Health*. New York: MD Publications

Rosen, G. 1993. *A History of Public Health*. Baltimore, MD: Johns Hopkins University Press.

Shattuck, L. 1948. *Report of the Sanitary Commission of Massachusetts, 1850*. New York: Cambridge University Press. (Original published in 1850)

US Public Health Service. 1979. *Healthy People: The Surgeon General's Report on Health Promotion and Disease Prevention*. Washington, DC: US Government Printing Office.

US National Library of Medicine. 2010. *Turning the Page Online. The Edwin Smith Surgical Papyrus*. Retrieved May 23, 2014, from http://www.nlm.nih/.../tu

US National Library of Medicine. *Smallpox: A Great and Terrible Scourge*. Retrieved from http://www.nlm.nih.gov/exhibition/smallpox/sp_variolation.html.

Chapter 4

Settings for Health Education and Health Promotion Practice

© John M. Fischer, 2013. Used under license from Shutterstock, Inc.

Health education professionals are specially trained to help individuals and communities reduce their health risks and increase the likelihood of living long, productive lives. Health education specialists perform their responsibilities in a variety of settings. The responsibilities and the health education process are generally the same, but the clientele, the needs, will vary according to the settings in which they serve. The fact that health education specialists practice in multiple settings allows the very important health education and health promotion services to be available to the greatest number of people with their many health challenges. This also means that the health education specialists will apply their competencies and will develop new competencies that meet the specific professional job descriptions for the specific settings and employers. Most professional preparation programs in health education/promotion usually prepare students for employment in schools, health care centers/hospitals, public/community health agencies, worksites/business, colleges/university, the military, international organizations, and the faith community. According to the Bureau of Labor, over 63,400 health education specialists were employed in the United States in 2010 (Bureau of Labor Statistics, 2012). All of these settings have their own unique needs, requirements for professionals, and barriers to success. They also have their own distinct reasons for providing health promotion/education.

School Health Education/Promotion

One of the most appropriate places for health education is the school. School health involves all the strategies, activities, and services offered by or in association with schools that are designed to promote students' physical, emotional, intellectual, and social development. Research has consistently demonstrated convincing links between good health and strong school performance (Murray et al., 2007). School health education primarily involves instructing school-aged children about health and health-related behaviors. The school setting offers a captive audience of students who can receive well-planned and effectively delivered health education and health education experiences. Unfortunately, these opportunities are not always used effectively and efficiently for greatest success in changing health behaviors for greatest improvements in health.

In the United States the historical efforts to control disease and promote health had strong beginnings in the schools. Initial impetus for school health stemmed from the terrible epidemics of the 1800s and the efforts of the Women's Christian Temperance Movement to promote abstinence from alcohol in the early 1900s. During this period leaders thought that educating children could establish disease prevention and health promotion habits early in life to continue throughout life (Butler, 2001). The quality of school health programs has often been compromised by the lack of qualified teachers and the lack of strict enforcement of education mandates. Most state departments of education do have mandates or regulations requiring health education in the school curricula for kindergarten through the 12th grade.

Today, school-based health education provides the opportunities to significantly influence positive health-related change in the lives of youth and address health and education goals through Coordinated School Health Programs (CSHP). The CSHP is currently known as the Coordinated School Health (CSH). The CSH puts both student health and well-being along with academic achievement at the center of its mission (Telljohann et al., 2012). The following are the components of CSH.

- Comprehensive school health instruction, built around the National Health Education Standards

- School health services

- Healthy school environment

- Nutrition services

- Community and family involvement

- Physical education

- School psychological, counseling/guidance, and social services

- Health education and promotion programs for faculty and staff

When properly implemented, CSH promotes wellness and motivation for health maintenance and improvement among students, their families, and the school staff because of the following features: CSH offers educational opportunities for the family and community, offers leadership and coordination through an effective management system, and provides planned ongoing in-service programs (Telljohann et al., 2012). The CSH requires continual assessment and evaluation for continuing relevance and success. All schools have implemented some components of the CSH, but it is rare when all eight components have been fully developed. Many school districts are concerned with financial challenges and are concerned about the cost of such efforts, but high quality school health education is cost effective when it is carefully planned and is based upon a realistic assessment of pupil needs, interests, and capabilities.

The goal of health education and health promotion in schools is to help students adopt and maintain healthy behaviors that they will apply throughout life. The school health education specialists must be well trained and prepared to deliver comprehensive standards-based curriculum. Most school districts offer health education, and thus need health teachers. However, some school districts hire individuals not specifically trained in health education. This can significantly reduce or eliminate the intent, effectiveness, and impact of the school health education goals and programming. Those health education specialists who want to be hired into school districts may perform substitute teaching, coaching, and volunteering in the schools to increase their chances for employment. While teaching is the primary function of the school health educator, school health education specialists are encouraged to take leadership roles in advocating for and developing school health policies. These policies may include food service options, safety measures, violence and suicide prevention, staff wellness, and community advisory committees.

Public/Community Health Education/Promotion

There is often confusion over the terms public health education/promotion or community health education/promotion. Health education specialists in both of these areas have similar skill sets, meet the competencies of the National Commission for Health Education Credentialing, and compete for similar jobs. The differences in public health and community health lie in their sources of funding and areas of focus. Public health programs are usually government funded through taxation that support initiatives and mandates serving individuals, local communities, states, and the nation in health education and health promotion. Community health programs are largely supported by community and voluntary health agencies that are funded by citizen donations, grants, and endowments. The health education specialists in both of these areas focus on the health of the community recognizing the health of the community is directly linked to the health of the community members. Voluntary health agencies and public health agencies are the most likely sources of employment for community health education specialists.

Community health agencies or voluntary health agencies play a larger role in the United States than in most other countries. Some examples of such agencies and organizations are the American Heart Association, the American Diabetes Association, the United Way, the American Cancer Society, etc. Voluntary health agencies are created to deal with health needs not met by governmental agencies. Much of their funding is used to provide services and support research for their areas of interests. Health education specialists are hired to plan, implement, and evaluate the education component of the agency's programs. Administratively, health education specialists may be involved in such duties as coordinating volunteers, budgeting, fund-raising, and serving as liaisons to other agencies and groups.

Public health education specialists are found in departments of public health that are formed to coordinate and provide health services to communities as mandated by laws and governmental directives. Health departments may be organized by the city, county, state, or federal government. In these departments, health education specialists serve in a variety of roles that will include assessment of populations, program planning, implementation, evaluation, grant writing and program administration. They will deliver direct services to the community and it's members through teaching, training, counseling, and consulting. They often serve as liaisons to other agencies and groups, building coalitions to address community health challenges. In public health, health education specialists perform their duties with diverse populations, addressing the needs of and partnering with people of various income levels, ages, races and ethnicities, cultures, genders, and political views. Within the public health environment they will work in concert with other health professionals to solve community health problems.

Worksite Health Education/Promotion

Worksite health promotion is defined as a combination of educational, organizational, and environmental activities designed to improve the health and safety of employees and their families (Cottrell et. al., 2012). Many businesses and organizations offer health care insurance to their workers. The costs of employee health benefits have increased for employers. The concerns for cost containment and the well-being of their employees have generated greater interests in the development and implementation of worksite wellness programs. These programs offer health promotion services for employees and their family members, often reducing the health care costs and health problems which are largely the result of behavioral issues. Health promotion programs at worksites differ greatly from site to site, because of differences in the businesses' goals, and types of employees. The proportion of employers providing worksite health promotion programs has increased over the years, with some kind of programming offered in over 80% of worksites with 50 or more employees, and almost all large employers with more than 750 employees (Cottrell et. al., 2012).

Health education specialists must be able to market a health promotion program to the management of a company, because the administrators are always concerned about getting the best return on their investments. The management of companies is most concerned about improving the health of their employees to reduce absenteeism, address an aging workforce, eliminate worksite injuries, reduce health insurance premiums, and to increase retention of employees, their job satisfaction and to improve morale. Companies are also interested in being perceived as innovators for their respective industries and among their employees. Worksite wellness programs that are successful, present the employers in a very positive light for the employees, their families and the community.

Health education specialists in worksite wellness are likely to have competencies that allow them to fulfill all of the health education responsibilities (assessment, planning, implementing, and evaluating programs and services), as well as expertise in physical fitness, diet and nutrition, stress management, etc. that are common areas of interest for employees. Working in worksite wellness programs, health education specialists will have duties that include the use of media in creating bulletin boards, newsletters, coordinating annual health fairs, conducting companywide screenings, and initiating and monitoring flu shot programs.

Passage of the Patient Protection and Affordable Care Act is expected to bring about significant changes for worksite health promotion in the form of increased opportunities to establish wellness programs and offer employee rewards in the form of insurance premium discounts. However, the legislation is presenting major challenges for employers who must support changes financially, resulting in the reduction in workforce for some companies.

Medical and Health Care Settings

Many positions exists for health education specialists in medical clinics, hospitals, community health care centers, and managed care organizations. Health education specialists in the medical care field serve as administrators, directors, managers, and coordinators, supporting and consulting on health education programs and services. Providing patient education is another way health education specialists have been used in a health care setting.

Health education specialists may provide worksite wellness programs and services to employees of the health care facilities. Because health insurance companies do not typically reimburse for patient education services; the hospitals, clinics, and physicians rarely offer health promotion and education services to their patients. HMOs have been most receptive to hiring health education specialists. Current changes in the medical care system, increased emphases on cost-cutting measures, and movement toward managed care should bring greater employment opportunities for health education specialists within the health care settings. In the various health care settings, health education specialist can expect to have expertise in grant writing, one-on-one or group patient education services, publicity, public relations, and employee wellness activities as some of the responsibilities beyond planning, implementing, and evaluating services and programs.

Health Education/Promotion in Colleges and Universities

The number and quality of health promotion programs have greatly increased on the campuses of universities and colleges. Many of these wellness centers are like health care centers with doctors and nurses on staff to care for minor health problems. However, the missions of most of these centers are to support the growth and development of students, to prevent diseases and to promote health among students and the university community. These wellness centers also support health promotion services for faculty and staff which is more like the functions of worksite health centers. Health education specialists are employed by university health services or wellness centers. They may be health education professionals with undergraduate degrees, but usually the master's degree in health education is preferred. If this professional is considered a member of the academic faculty, a doctoral degree and prior experience are usually required with major responsibilities for teaching, community and professional service, and scholarly research.

Health education specialists will have major responsibility for planning, implementing, and evaluating health promotion and education programs for program participants, which will include students, faculty, and staff. Other duties will include developing health education materials, maintaining a resource library, one-on-one counseling with students, developing and coordinating a peer education program, speaking to student groups, and planning special events.

International Opportunities

A variety of positions exists in international organizations for professionals with health education training. Many positions exist to help residents in developing countries to improve their health and the quality of their lives. Often these positions require special dedication due to unusual and sometimes difficult, working or living conditions. Working in international situations requires knowledge of and sensitivities to indigenous cultures. Working internationally requires examination of different health conditions, social conditions and political environments. Health education specialists must be willing to try culturally appropriate interventions to encourage the communities' participation in the planning and implementation process and to achieve successful behavior changes.

The Military

Our government has always been committed to the health of our armed forces. A healthy military provides greater safety and protection for the citizens of this country. The nutritional status and physical fitness have always been of great interests. The military then provides an important setting for health education and health promotion for the military forces and their families. The military focus in health promotion is to optimize the total effectiveness and efficiency of the armed forces. The military is also concerned about cost containment related to treating diseases, injuries, and disabilities. Health promotion helps to reduce those costs.

Health education and health promotion in the military is similar to the work that is performed in worksite wellness programs. Many of the functions and responsibilities of the health education specialists in the military will be similar to those of the health education specialists in worksite wellness programs. These specialists in the military may come from the military health professionals or they may be civilians hired to perform health education services for the military. The professional preparation and responsibilities are the same as the other health education specialists in diverse community and health care services.

The Faith Community

Formal communities of faith are important and significant settings for health education and health promotion. Early in the history of human beings there existed strong relationships between peoples' faith and religious practices and their health. Those same connections exist today among many of our citizens and communities. It appears that these communities of believers will again be important to improving the health and quality of life of these citizens.

The faith community itself is mobilizing and focusing on health promotion interventions among their congregants and the communities. Significant research findings show that active faith or religiosity improves immunity to communicable diseases, reduces the incidence of many chronic diseases, extends the survival rate of surgery patients, improves social interaction, reduces stress and anxiety, and generally makes people healthier and happier (Breckon et. al., 1998; Butler, 2001). Anyone seeking employment in faith-based organizations should research the beliefs and goals of such organizations thoroughly to avoid misunderstandings and conflicts. Besides the competencies and responsibilities of the professional health educator, an interfaith organization described six characteristics of health education specialists who would serve faith communities (Interfaith Health Program, 1997):

- The ability to listen to the community;

- The possession of natural leadership ability;

- Respected by the community;

- Actively participate in the health education process with the community;

- Demonstration of honest concern for the health and wellness of others;

- Understanding that health goes beyond just medicine and incorporates the spiritual well-being in the total health of individuals.

Non-Traditional Health Education/Promotion Positions

The professional trained in the responsibilities and competencies for health education will find career potential in a number of less traditional fields. There are many opportunities available to health education specialists who are committed to informing, teaching and training people in health promotion and health education in nontraditional fields. Sales positions related to health, such as pharmacy sales, fitness equipment sales, and sales of health-related textbooks offer great opportunities for health education specialists. Journalism and broadcasting provide career opportunities for health or medical reporters and for authors of health articles in newspaper, magazines, or web-based services. The criminal justice and mental health systems can provide careers working as a teacher, drug educator, sexuality educator, or counselor.

Application Opportunity

1. Find and document the following organizations' websites and urls.

   - U.S. Bureau of Labor Statistics: Health Education Specialists or Health Educators

   - Centers for Disease Control and Prevention: Workplace Health Promotion

   - National Association for Worksite Centers

   - American School Health Association

   - Peace Corp

2. For each of these five organizations, briefly describe the information and/or opportunities that are available for those trained for the responsibilities and competencies of health education specialists.

References

American School Health Association. 2013. *What is School Health?* Retrieved May 22, 2013, from http://www.ashaweb.org/i4a/pages/index.cfm?pageid=3278.

Association of Schools of Public Health. 2013. Careers in Public Health. Retrieved May 12, 2013 from http://www.whatispublichealth.org/careers/index.html.

Breckon, J., J. R. Harvey, and R. B. Lancaster. 1998. *Community Health Education: Settings, Roles, Skills for the 21st Century.* Gaithersburg, MD: Aspen Publishers.

Bureau of Labor Statistics, US Department of Labor, *Occupational Outlook Handbook, 2012-13 Edition*, Health Educators. Retrieved on June 01, 2013 from http://www.bls.gov/ooh/community-and-social-service/health-educators.htm.

Butler, J. T. 2001. *Principles of Health Education and Health Promotion.* Belmont, CA: Wadsworth/Thomson Learning.

Centers for Disease Control and Prevention (CDC). 2013. *Career Opportunities in Global Health.* Retrieved April 10, 2013, from http://www.cdc.gov/globalhealth/employment/pdf/Global%20Health%20recruitment%20 brochure(links).pdf.

Cottrell, R. R., J. T. Girvan, and J. F. McKenzie. 2012. *Principles and Foundations of Health Promotion and Education.* Boston: Benjamin Cummings.

Daitz, S. J. 2007. "Health Education Careers at Nonprofit Voluntary Health Agencies." *Health Education Monograph* 24 (1): 4–6.

Interfaith Health Program, The Carter Center. 1997. *Starting Point: Empowering Communities to Improve Health—A Manual for Training Health Promoters in Congregational Coalitions.* Atlanta, GA.

Murray, N., B. Low, A. Cross, and S. Davis. 2007. "Coordinated School Health Programs and Academic Achievement: A Systematic Review of the Literature." *Journal of School Health* 77 (9): 589–600.

National Task Force on the Preparation and Practice of Health Educators. 1985. *Framework for the Development of Competency-Based Curricula for Entry Level Health Educators.* New York: National Commission for Health Education Credentialing, Inc.

National Task Force on the Preparation and Practice of Health Educators. 2013. *Health Education Profession.* Retrieved on April 10, 2013 from http://www.nchec.org/credentialing/profession/.

Telljohann, Susan K., C. W. Symons, B. Pateman, D. M. Seabert. 2012. *Health Education: Elementary and Middle School Applications*, 7th edition. New York: McGraw-Hill Companies, Inc.

Totzkay-Sitar, C., and S. Cornett. 2007. "Health Education Options in Health and Medical Care." *The Health Education Monograph* 24 (1): 7–10.

Chapter 5

An Overview of Changing Health Behaviors

© iQoncept, 2013. Used under license from Shutterstock, Inc.

The health education process is at the core of establishing and changing behaviors for successful health impacts and outcomes. The health education process includes needs assessments, program planning, program implementation, and program evaluation. The health education specialist has great responsibility in planning effective interventions that result in responsible behavior change for improved health and quality of life. Goals and measurable objectives at various levels in a health promotion program enable the health program planners to have clear direction for the desired change or outcome to be accomplished in the program. Measurable objectives are the most important constituents of planning that direct the appropriate selection of strategies and methods for the intervention. However, the formation of objectives and the selection of strategies and methods will also depend on the effective application of learning principles, theory, and models.

Learning Principles

Health education specialists, like other educators, seek to either change human behavior or establish preferred behaviors. Learning principles are general guidelines for action, which may be based on history, precedent, or research results. When principles are based on accumulated research, they can provide hypotheses for how the health professional can achieve the desired outcome for a target population. However, at their worst they can be so broad and non-specific that they can misrepresent reality. Green and Lewis (1986) and Butler (2001) provide learning principles that can guide planning for establishing or changing behaviors in health education. An overview of those principles is provided here:

- Learning is not a single event, it is continuous.

- If several of the human senses are utilized then learning is facilitated.

- People learn by doing, by being actively involved in the learning process.

- The learner's motivation is required for learning to occur.

- Learning is enhanced with immediate responses or reinforcement.

- We cannot teach another person, we can only facilitate their learning.

- A person learns only what he or she perceives as relevant.

- Learning experiences that involve changes in the self will be resisted if they are inconsistent with the self; relaxation of the self is required so that learning can be facilitated.

Gilbert et. al., (2011) also provide some basic educational principles that can help planners choose appropriate methods and sequence methods for interventions:

- Repetition is usually required for learning to occur. At least three exposures to the content are recommended.

- Learning is an active process involving dynamic interaction of the learner and the content being learned.

- Learning usually advances from the simple to the complex, from the known to the unknown and from the concrete to the abstract.

- Transfer learning is not automatic; so teaching should focus on transfer which is the ability to apply prior knowledge or skills to new situations.

- Behaviors and skills that are being taught must be practiced.

- Periods of practice with intermittent periods of rest result in more efficient learning.

Sometimes broad and non-specific principles may generate multiple interpretations and are unreliable. Theory goes beyond principle (Glanz, 1997).

Theories and Models in Health Education and Health Promotion

Health promotion and health education planning have foundations based in a multidisciplinary field of practice. Health promotion planning is most likely to be effective and successful when the process and plan is theory-based and theory-driven. The foundations of health promotion have evolved from various fields of practice such as biological, sociological, behavioral and health science disciplines. These disciplines, especially the social and behavioral sciences offer foundational theories and models that can guide the health education specialists in trying to explain existing human behavior, predict future behavior, and to plan interventions to bring about desired changes in health behavior and health status for individuals and communities. These theories are meaningful in health education and health promotion when accompanied by the specialists' strong foundations in biological sciences, epidemiology, biostatistics, and cultural competence.

Helping individuals, families, and communities establish responsible health behaviors is the central concern of health promotion and health education. Health behaviors are the actions of individuals, groups, organizations, and communities, and their associated determinants, correlates and consequences, i.e., social change, policy development and implementation, and enhanced quality of life (Glanz et. al., 1997). Theories provide tools to the health education specialist to use in examining health problems and in planning interventions to solve health problems.

Theory Defined

Glanz et. al., (1997) state that "a theory is a set of interrelated concepts, definitions, and propositions that presents a systematic view of events or situations by specifying relations among variables in order to explain and predict the events of the situations." A theory offers a general and simplified explanation of "why people act or do not act to maintain and/or promote the health of themselves, their families, organizations, and communities (Cottrell et. al., 2012, p. 100)." Theories have three important characteristics. They have generality, so that they can be applied broadly to a variety of health issues. Secondly, they are testable. Credible theory is supported by a strong research foundation that tests the theory in real health issues and applications. Thirdly, theories are abstract. According to Blalock (1969), theory does not represent a real system in the social sciences nor in health promotion and education; it only approximates reality. It is important to remember that theory deals with the ideal more than with the real.

> *Like empty coffee cups, theories have shapes and boundaries, but nothing inside. They become useful when filled with practical topics, goals, and problems* (Glanz and Rimer, 2005).

Theories can be classified as explanatory theories or theories of the problem, and change theories or theories of action (Sharma & Romas, 2012). Explanatory theory describes the reasons for why a problem exists, guiding the health education specialists' search for factors that contribute to a problem and that can be targeted for change. Examples of explanatory theories include the Health Belief Model and the Theory of Planned Behavior. Change theory guides the health education specialists in developing meaningful health interventions for defined health problems. It presents the concepts that can be translated into interventions, methods, and strategies, and offers a basis for program evaluation. Change theory helps program planners to be explicit about their assumptions for why a program will work. Two examples of change theories include Community Organization and Diffusion of Innovations.

While only a limited number of theories are presented in this textbook, theories, and models from a variety of disciplines explain problems, explain behaviors, and suggest ways to achieve behavioral change. A theoretical foundation provides researchers and program planners with a perspective from which to organize knowledge and to interpret factors and events. By telling the program planner the what, how, when, and why of a given health issue, theories can help guide program development in health education and health promotion. The "what" tells the planner the elements that should be considered as the targets for the intervention. The "why" informs the planners about the processes by which changes occur in the target variables. The "when" tells the planner about the timing and sequencing of planned interventions in order to achieve maximum effects. The "how" describes the methods and activities the planner will use to focus interventions; it includes the specific means of inducing changes in the explanatory variables. (Glanz, Lewis, & Rimer, 1990)

Models

Models are similar to theories when the theories are in the early development. Models are presented without the empirical evidence that is required for a theory. They may actually draw on a number of theories to help understand a particular problem in a certain setting or context. They are not as specified as theory. Models can be eclectic in the choices of theories that are used in them. Models can be used for guidance in the planning process. Many models are utilized to inform the program planning process, such as, PRECEDE-PROCEED (Green and Kreuter, 2005), social marketing, ecological planning approaches (Green et. al., 1994; Glanz et. al., 2005). In these cases, the models can serve as the vehicles by which the theories are applied. As previously stated, an example of a model used extensively for guidance in program planning is the PRECEDE-PROCEED (Green and Kreuter, 2005). This model provides guidance for planning at the macro level, helping health education planners identify the behaviors that must be targeted, what resources are available to use, how to mobilize the community, etc. Theories can provide guidance at the micro level, helping to identify the attitudes to change for health behavior change, the activities that are best for the targeted audience, which methods to employ, etc. (Sharma, 2012). There are models that have been thoroughly tested and are considered theories, but still have the word "model" in their names. The Health Belief Model and the Transtheoretical Model are examples of models that have undergone significant testing and have generated significant research findings supporting their use in program planning.

Theory Components

The critical components of a theory are constructs, concepts, variables, and constants. See Figure 5.1. Constructs are the building blocks of

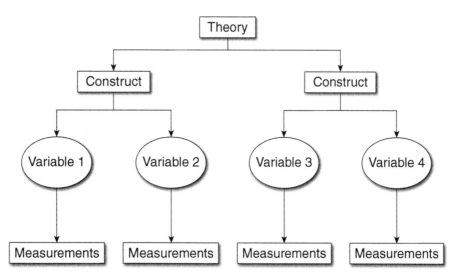

Figure 5.1 Conceptual representation of a theory

a theory and represent the primary elements and major components of a theory. Constructs are described as latent variables that lack empiricism; which means they cannot be observed through taste, touch, vision, smell, or hearing. Constructs organize and combine concepts or variables into one group or under one subheading in a theory. Constructs are specific and can be used only within the context of a given theory. Constructs are concepts and variables that have been developed or adopted for use in a particular theory (Kerlinger, 1986). Cornish (1980) described a concept as a generalized idea, a mental map or an image of some phenomena. A group of concepts under a given construct must have cohesion that is logical and real (Ledlow and Coppola, 2012). Actually concepts are variables or constants in a theory. Variables are defined as the empirical counterparts or the operational forms of constructs; meaning that they can be measured or observed by the senses (Green and Lewis, 1986; Glanz et. al., 1997). They are universally described and recognized. Variables can be measured and the measurements can vary or change. An example would be "weight." The variables direct how constructs in a given situation are to be measured. According to Glanz and Rimer (2005), variables should be matched to constructs when determining what should be measured in the evaluation of a theory-driven program.

Constants are concepts that do not vary or change. Sex can be a constant in some situations. In a program or research on the course of pregnancy, the sex of all participants would be female, a constant. However, in a program or research on heart disease, sex would be a variable that would identify participants as male or female.

The success of a program in health education and health promotion will depend on the health educators' uses of the most appropriate theories, models, and related practice strategies for a given health issue. Differing theories apply to different units of practice: individuals, groups, organizations, and communities. The selection of the theory begins with the problem definition, the hypothesis, the goal, the unit of practice, and the context of the practitioner's activities.

The use of theory in explaining, understanding, and predicting human and health behavior and in designing health promotion and health education programs is based on the belief that there are some commonalities across populations in factors that influence behavior and that there is consistency and predictability in the relationships among these factors. A great body of research and professional literature demonstrates that socioeconomic, racial, ethnic, and cultural differences among individuals and population groups have significant influence on the theoretical relationships among factors that determine health behaviors and health status. Socioeconomic, racial, ethnic, and cultural factors will often represent the beliefs, knowledge, attitudes, values, and skills that individuals and populations will bring to the program's methods and learning experiences. So regardless of the principles, theories, and models used, the socioeconomic, racial, ethnic and cultural factors and influences must also be considered in selecting interventions and methods. It would be a fatal program and professional error to assume that all individuals are the same and will fit into some theoretical box for the planners' purposes.

Learning and Behavior

Behavioral change will occur through developmental maturation, through learning or through both processes. Developmental maturation is the process manifested as an individual grows to fulfill his/her genetic human blueprint. Learning brings about changed behavior through experiences, insights, and perceptions. The health education specialist must be knowledgeable about both processes in helping individuals to achieve improved health outcomes. This chapter focuses on learning for behavior change and the theories that assist the professional in explaining and supporting behavioral change for improved health.

Generally, the professional literature supports that learning is more than an accumulation of knowledge. Learning is defined as a change in knowledge, skills, beliefs, attitudes, values, and behavior as a result of experience. Learning is required for survival and success. It influences decision-making about a wide range of health behaviors. However, learning is not the only influence on behavior. There are those factors that require the individual and/or communities to balance influences on their behavior: influences from personal preferences, family, friends, media, school, work, religion, culture, ethnicity, etc. These will be addressed in the discussion on the social ecological model.

Learning for behavior change involves more than the accumulation of knowledge or the collection of information. Learning actually occurs in three domains: cognitive domain, affective domain, and the psychomotor domain. The cognitive domain involves acquiring knowledge and information on an intellectual level, developing relationships with facts, truth, and principles. In health education the goal is behavior change which requires more than cognitive learning. In the cognitive domain there are certain educational objectives that must be achieved. The *Bloom's Taxonomy of Educational Objectives* (Bloom, 1956), has been instructive for educators for many years. Bloom provides a listing of cognitive objectives with examples of the cognitive abilities required for each. The following is a sampling of these cognitive abilities for each level of cognitive development.

1. *Knowledge:* naming, defining, describing, listing, identifying, matching, selecting, reproducing, labeling

2. *Comprehension:* explaining, describing, interpreting, converting, defending, distinguishing, generalizing, estimating, paraphrasing, predicting

3. *Application:* illustrating, predicting, applying, computing, changing, discovering, modifying, using, preparing, producing, relating, solving

4. *Analysis:* analyzing, categorizing, classifying, differentiating, discriminating, distinguishing, inferring, selecting, separating

5. *Synthesis:* concluding, proposing, synthesizing, composing, compiling, creating, designing, explaining, planning, revising, summarizing

6. *Evaluating:* contrasting, comparing, evaluating, appraising, concluding, describing, explaining, justifying, summarizing, supporting

While knowledge is necessary in the learning process, it is not sufficient to promote changed behavior in health. Health education specialists know that learning must also be reflected in attitudes, beliefs, values, and skills.

The affective domain relates to emotions, feelings, and attitudes. The primary goal of health education and health promotion is for people to voluntarily undertake responsible health behaviors. That means people determine what is best for them. Their choices will be personal and individual, influenced by their feelings, emotions, and attitudes about any given health issue. To force individuals to make choices against their wishes is unethical. Therefore the health education specialist through ethical programming and support services can assist populations in rational decision-making that honor their feelings, emotions, and attitudes. Appropriately planned and delivered learning experiences and new information may result in rational changed feelings, emotions, values, and attitudes about given health issues. Rational affective domain development coupled with knowledge produces attitudes, beliefs, and values that support establishing and changing health behaviors.

The psychomotor domain involves human motor skills and coordination. This domain involves the development of behavioral patterns and skills made by choice. The choices in the psychomotor domain will depend on selecting and developing specific behaviors and skills from among several alternatives. The decision-making and skill development depends on knowledge, attitudes, beliefs, and feelings, illustrating how the cognitive and the affective domain work together to affect the psychomotor domain. In other words, people will perform behaviors to support improved health, if they have the required knowledge, the emotions, and attitudes to support their desire to perform the behaviors. The work of the health education specialist is to provide learning experiences and support that help people develop the knowledge, the attitudes, beliefs, emotions and skills to voluntarily make the decisions to behave in health-enhancing ways.

Traditionally, learning and behavior are conceptualized as S-O-R: stimuli (S) are processed by the organism (O) and then produce a response (R). Learning is the result or product of stimuli, much of which are planned educational experiences. However, most stimuli are unplanned experiences and part of everyday life, coming from many places in the organism's environment. Some stimuli are planned experiences and are actually designed to influence behavior and to create new knowledge, perceptions, attitudes, feelings, experiences, and skills. Examples of such planned experiences include advertisements, marketing campaigns, and planned educational activities.

The manner in which the organism processes the stimuli determines the responses.

Stimuli (S) ⟶ Organism (O) ⟶ Response(R)

Figure 5.2 Conceptualization of the stimuli, organism, and response

The existing knowledge, previous experience, current attitudes, and even the mood, personality, gender, and socialization of the individual influences how she or he receives and processes a stimulus. The wide variation in how individuals are influenced by stimuli is partly the product of inherent human individuality, partly the product of learning, and partly the product of environmental circumstances and ongoing individual life events. The many competing stimuli are a challenge to consistency in human behavior. So humans are not passive recipients of stimuli, but active processors of stimuli. Individual responses to specific stimuli are not always immediate or predictable and are influenced by factors associated with being human—personality, capabilities, cognitive characteristics, and situational factors (Simons- Morton et. al., 1995).

Social Ecological Model

If health education specialists are to help populations become healthier, they will have to address many factors that impact health behaviors. It is not enough to address the individual and his or her behaviors only, health education specialists must reach beyond the intrapersonal level. In the Social Ecological Model of health behavior, the dimensions of health interact with the determinants of health at five hierarchical levels of influence: intrapersonal, interpersonal, organizational, community, and societal (or public policy). The health education specialist's ability to help populations change their behavior for improved health will depend on how these various levels of influence interact and impact the individual and how the individual impacts these various systems and levels of influence. The social ecological model is part of the ever expanding multi-level theories on health behavior change and has given rise to various versions of ecological perspectives. These ecological perspectives are most useful for examining behavior theories in the context of social, environmental, and cultural factors affecting disease and health interacting with various levels of influence that impact the individual and his/her health choices and behaviors. These interactions and the levels of influence must be considered in designing health education and health promotion interventions that successfully help health promotion program participants change behavior. Secondly, the model helps the investigator to plan strategies that target these multiple levels of influence on changing health risk factors and health behaviors for the individual, groups, and communities. These levels of influence include the following descriptions, but are not limited to these. McLeroy et. al. (1988) begin with the individual, but also include all the levels with which the individual interacts.

- Intrapersonal level (Individual characteristics that influence behavior): genetics, knowledge, attitudes, beliefs, values, skills, and self-efficacy.

- Interpersonal level (Family, friends, peers): Interpersonal processes and groups that provide identity and support to the individual.

- Organizational level (Churches, other organized worship centers, stores, community organizations): Providing context, rules, regulations, policies, and structures that constrain or promote behaviors for the individual, groups, and communities.

- Community level (Social networks, Community norms, Community regulations): At the community level, greater efforts are made to create healthful environment by addressing unemployment, homelessness, poverty, housing, violence, substance abuse, sedentary lifestyle that impacts the individual and the community.

- Public policy (Local, state, federal): Policies and laws that regulate or support healthy practices/actions.

Often planners and researchers combine the levels of organizations, community, and public policy into one category or level of community.

Many of the efforts to help individuals improve their risk status have centered on changing behavior at the intrapersonal levels. These have met with varying levels of success and failure. The problem is that research with multicultural populations has shown that interventions must do more than enhance the individual's knowledge and skill sets; they must also provide trusted social support in a safe environment. Family and peer support, organizational support and relevance, community factors, and cultural relevance are indeed important determinants of health for the target populations. The ecological approach or perspective demonstrates how more than one theory may be used to address health issues that are multilevel.

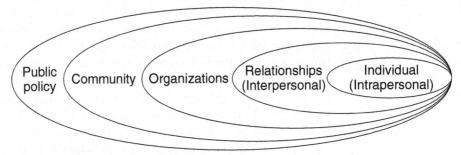

Figure 5.3 Social Ecological Model

© Kendall Hunt Publishing Company

Theory at the Intrapersonal Level

Lewin's Field Theory

Kurt Lewin along with other field theorists proposed that humans, when exposed to various stimuli, will usually organize the various stimuli into meaningful wholes or gestalts, influenced by context and overall effect. They then respond to these meaningful wholes or gestalts according to their relevance to important personal needs and goals. So each individual interprets a stimulus in terms of the whole field within which the stimulus is presented and the person's perceptual context that is shaped by personal total experiences.

Field theory is important to health promoters and health educators, because it shows that each person interprets stimuli from their own personal perceptual context. In providing learning experiences, it is important not only to consider the content but also the context in which the content is delivered to the learner. This explains why the same stimulus may be highly motivating for one individual but not to another.

Lewin proposed an especially useful theory and tool called force-field analysis. Force-field analysis proposes that the forces that exist in group situations are subject to systematic analysis, and that the continuing forces within a group situation influence one another (Butler, 1997). Behavior results from two sets of forces: change or driving forces and resisting or restraining forces. With change forces, the individual or group is pressured to move toward a goal. The resisting forces will cause the individual or group to resist change. These two sets of forces work against each other constantly.

So what might be the outcomes of these sets of forces working against each other? If the total influence of the change and resisting forces is equal, there is no action by the individual or group, and no change. When the change forces are stronger than the resisting forces, individual or group behavior is changed to achieve the goal. When the resisting forces are stronger, then there is no movement toward the goal. The health education specialist can use the force field analysis to plan interventions and methods that would do the following:

- increase the influence of the driving or change forces

- reduce the influence of restraining or resisting forces

- both increase change forces and decrease the resisting forces

The health education specialist would have to identify the change forces and resisting forces acting on the target population. This information may be apparent from the needs assessment. Then the planner would determine methods for increasing the change forces and reducing the resisting forces. Focus groups, surveys and interviews in the target population can reveal valued insights that would help the planner. Most importantly, involving representatives of the target population in the planning process will certainly inform and help identify and develop the methods that will influence the change forces and the resisting forces.

Table 5.1 Smoking cessation: An example of force-field analysis

Change forces	Resisting forces
• knowledge of the health risks of smoking on the individual and his or her family • inconvenience caused by laws restricting smoking in public places • growing social isolation of smokers	• pleasure that comes from smoking • reinforcement and acceptance by their peers • difficulty of withdrawal from an addictive drug

In this situation of smoking cessation, the health education specialist may use intervention strategies and methods that would encourage family members to support a loved one's decision to stop smoking; initiate and support smoking cessation programs in the community; or increase legislation to make smoking in public more restricted. These efforts would enhance the change forces. The resisting forces can be minimized by encouraging membership in peer groups that accept and support non-smokers, and giving smokers access to the physicians who can prescribe nicotine patches to reduce withdrawal problems. Addressing both the change forces and the resisting forces will be far more effective than addressing just one set of forces.

The Health Belief Model

The Health Belief Model (HBM) was developed in the 1950's by social psychologists in the US Public Health Service as a way of explaining the overwhelming failure of people to participate in disease detection and disease prevention programs. The HBM has its basis in Lewin's decision-making model. It has been used to describe and explain several health behaviors (Janz and Becker, 1984).

HBM proposes that health-related action depends upon three categories of factors.

- the presence of sufficient motivation or health concern to make health issues relevant or prominent

- the belief of one's susceptibility or vulnerability to a serious health problem, condition, or perceived threat

- the belief that adhering to a particular health recommendation or health behavior would be beneficial in reducing the perceived threat at a personally acceptable cost. The cost relates to the perceived barriers that must be overcome to follow the recommendation (Rosenstock et. al., 1988; McKenzie and Smeltzer, 2001)

The HBM has been applied to many health behaviors to address an individual's beliefs about health and their health—specific behaviors. According to the model, the beliefs that mediate health behavior are (1) perceived susceptibility for contracting the health problem, (2) perceived severity of the health threat, (3) the perceived benefits of available and effective actions that reduce the health threat, and (4) the perceived barriers of costs or the negative aspects associated with engaging in the health behavior. Cues to action are the necessary triggers for the initiation of behavior.

According to the HBM (Rosenstock, 1974), in order for a person to take action or perform a health behavior to avoid disease or illness, he or she must believe that:

1. the individual is personally susceptible to the disease or illness

2. if the individual has the health problem, it will be severe enough to negatively affect his or her life

3. taking the recommended action or performing a recommended health behavior will have beneficial effects

4. the barriers to taking action or taking on the new behavior do not overwhelm the benefits

An HBM Application:

Carla is a health education specialist assigned to conduct classes on HIV/AIDS prevention with a group of twenty 15 and 16 year old girls. Throughout the presentation she notices restlessness and boredom. As she finishes her presentation, she questions the young ladies and finds out that they do not think her message is appropriate for them. They inform her that none of them are involved in doing drugs, and that HIV/AIDS is a problem for gay men and IV drug users.

Carla makes changes in her methods for the next session with the girls. She begins class with a video presentation on HIV/AIDS prevention that featured teenage girls and boys who had contracted HIV through heterosexual sexual intercourse. Then she introduced a young adult woman from the local speakers' bureau who had contracted HIV through heterosexual intercourse while in college. The guest speaker shared with the girls how HIV had changed her life and her dreams. That session had a very sobering effect on every girl in the class and they wanted Carla to tell them more about how to avoid the disease.

Carla was able to change methods that made her message more relevant to her target audience. She chose a video with characters and a speaker that were closer in age to the girls. The chosen methods forced the girls to heighten their perceived susceptibility to HIV/AIDS. They also began to consider the perceived benefits of changing behavior to prevent the disease. Carla understood through the Health Belief Model that helping the girls recognize their personal susceptibility, the severity of the disease, and the perceived threat of the disease would improve the likelihood of changing their behavior to personally prevent the disease in their own lives.

The Transtheoretical Model and Stages of Change

The Transtheoretical Model, or the Stages of Change, is a model that explains the stages that the majority of people seem to experience as they attempt to change health behaviors over time. Having its roots in psychotherapy, James Prochaska developed this model after he completed comparative analyses on eighteen therapy systems and a critical review of three hundred therapy outcome studies. As a result of his research Prochaska found that there were some common processes involved in behavior change. The Transtheoretical model explains that people move from precontemplation to contemplation, to preparation, to action and into maintenance (Prochaska, 1979, 1984; Prochaska and Di Clemente, 1983). These stages are precontemplation, contemplation, preparation, action, and maintenance and are defined below.

1. Precontemplation Stage: The time frame in which people are not thinking about making a change in their behavior during the next six months.

2. Contemplation Stage: The timeframe in which people become aware that a problem exists, are seriously thinking about making a change, but have not made a commitment to action.

3. Preparation Stage: People actively plan change within the next month.

4. Action Stage: People are obviously making changes in their behavior, experiences, and/or environment in order to correct a health problem.

5. Maintenance Stage: Change that starts in the action stage continues through six months after taking the obvious action that started the change in the behavior.

Besides the construct of the stages of change, the Transtheoretical Model also presents the construct for the processes of change (Prochaska et. al., 1997). The processes of change are the covert and overt activities that people use to progress through the stages of change. The health education specialist will find the construct for processes of change to be important guides for developing intervention strategies. They include for the individual:

- Consciousness raising: finding and learning new facts, ideas, and tips that support the healthy behavioral change

- Dramatic relief: experiencing the negative emotions (fear, worry, anxiety) that go along with unhealthy behavioral risks

- Self-reevaluation: realizing that the behavioral change is an important part of one's identity as a person

- Environmental re-evaluation: realizing the negative impact of the unhealthy behavior or the positive impact of the healthy behavior on one's proximal social and physical environment

- Self-liberation: making a firm commitment to change

- Helping relationships: seeking and using social support for the healthy behavioral change

- Counter-conditioning: substituting healthier alternative behaviors and cognitions for the unhealthy behaviors

- Stimulus control: removing reminders or cues to engage in the unhealthy behavior and adding cues or reminders to engage in the healthy behavior

- Social liberation: realizing that the social norms are changing in the direction of supporting the healthy behavioral change

As health education specialists help people progress through the stages of change, they must understand and apply the processes of change. The most basic principle is that different processes of change must be applied at different stages. Prochaska, DiClemente and Norcross (1992) discovered that in the early stages, people apply cognitive, affective and evaluative processes to move through the stages of change. However, in the later stages people are more involved with commitments, conditioning, contingencies, environmental controls, and support for progressing toward maintenance.

The Transtheoretical Model has been used in addressing addictive behaviors, smoking cessation, condom use, weight control and HIV prevention (McKenzie et. al., 2013). People move through behavior change at different rates. The progression through the stages of change is not linear.

The majority of people undergoing change will have relapses, which is part of the change cycle. This reminds the health education specialist that not all people are ready for change at the same time, nor do they take action for change at the same time. The model also helps the health education specialist to identify people who are ready for making changes in their health behavior, and for predicting who may be successful in changing behavior. Health education specialists can be proactive in designing programs that help individuals to become ready for change.

The Theory of Reasoned Action

The Theory of Reasoned Action developed by Fishbein and Ajzen (1975) attempts to explain volitional behaviors. It provides a way to study attitudes towards behaviors. The theory distinguishes among the constructs of attitude, belief, behavioral intention, and behavior. According to the theory, the most important determinant of behavior is a person's behavioral intention. A person's intention to engage in a particular behavior is formed by two elements:

- The person's own attitude toward performing the behavior

- The subjective norm, i.e.,

  - The person's beliefs about what significant others think the individual should do

  - How important the relevant other's opinions are to the person

The construct of subjective norm deals with the person's beliefs about what relevant others think the person should do. So a person's decision to perform a given behavior is partly dependent on what he or she believes others think he or she should do, and that the person cares about what these others think. An example of the theory of reasoned action's construct of subjective norm in health promotion is the employee who wants to enroll in a worksite weight control program, because he believes his employer wants him to do so.

The Theory of Planned Behavior

Theory of reasoned action is most effective in "dealing with purely volitional behaviors, but complications are encountered when the theory is applied to behaviors that are not fully under volitional control (McKenzie and Smeltzer, 1997)." Even when an individual wants to change a behavior to improve health and the intent is high, other non-motivational factors could prevent successful behavior change. The theory of planned behavior as an extension of the theory of reasoned action, addresses this problem. The theory of planned behavior includes the constructs of (1) attitude toward behavior, (2) subjective norm, and (3) perceived behavioral control. The perceived behavioral control reflects the person's belief about the ease or difficulty in performing a behavior, past experiences, and anticipated barriers and obstacles. Perceived behavioral control has motivational implications for behavioral intentions. Perceived behavioral control must be strong for behavioral change to occur. If the attitude toward the behavior and the subjective norm are high and the person's perception of control over the behavior is low, then there is likely to be little success in adopting the new behavior. In matters such as smoking cessation or weight reduction, volition and motivation are not enough. The person must believe that he or she has control over whether or not he or she can really change behaviors for successful health outcomes.

Theory at the Interpersonal Level

Social Cognitive Theory

Social Learning Theory (SLT), as the theory was originally named, explains human behavior in terms of a continuous interaction among cognitive, behavioral and environmental determinants (Parcel and Baranowski, 1981). SLT proposed that a person's behaviors are responses to which other people apply reinforcements. Reinforcement can be used to change a person's behavior directly or vicariously by observing others being rewarded for their behavior and then copying their rewarded behavior. Bandura and Walters (1963) concluded that individuals change their behaviors because they desire to emulate role models who are being rewarded for their behaviors. While there are several versions of the Social Learning Theory, there are basic tenets.

1. Response consequences (such as rewards or punishments) influence the likelihood that a person will repeat a particular behavior in a given situation.

2. Humans can learn by observing others, and they also learn by participating in an act personally. Learning by observing others is called vicarious learning.

3. Individuals are most likely to model behavior that they observe in others with whom they identify and respect. Identification with others is a function of the degree to which a person is perceived to be similar to one's self, in addition to the degree of emotional attachment that is felt toward an individual.

Albert Bandura added to the theory, the constructs of self-efficacy, modeling or vicarious learning, reciprocal determinism, and that there can be significant temporal variation in time lapse between cause and effect. Through Bandura's work (1986), his version of Social Learning Theory became known as Social Cognitive Theory (SCT). Bandura (1986) stated that the Social Cognitive Theory expresses learning to be an internal mental process (cognitive process) that may or may not be reflected in immediate behavioral change. SCT considers the role of personal factors (e.g., beliefs, attitudes, expectations, and memory) in addition to the environmental and behavioral aspects of learning. SCT approaches human behavior in terms of a continuous interaction among personal, behavioral, and environmental determinants. An underlying assumption is that behavior is dynamic and depends on the environment and personal constructs which influence each other simultaneously. The continuing interaction among a person, his or her behavior, and the environment is called *reciprocal determinism* and is illustrated in Figure 5.4.

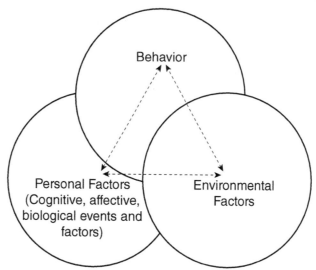

Figure 5.4 Reciprocal Determinism: Interactional, triadic, reciprocal model between environment, personal factors, and behavior

© Kendall Hunt Publishing Company

Bandura introduced constructs for application in SCT. These are especially important in health promotion interventions. See Table 5.2.

Table 5.2 Social Cognitive Constructs and Definitions.

SCT constructs	Definitions
Knowledge	The learning of facts and gaining greater insights related to an action, idea, object, person, or situation
Outcome expectations	The anticipation of the desired outcomes that would follow as a result of engaging in the behavior that is being addressed
Outcome expectancies	The value that a person places on the probable outcomes
Situational perception	How one perceives and interprets the environment or situation in which one is surrounded
Environment	The physical and social circumstances in the environment that surrounds a person
Self-efficacy	The confidence in one's ability to establish or change a behavior
Self-efficacy in over-coming impediments	The confidence that one has in overcoming barriers while performing the targeted behavior
Goal setting or self-control	The ability to set goals for chosen behaviors and developing plans to accomplish these goals
Emotional coping	The techniques that one uses to control emotional and physiological challenges associated with the establishment of new behaviors

A number of techniques based on SCT have been developed and have been determined to be effective in health education and health promotion for inducing behavior change (Butler, 2001).

- *Revising expectations*
  This technique involves helping individuals and populations revise how they view outcomes of their behaviors realistically. An illustration of this technique is in helping adolescents see that "everyone" does not do drugs and that they can make different choices. With reliable learning experiences and new knowledge, they will see the expected outcomes of refraining from drug use will improve their health and provide greater life options from which they can choose. Revising expectations is commonly used by health educators.

- *Modeling (imitation)*
  The process of modeling provides knowledge about the healthful behavior and provides concrete examples of how to do it. Learners can learn the new behavior by observing others successfully execute the behavior.

- *Building self-efficacy*
  The health education specialist must be aware of the learner's knowledge, skills, and perceptions of their abilities. Using this information, the learner is assisted in setting realistic goals for developing new behaviors. The learner's process for behavior change is taking small steps to accomplish the goal. Each step enables the learner to be successful and grow in self-efficacy.

- *Contracting*
  In this technique, the learner and at least one other person agree by written contract to achieve a specific behavior. Specific conditions for successful completion of the contract are indicated: the specific behaviors, conditions for measuring successful completion and fulfillment of contract terms, the timeframe, rewards or consequences. This technique usually requires recordkeeping by the participants and the health education specialist.

- *Self-monitoring*
  Self-monitoring is one technique that requires the learner to think about the processes required to achieve behavior change and to set realistic goals. The learner must then monitor his or her progress in achieving the targeted behavior. Self-monitoring is actually like having a contract with oneself.

Theory at the Community Level

Health education/promotion professionals will plan what they believe is an effective program and will want to be sure that the target population will participate in the program for its duration. Therefore health education specialists require skills in marketing and psychology in order to attract the target population and keep them involved in order for behavior change to occur. In marketing a product, the process would come down to offering benefits that the consumer is willing to pay a price for and with which the consumer would be satisfied. In health promotion, program planners would like to exchange costs and benefits with those in the target population. Health educators would like to exchange the benefits of participation in health promotion programs (the objectives or outcomes of the programs they planned) for the costs of the program, which come from the participants, such as their time, money, and effort. Unlike applying marketing principles to a line of clothing or a new car, health promotion programs are health enhancement programs that do not have material objects, but instead they market awareness, knowledge, attitudes, skills, and behavior. For this reason, the marketing of health promotion programs falls into a special type of marketing called social marketing.

Social Marketing

Social marketing, while based on commercial marketing principles, is indeed different when applied to health education and health promotion. Social marketing is a process for influencing human behavior for the purpose of benefiting society and not for commercial purposes or profit. It is used in a variety of situations to influence behaviors and choices on a large scale. In health promotion it can be used to influence the use of health education programs, increase health care utilization, or to communicate campaigns to encourage individuals and groups to change attitudes and behaviors.

Social marketing process is used for planning programs or interventions for large defined populations and its process is similar to the traditional health education program planning process. While there are some differences in terminology, both processes include assessment of potential consumers or target audience, setting specific goals and objectives, planning, implementing, evaluating, and modifying the intervention or campaign. The marketing concepts used in social marketing are consumer orientation, exchange or exchange theory, market segmentation and consumer analysis, demand, competition, the marketing mix, positioning, consumer satisfaction, and brand loyalty (Bensley and Brookins-Fisher, 2009).

Consumer orientation means that the health education specialist or planner is focused on meeting the needs and desires of the consumers in the process of helping them achieve behavior change. In health education, the most important activity is learning as much as possible about the consumer. The health educator must remember that consumers make voluntary choices about changing behaviors or making choices among competing products, offerings and ideas. The more that is known and honored about the consumers will influence the voluntary choices that they make and the success of the programs or services.

Exchange theory implies the transfer or transaction of something valuable between two individuals or groups. In social marketing, the emphasis of this transaction is voluntary and underscores the benefits to the consumer. If a program's participants are encouraged to increase physical activity, the costs to the participants might be their loss of family time, loss of time for television watching, loss of free time, and money paid for transportation to the program site, etc. The benefits for their increased physical activity must be more attractive than the costs. These benefits may be feeling healthier, having more energy, desired weight loss, etc.

Market segmentation or audience segmentation and consumer analysis is central to a social marketing plan. The social marketer identifies distinct groups of people or segments who are similar to each other in various characteristics and are expected to respond to messages in similar ways. These segments may be based on geographic factors, demographic factors, medical history factors, personality characteristics, attitudinal factors, behavioral factors, etc. After identifying the segments, knowledge, attitude, and behavior data are collected from the target audience by using qualitative methods such as focus groups, in-depth interviews, case studies, or quantitative studies using surveys.

The key constructs in social marketing are product, price, place, and promotion and are also referred to as the marketing mix. Product is the desired behavior or offering that is intended for the target audience or consumers to adopt. Price is the tangible and/or the intangible things that the consumer has to give up in order to adopt the new idea or product. Place is where the target audience will perform the behavior. Promotion is the mechanism or methods by which the health education specialist gets the message across to the consumers. A promotion may include a mix of advertising in various media formats, incentives, face to face selling by spokespersons, and public relations that are best suited for the consumers.

Experts in the field of social marketing have added other constructs to the marketing mix that address the social and non-profit funding base of social marketing. These components include publics, partnership, policy, and purse strings.

Publics refer to the primary and secondary external and internal stakeholders that must be considered in planning a social marketing campaign that seeks to change behavior. Partnership addresses the importance of collaborating and partnering with other organizations that can bring expertise and resources to complex problems. Policy relates to the laws, and policies that can affect the context and environment in which the behavioral change must occur. Purse strings deal with various funding sources that are needed to support the social marketing campaign.

Other constructs to be considered in the social marketing campaign are positioning, consumer satisfaction and brand loyalty. In commercial marketing, positioning is creating a personality for the product that the consumer recognizes and expects to take care of their need or problem effectively. The same is true for positioning in social marketing. The proper positioning becomes clear to the planners as they learn about the consumers and their needs, desires, and resources. Consumer satisfaction is the goal of social marketing. Consumers want at least what they expect from the product or service and more than they expect is even better. Satisfied consumers will share their positive experiences with others. Dissatisfied consumers will also share their negative experiences with others. Brand loyalty is the consistent selection and preference for a particular product or service that has proven itself to be effective, satisfactory and reliable over time.

Andreasen (1995) reminds those who design social marketing campaigns that the process is challenging. He recommends six stages for social marketing for producing successful campaigns:

1. *Listening stage* in which background analysis and listening to the target audience is done (the assessment stage).
2. *Planning stage* in which the marketing mission, goals, objectives, and strategy are clearly defined.
3. *Structuring stage* in which marketing organization, procedures, benchmarks, and feedback mechanisms are established.
4. *Pretesting stage* in which key program elements are tested.
5. *Implementing stage* in which the strategy is put into effect.
6. *Monitoring stage* in which program progress is tracked and evaluated.

These stages for social marketing are very similar to the health education process that will be presented later in this textbook.

Diffusion of Innovations Theory

Diffusion of Innovation theory is strongly based in marketing theory, but also involves the communication channels necessary to promote an innovation. Diffusion refers to the process by which new ideas, objects or practice are adopted by individuals in target populations. Diffusion theories view communication as a two-way process, rather than one of merely "persuading" an audience to take action. There is a two-step flow of communication, in which opinion leaders mediate the impact of mass media and emphasize the value of social networks, or interpersonal channels, over and above mass media, for adoption decisions. For an example, health professionals and community leaders are especially important allies and communication channels for new ideas, practices, programs and products to improve health. As they repeat the same information that is provided through mass media channels, the chances that the target audience will act positively toward the innovation increases.

There are four constructs in the diffusion of innovations theory (Rogers, 2003). The first is innovation. Innovations are new ideas, practices, services, or products that are offered to individuals and groups who perceive them as new. It does not matter how long the idea, product or practice has existed, what is important is that the target population views it as new. A limited number of attributes for an innovation are presented in Table 5.3.

Table 5.3 Attributes of Innovations

Attributes	Definition	Application
Relative Advantage	The degree to which an innovation is seen as better than the idea, practice, program, or product it replaces	Point out unique benefits: monetary value convenience, time saving, prestige, etc.
Compatibility	How consistent the innovation is with values, habits, experience, and needs of potential adopters	Tailor innovation for the intended audience's values, norms, or situation.
Complexity	How difficult the innovation is to understand and/or use	Create program/idea/product to be uncomplicated, easy to use and understand.
Trialability	Extent to which the innovation can be experimented with before a commitment to adopt is required	Provide opportunities to try on a limited basis, e.g., free samples, introductory sessions, money-back guarantee.
Observability	Extent to which the innovation provides tangible or visible results	Assure visibility of results: feedback or publicity.

The second construct is communication channels. Communication channels are the links between those who have knowledge and expertise regarding the innovation and the individuals and population who have not adopted the innovation. Time is the third construct. Time is the interval between the target population's awareness of the innovation and the adoption of the innovation. Finally, the fourth construct for this theory is social system, which addresses how people relate to each other as individuals, families, groups, organizations, and communities. In this theory it is important to know how similar group members are. Similarity of group members is homophily. Innovations generally spread faster among individuals and groups that have much in common and are more similar, enhancing the diffusion of the innovation.

Other aspects of the social system are the social networks, change agent, and opinion leaders. Social networks are physical or virtual person-centered webs of social relationships that lend support, friendship and communication. Social networks may actually govern the pace at which innovations are adopted. The change agent is the person who positively influences the potential adopter. This person or persons may be the health education specialist or other influential health provider. Change agents will be involved in promoting the intervention and innovation. Opinion leaders are individuals who are influential in communities and can effectively influence the beliefs and actions of their colleagues, positively or negatively. Opinion leaders' support should be solicited early and they should be recruited to the program early.

Diffusion theory can demonstrate the process of marketing innovations or health promotion interventions, as health education specialists examine how their program will be adopted. When the consumers adopt an innovation they are referred to as adopters.

Rogers (1983) explained the diffusion of innovation in populations, or the adoption patterns of the innovation by adopters, based on when

Diffusion of Innovations

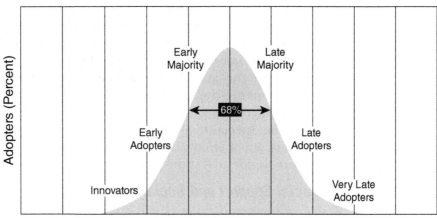

Figure 5.5 Adopter categories and the bell-shaped curve

they adopt innovations. Rogers used a bell-shaped curve divided into adopter categories to describe this phenomenon.

The value of the diffusion theory in health promotion programs is its ability to distinguish the characteristics of people in the target population and consistently predict how people will participate in the health promotion innovations. The diffusion of innovation theory, as represented by the normal bell-shaped curve, identifies innovators as those persons who fall in the portion of the curve that is left of -2 standard deviations from the mean. Innovators who are 2% to 3% of the target population would probably become involved with a health program because they heard about it and wanted to be the first participants. They are usually ahead of their time.

Early adopters represent about 14% of the target population, -2 to -1 standard deviations on the curve. Early adopters are those people who are usually interested in the innovation, but they are not the first to sign up. They usually wait on the innovators so that they can be sure the innovation is useful. Early adopters are seen as opinion leaders by the target population and respected by that population.

The next two groups, early majority and late majority, represent between -1 standard deviation and the mean and between the mean and +1 standard deviation. Each of these groups is about 34% of the target population. The early majority takes more time to deliberate before making a decision. The late majority takes even more time for making the decision, because they are more skeptical and are not likely to become involved until most members of the target population are participating in the health promotion program.

The late adopters and the very late adopters, also known as laggards, are the 16% of the target population represented by the part of the curve greater than +1 standard deviation. Laggards are not usually interested in new innovations, so they would be the last to participate. The very late adopters are also populations that are hard to reach. They may not even become participants in the health promotion program. Laggards may have limited communication networks.

While adoption, the continuation or integration of the innovation into the lifestyle of the target population is very important, the health education specialist must really know the characteristics of the target population and the attributes and characteristics of the innovation. Some innovations are simple while others are complex. As with all theories and models there are some disadvantages in using this theory, if the health education specialist does not know her or his target population. How populations adopt innovations is greatly affected by socioeconomic status, culture, residential status, etc.

Social Support and Social Network Theory

Cohen and Wills (1985) reviewed and organized the literature on social support and well-being. They tried to determine whether the positive association between social support and well-being may be attributed more to an overall beneficial effect of support (director model) or to a process of support that protects persons from the potentially adverse effects of stressful events (buffering model). The research studies were divided by whether a measure assesses support structure (the existence of relationships) or function (the extent to which one's interpersonal relationships provide particular resources).

Numerous studies have demonstrated that the extent and nature of one's social relationships affect one's health (House et. al., 1988). An understanding of the impact of social relationships on health status, health behaviors, and health decision-making can contribute greatly to the development of effective interventions for preventing the onset of diseases and promoting health. Various conceptual models and theories have guided research in this area, but there is no one theory or model that actually explains the linkage. Social network is a person-centered web of social relationships. The provision of social support is one of the important functions of social relationships. Therefore social networks are linkages between people that may (or may not) provide social support and that may serve other functions in addition to support.

The structure of social networks can be described in terms of characteristics such as:

- **Reciprocity:** the extent to which resources and support are both given and received in a relationship

- **Intensity:** the extent to which a relationship is characterized by emotional closeness

- **Complexity:** the extent to which a relationship serves a variety of functions

- **Homogeneity:** the extent to which network members are similar in terms of demographic characteristics such as age, race, and socioeconomic status

- **Geographical dispersion:** the extent to which network members live in close proximity to the focal person

- **Density:** the extent to which network members know and interact with each other

House (1981) defined social support by the functional content of relationships.

- **Emotional support:** the provision of empathy, love, trust, and caring

- **Instrumental support:** provides tangible aid and services, that directly assists a person in need

- **Informational support:** provides advice, suggestions, and information that a person can use in problem-solving

- **Appraisal support:** provides information that is useful for self-evaluation purposes that is constructive feedback, affirmation, and social comparison

While the four types of support can be presented conceptually as separate, in reality relationships that offer one type of support will also provide the other types of support. Heaney and Israel (1997) hypothesized a direct interplay of social networks and physical, mental and social health, each affecting the other in a bidirectional feedback loop. They reasoned that social networks would offer persons close relationships and the esteem of others, a sense of belonging, and self-esteem that would tend to improve health regardless of the effects of other factors on health. Similarly, they hypothesized that individual coping resources, organizational and community resources, and health behaviors would also have a bidirectional interplay with health. Furthermore, the degree of individual coping resources would affect stress, and so would the degree of organizational/ community resources. Individual coping resources might include the ability to problem-solve, to access new contacts and information, and increased perceived control. Organizational/community resources might be reflected in community empowerment.

Heaney and Israel (1997) proposed that strengthening social networks and enhancing the exchange of social support may increase a community's ability to garner its resources and solve problems. The work by Minkler (1990) and Eng and Parker (1994) documented that several community interventions have shown how intentional network building and strengthening social support within communities are associated with enhanced community capacity and control for changes in health status. The availability of improved individual or community resources increases the likelihood that stressors will be dealt with so that adverse health consequences are reduced. This is known as the buffering effect. Also, social networks and social support may mediate the frequency and duration of exposure to stressors. Finally, social networks and social support have potential effects on health behaviors. By mediating behavioral risk factors, preventive health practices and illness behaviors, social networks, and social support may have an impact on the incidence of, diagnosis of, and recovery from disease.

The use of social support and social network theory can help the health professional in designing effective interventions and methods to change health behaviors and health status for individuals and communities. Heaney and Israel (1997) suggest the following types of possible social network interventions with examples of activities and methods.

- *Enhancing existing social network linkages:* training of network members in skills for support provision; training of indigenous individuals in mobilizing and maintaining social networks; systems approach (i.e., marital counseling, family therapy, mediation services, etc.)

- *Developing new social network linkages:* creating linkages to mentors; developing buddy systems; coordinating self-help groups

- *Enhancing networks through the use of indigenous natural helpers:* identification of natural helpers in the community; analysis of natural helpers' existing social networks; training of natural helpers in health topics and community problem-solving strategies

- *Enhancing networks at the community level through participatory problem-solving:* Identification of overlapping networks within the community; examination of social network characteristics of members of the selected need or target area; facilitation of ongoing community problem identification and problem-solving

Health professionals have effectively used these interventions to identify, recruit and train people who are natural helpers in the target population and assist individuals in a specific social network and community. The natural helpers are often referred to as lay health advisors or community health advisors. They are trained to provide information on specific health issues, information on and access to health and community resources and services, emotional support, and provide leadership in community problem solving.

A Framework for Planning Practice and Research

Frameworks are planning tools, which incorporate theories or models or parts of them. One of the most popular of the planning frameworks used in health education/promotion program planning is the PRECEDE-PROCEED Model. While there are other frameworks and models that can be used for program planning, PRECEDE-PROCEED is one of the well-developed planning tools that can be used to integrate diverse theoretical frameworks.

PRECEDE-PROCEED Model

Green and Kreuter (2005) designed PRECEDE-PROCEED as a planning model for health education and health promotion programs. It is an ecological approach to planning for health promotion interventions. The model originated in the 1970s. The acronym PRECEDE stands for predisposing, reinforcing, and enabling causes in educational diagnosis and evaluation. PROCEED is the acronym for policy, regulatory, and organizational constructs in education and environmental development. One of the strong principles upon which the model is based is the principle of participation. The principle emphasizes active participation of the target audience in defining their own issues, priorities, and goals in developing and implementing solutions for those issues. Achieving healthy behavioral change is greatly enhanced by the active participation of the target population. At every phase of the model, the health professional must include the target population (Green and Kreuter, 1991). In 2005, PRECEDE-PROCEED model was updated and now has eight phases in the planning process instead of the nine original phases in the planning process (Green and Kreuter, 2005). According to Green and Kreuter (2005, p. 18), the most important hallmarks of the PRECEDE-PROCEED Model are: "(1) flexibility and scalability, (2) evidence–based process and evaluability, (3) its commitment to the principle of participation, and (4) its provision of a process for appropriate adaptation of evidence-based 'best practices'. "

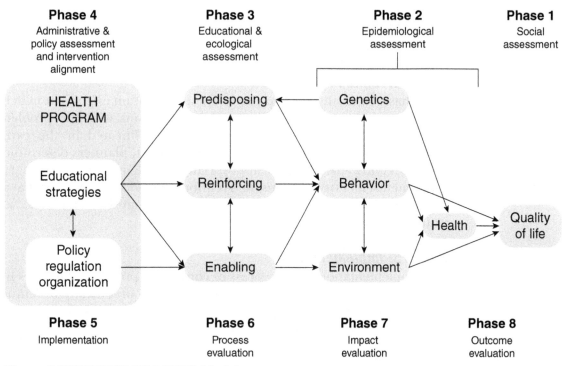

Figure 5.6 PRECEDE-PROCEED Model

Green, L. W. & Kreuter, M. W. (2005). *Health program planning: An educational and ecological approach (4th ed.).* Boston: McGraw-Hill.

Phase 1: Social Assessment

The social assessment phase assesses the quality of life in a community. The social assessment looks at both the objective and subjective data that reveals high-priority problems and/or aspirations for the common good of the population. From both primary and secondary data, economic and social indicators and the population's documentation define the individuals' and community's quality of life.

Phase 2: Epidemiological Assessment

The epidemiological assessment phase delineates the extent, distribution, and causes of a health problem found in the defined population. The planners use data to identify and rank health goals or problems that may contribute to problems identified in phase 1. This phase includes mortality, morbidity, and disability data as well as genetic, behavioral, and environmental factors. It is important that planners rank the health problems because there are rarely enough resources to address all problems.

Phase 3: Educational and Ecological Assessment

The educational and ecological assessment is the explanation of the specific health-related actions that will most likely cause positive health outcomes. Phase 3 identifies and classifies factors that can influence a given health behavior into predisposing, enabling and reinforcing factors. These factors can facilitate or hinder behavioral change in the individuals targeted by the plan.

Phase 4: Administrative and Policy Assessment and Intervention Alignment

Phase 4 actually has two parts. The intervention alignment matches appropriate methods, strategies, and interventions with the problems, projected changes and outcomes that were delineated in the earlier phases. The administrative and policy assessment, planners determine if resources and capabilities are appropriate and adequate for the program components, identify previous interventions and address any gaps that are apparent, and then map the specific interventions, methods, and strategies.

Phase 5: Implementation

Implementation is the process of converting program objectives into actions through policy changes, regulation, and organization. Planners address any factors that impede the intervention's progress in serving the target population. The intervention or program begins.

Phase 6: Process Evaluation

Process evaluation is the assessment of policies, materials, personnel, performance, quality of practice or services, the experiences of the target population in receiving program service, other inputs, and implementation experiences.

Phase 7: Impact Evaluation

Impact evaluation assesses immediate effects of the intervention on targeted behaviors and/or environments. The impact assessment determines program effects on intermediate objectives that include changes in predisposing, enabling, and reinforcing factors.

Phase 8: Outcome Evaluation

Outcome evaluation determines the effects of the program on its ultimate objectives, including changes in health, social benefits and/or the quality of life.

The health education specialists have major responsibilities for planning, implementing and evaluating health education and health promotion interventions. Planning models certainly help the professionals Zeffectively and efficiently fulfill these responsibilities. Planning models like the PRECEDE-PROCEED Model help the planner to grasp three fundamen-tal assumptions: (1) all planning must begin with appropriate assessments; (2) health and health risks have multiple causes and (3) efforts to address health and health risk change must be multilevel and multidimensional.

Application Opportunity

Mark is a health education specialist designing a drug prevention program for young adolescent males. He has been directed to develop the program based on the Social Cognitive Theory in order to teach them refusal skills for avoiding the use of drugs. He has asked you to assist him in this assignment. As part of Mark's assessment with these young men Mark conducted a focus group, asking them questions for discussion about drug use in their community. They talked about their friends, relatives, and neighbors who used drugs from early ages. Some of them thought that they might eventually succumb to that same lifestyle, since everybody else does.

1. As a health education/promotion professional, describe at least 2 concerns that you have for this group of young men.

2. Using the social cognitive theory, what would be four (4) factors or constructs that you would consider as you plan an intervention for this population?

3. Using the social cognitive theory, design a draft of a health education/promotion program using any or all of the four (4) factors that you identified in item 2 above.

References

Andreasen, A. R. 1994. "Social Marketing: Its Definition and Domain." *Journal of Public Policy & Marketing* 13 (1): 108–114.

Bandura, A., and R. H. Walters. 1963. *Social Learning and Personality Development*. New York: Holt, Rinehart and Winston.

Bandura, A. 2004. "Health Promotion by Social Cognitive Means." *Health Education and Behavior* 31: 143–64.

Bensley, R. J. and J. Brookins-Fisher (editors). 2009. *Community Health Education Methods: A Practical Guide (3rd edition)*. Sudbury: Jones and Bartlett Publishers.

Butler, J. T. 1997. *Principles of Health Education and Health Promotion (2nd edition)*. Englewood: Morton Publishing Company.

Butler, J. T. 2001. *Principles of Health Education and Health Promotion*, 3rd ed. Belmont, CA: Wadsworth/Thomas Learning.

Cohen, S., and T. A. Wills. 1985. "Stress, Social Support, and the Buffering Hypothesis." *Psychological Bulletin* 98 (2): 310–57.

Coreil, J. 2010. Social and Behavioral Foundations of Public Health. Los Angeles: Sage Publications, Inc.

Cottrell, R. R., J. T. Girvan, and J. F. McKenzie. 2012. *Principles and Foundations of Health Promotion and Education*. Boston: Benjamin Cummings.

Eng, E., and E. Parker. 1994. "Measuring Community Competence in the Mississippi Delta: The Interface Between Program Evaluation and Empowerment." *Health Education and Behavior* 21 (2): 199–220.

Fishbein, M. and I. Ajzen. 1975. *Beliefs, Attitudes, Intention and Behavior: An Introduction to Theory and Research*. Reading MA: Addison-Wesley.

Gilbert, G. G., R. G. Sawyer, & E. B. McNeill. 2011. *Health Education: Creating Strategies for School and Community Health (3rd edition)*. Sudbury: Jones and Bartlett Publishers.

Glanz, K., F. M. Lewis, & B. K. Rimer (Eds.). 1997. *Health Behavior and Health Education: Theory, research, and practice (2nd edition)*. San Francisco: Jossey-Bass.

Glanz, K., and B. K. Rimer. 2005. *Theory at a Glance: A Guide for Health Promotion Practice*. National Cancer Institute, National Institutes of Health, US Department of Health and Human Services. NIH Pub. No. 97–3896. Washington, DC: NIH.

Green, L. W., and M. W. Kreuter. 1999. *Health Promotion Planning: An Educational and Ecological Approach*, 3rd ed. San Francisco, CA: Mayfield.

Green, L. W., and M. W. Kreuter. 2005. *Health Program Planning: An Educational and Ecological Approach*, 4th ed. Boston: McGraw-Hill.

Hanson, D., J. Hanson, P. Vardon, K. MacFarlane, J. Lloyd, R. Muller, et al. 2005. "The Injury Iceberg: An Ecological Approach to Planning Sustainable Community Safety Interventions." *Health Promotion Journal of Australia* 16 (1): 5–10.

Heaney, C. A., and B. A. Israel. 1997. Social Support and Social Networks. In K. Glanz, B. Rimer, and F. Lewis, eds. *Health Behavior and Health Education: Theory, Research, and Practice,* 2nd ed. San Francisco, CA: Jossey-Bass, pp. 179–205.

House, J. S., D. Umberson, and K. R. Landis. 1988. "Social Relationships and Health." *Science* 241 (4865): 540–45.

House, J. S., D. Umberson, and K. R. Landis. 1988. Structures and Processes of Social Support. *Annual Review of Sociology* 14: 293–318.

Janz, N. K., and M. H. Becker. 1984. "The Health Belief Model—A Decade Later." *Health Education Quarterly* 11 (1): 1–47.

Ledlow, G. R., and M. N. Coppola. 2011. Leadership for Health Professionals: Theory, Skills, and Applications. Sudbury, MA: Jones & Barlett Learning.

McKenzie, J. F., and J. L. Smeltzer. 1997. *Planning, Implementing, and Evaluating Health Promotion Programs: A Primer (2nd edition).* Boston: Allyn and Bacon.

McKenzie, J. F., and J. L. Smeltzer. 2001. *Planning, Implementing, and Evaluating Health Promotion Programs: A Primer,* 3rd ed. New York: Macmillan.

McKenzie, J. F., B. L. Neiger, and R. Thackeray. 2013. *Planning, Implementing, and Evaluating Health Education Programs: A Primer.* Boston: Pearson Education.

Minkler, M. 1990. "Improving Health Through Community Organization." In K. Glanz, F. M. Lewis, and B. Rimer, eds. *Health Behavior and Health Education: Theory, Research, and Practice.* (pp. 257–287). San Francisco, CA: Jossey-Bass.

Parcel and Baranowski. 1981. "Social Learning Theory and Health Education." *Health Education* 12 (3): 14–18.

Prochaska, J. O. 1979. *Systems of Psychotherapy: A Transtheoretical analysis.* Homewood, IL: Dorsey Press.

Prochaska, J. O., & DiClemente, C. C. 1983. "Stages and Processes of Self-change of Smoking: Toward an integrative model of change." *Journal of Consulting and Clinical Psychology* 51 (3): 390–395.

Prochaska, J. O., DiClemente, C. C., & Norcross, J. C. 1992. "In Search of How People Change: Applications to Addictive Behaviors." *American Psychologist* 47 (9): 1102–1114.

Prochaska, J. O., & W. F. Velicer. 1997. "Introduction: The Transtheoretical Model." *American Journal of Health Promotion* 12 (1): 6–7.

Rogers, E. M. 1983. *Diffusion of Innovations,* 3rd ed. New York: Free Press.

Rogers, E. M. 2003. *Diffusion of Innovations,* 5th ed. New York: Free Press.

Rosenstock, I. M., V. J. Strecher, and M. H. Becker. 1988. "Why People use Health Services." *Milbank Memorial Fund Quarterly* 15 (2): 175–183.

Sharma, M., and J. A. Romas. 2012. Theoretical Foundations of Health Education and Health Promotion, 2nd. ed. Sudbury, MA: Jones & Barlett Learning.

Wills, T. A. 1985. Supportive Functions of Interpersonal Relationships. In S. Cohen & L. Syme. Social support and health. pp. 61–82. Orlando, FL: Academic Press.

Section II

Chapter 6

Health Professions

kurhan / Shutterstock.com

What Is a Health Care Professional?

A health care professional is any person who is involved in the systematic delivery of some type of heath care to people, families or communities. Some health care professionals are directly involved in "hands on" patient care, some work in an administrative setting, and others work in support services. Most health care professionals have some type of specialized training and many must obtain a certification or license appropriate for their occupation. For example, phlebotomists usually enter the field with a nondegree award from a phlebotomy program. Certification usually requires taking a written exam and may include showing proficiency in such areas as drawing blood. This portion of the book describes what health care professionals are.

Where Do They Work?

Health care professionals work in many different settings. Professions with patient contact work in many different settings. Many of these sites are owned by the federal government, state and local government, and non-profit organizations. Some of those settings include the following:

- Inpatient facilities such as hospitals, long term acute care services (LTACs), nursing homes and assisted living facilities

- Outpatient facilities such as primary care facilities (physician's offices and services including ambulatory clinics, blood banks, EMS and ambulance services, clinical medical laboratories, and diagnostic facilities, dental laboratories, family planning services, home health, opticians, poison control centers, community health centers, neighborhood health centers, health maintenance organizations (HMOs), volunteer health agencies (such as the American Health Association and the American Cancer Society), and professional health associations.

There are many health care professionals who have little or no direct patient contact. Often we consider these jobs to be "behind the scene" but are vital to the health care industry. Some of these jobs can be found in the following:

- Pharmaceutical companies
- Durable medical equipment companies
- Household health supplies manufacturers
- Diagnostic laboratories
- Prosthetics
- Hospital and health facilities suppliers
- Health care administration

There are many new opportunities for health care professionals. These jobs can be found in information technology. Since electronic medical records (EMRs) are required for reimbursement for many government agencies for services rendered, new ways to store and transmit that data are constantly being developed. Often large medical systems have many different clinics and hospitals that all must be securely linked together. Other fast growing fields include biomedical engineering. At this time, engineers are implanting chips in paralyzed peoples' brains that allow them to move their limbs. Some research facilities are trying to create body suits for quadriplegics that allow them to walk and stand up. In addition, more professionals are needed to create new diagnostic and treatment equipment. 20 years ago, when a person went to get a MRI, it would take several hours and many patients became very scared because they were in a thin tube and could not move for long periods of time. Now we have MRIs that take only a few minutes and can be done in an open room.

One of the big problems we have in places for health care professionals to work is **maldistribution**. Maldistribution means that there are areas in the country where there are very few or not enough health care workers. Often these can be found in the very low socio-economic portions of a large city or in rural areas. This makes it very difficult for populations that live there to get medical attention. There are a variety of reasons for this issue, but it usually stems from the fact that few physicians want to live in run down areas of town or in a very rural area. There is one area in Texas where the closest doctor is over 75 miles away!

What are the job projections for health care professional in the U.S.?

Occupation in health care is the fasting growing segment of the United States' labor force. Between 2000 and 2010, health care employment grew by more than 25% while during the same period, U. S. Employment dropped by over 2%. That trend is projected to continue to rise as the health care sector is projected to add over 4.2 million jobs between 2010 and 2020. 63% of those jobs will be in ambulatory settings (offices of health practitioners, home health, and other non-institutional settings). In 2010, there were more than 19 million health care professional jobs. This accounted for over 13% of the total U.S. workforce.

The U.S. Bureau of Labor Statistics predicts that by the year 2020, nearly one in nine jobs in the U.S. will be in the health sector. One of the reasons for this is the growth of the population over 65 due to the aging of the baby boomers. As people age, they usually need more health care including physician visits, medications, physical therapy, diagnostic tests, surgeries, and hospitalizations.

The fastest growth is projected to be in home health care. Home health care usually consists of nursing, physical therapy, and occupational therapy services. By using home health care, older adults can stay in their own homes and will be less likely to need more advanced care. Research shows that with proper home health care, many older adults stay more active and healthier when they can stay in the environment to which they are accustomed. Home health care jobs are expected to have an annual growth of more than 8% between 2010 and 2020. Jobs in health practitioners' offices (such as physicians, nurse practitioners, and physical therapy) is projected to grow more than 3% annually between 2010 and 2020.

How Do I Find a School?

There are several to ask when deciding where to go to school. The first thing to decide is what kind of schooling does one need? Does one need a two year or a four college or university and what type of degree do I need? Does one need to find a technical institute for vocational training or a will I only need a certificate program like the previously mentioned phlebotomist? Will one need to attend medical school, dental school, nursing school, physical therapy school or occupational school? Can the hospital provide training in the hospital? Should one consider a military school for training? What is the difference between a public school and a private school? As we go through the different health care professions in this book, we will learn about what type of schooling is needed for each one.

Another factor in deciding where to attend school is cost. Private schools usually cost much more than private schools. One must ask if there are scholarships and grants to attend a particular school. Often military institutions pay a students a salary while they attend school along with their tuition and schooling expenses. In return, students will repay the military by spending time working for the military before they go to different institutions. The military will also pay for students to attend public institutions such as medical school or graduate schools. While attending school, students draw full salary and must pay back the military by spending time working for the military. An example of this is a safety officer in the U.S. Navy had a master degree in medical technology. He wanted to get a doctorate in epidemiology. The Navy paid him his regular salary for the three years it took to complete his doctorate degree and when he graduated, the Navy required him to stay in the Navy for three more years to pay them back. He received a promotion, a raise in pay, and a free education! Another first year medical student was struggling with paying bills for his family and paying for tuition. He joined the U.S. Air Force and they finished paying for his schooling. He went in as a 2nd Lieutenant and received the full pay of that rank. When he graduated from medical school, he was promoted and went to work at a large military hospital where he did his internship and residency. He was so impressed with the program, he stayed and did a fellowship in cardiology. For every year of his medical school, he had to pay the Air Force back one year. At this time, the federal government is funding some schooling for students who want to work in rural and underserved areas. For many students, this is a much better option than taking on hundreds of thousands of dollars in student loans.

A further factor in selecting a school is location. If a student does not have a spouse or children, then often he or she is considered more mobile and can move across the country more easily. Often students want to stay in their home state for professional school so they will not have to pay extra out-of-state tuition. There have been students who wanted to go to exotic locations for professional school. Students who go out of the country for professional schools often have to take extra exams to prove their education was as competent as U.S. institutions.

Discussion

Before a person enters college, should he or she decide what kind of career they want? How will that help? What is he or she changes his or her mind?

Why do you think there is a maldistribution of health care? Why do health care professionals tend to avoid certain areas?

Do you think technology will change the way health care is delivered in the future? Why or why not? How will technology affect the way we learn about health in the future? Is this a good thing or a bad thing?

References

U. S. Bureau Labor Statistics: http://www.bls.gov/ooh/healthcare/home.htm

Chapter 7

Health Professions with Patient Contact

michaeljung / Shutterstock.com

Introduction

Sherry has a bad sore throat. She has been sick for a couple of days with a fever. She calls her doctor's office to make an appointment and speaks with Reagan. Sherry then goes to the office and is greeted by Ben. Ben works at the front desk for a busy group of family physicians. He is one of the people who greet patients when they come into the clinic and gets their name and insurance information. For new patients, he hands them a form to complete that gives their medical history and other pertinent information. When a room is ready, Tina, the medical assistant, calls Sherry patient back and takes and records her blood pressure, pulse, weight and height and then leads Sherry to a room. The physician, Dr. Feelgood, then comes in to examine Sherry and decides she needs to have some blood tests. Dr. Feelgood makes a note on the computer about the blood tests and once the visit is finished, she leaves the room. Tony, Dr. Feelgood's nurse, comes in with paperwork for Sherry's blood work and for her to check out of the doctor's office. Sherry stops by the laboratory on her way out and gives the phlebotomist, Chuck, her paper work for her blood tests. Chuck draws her blood and tells her the nurse will give her a call as soon as the tests are complete. Sherry then goes to the checkout desk where she gives Kim her paperwork and pays her bill.

How many of the people in the above scenario had direct communication or contact with Sherry? All of them did. They are called healthcare providers with patient contact. There were people who worked for the practice that may never see patients and are usually involved in administrative duties. The healthcare providers who have patient contact are what we will study in this chapter. It is a long chapter but is divided into small sections so do not be discouraged about the chapter length. All of the information in this chapter was obtained from the U.S. Bureau of Labor Statistics and can be found at http://www.bls.gov/ooh/healthcare/home.htm.

Physicians and Surgeons

Perceptions

Physicians and surgeons, also called doctors, are what many people think of when they hear the word medicine. We all have different perceptions of physicians, some are positive and some are negative depending on our past experiences with them. Many people believe that all physicians are fabulously wealthy and can control everything about a patient's health and the way they administer medicine. Most people realize that physicians are usually very intelligent and knowledgeable and think they can help them conquer a health issue or stay healthy. Often, lay people (people who do NOT work in healthcare) do not realize how hard a physician works.

Realities

Physicians and surgeons practice medicine. In reality, physicians and surgeons work long, hard, irregular hours. Many are deeply in debt paying for the many years of expensive education they had to attain in order to be a physician, but there is almost always a job available for them, especially in rural or low-income areas. Acceptance to medical school is highly competitive. Not only do students have to take and excel in many grueling science courses, but they must be well-rounded in other areas of life, such as knowing communication skills and being able to work with people.

Physicians diagnose and treat human illnesses or injuries by examining patients, taking medical histories, and ordering, performing, and interpreting diagnostic tests. Physicians also utilize health promotion techniques when they counsel their patients on proper eating habits (diet), hygiene, preventive healthcare (such as receiving immunizations), and lifestyles. Surgeons perform surgery or operate on their patients to treat diseases, such as removing cancerous tumors or removing a bad appendix, to treat injuries, such as repairing a broken bone, and to treat deformities such as fixing a cleft palate or separating conjoined twins. Surgeons are physicians who specialize in surgery.

Types of Physicians

There are two types of physicians: MD (Medical Doctor) and DO (Doctor of Osteopathic Medicine). MDs are known as allopathic physicians. Dos are commonly called osteopaths. Osteopathic medicine started during the Civil War when physicians were using dangerous substances as medications. An MD named A. T. Still thought these substances were overused and resulted in more deaths and complications than needed. He founded a DO school based on using more holistic (whole-person) patient care for healing and prevention and place emphasis on the musculoskeletal system. DOs and MDs practice the same type of Western medicine, the same types of diagnosis and treatments, and do the same types of surgeries. Often it is difficult to tell the difference between the two unless you look at the initials after their names. DOs are more likely to be family physicians (called primary care physicians), but DOs who are specialists exist in all specialties.

Duties and Job Tasks

Physicians and surgeons have many different types of duties and job tasks. Some of those tasks are described in the following:

- *Taking a patient's medical history.* Both MDs and DOs take medical histories. A medical history gives the healthcare provider information about that patient's health status, their past health status, and current medications they may take. Some physicians prefer to have patients complete a form describing various systems in the body and health concerns and some physicians, especially in some specialties, prefer to take the history personally. They will sit with the patient and ask them questions about their medical past. The big drawback to this is it takes up a large amount of time and most primary care physicians do not have that luxury as they see many patients in a day.

- *Updating charts and patient information to show current health status and treatments.* With the invention and adoption of electronic medical records (EMR) many physicians will update the information directly on their computers or tablets when they receive it from the patient. Before EMRs, many physicians would dictate their notes on patients into a recording device and someone would transcribe those notes for the patients' charts. EMRs have shown to improve accuracy and save time for physicians that could be spent on patient contact or care.

- *Ordering tests for other healthcare providers and/or staff to perform.* It would be nice if patients could walk into a doctor's office and the doctor take one glance at them and determine the cause of their malady or the correct treatment. Often, physicians must order some type of test, such as an x-ray or a blood test to determine the proper diagnosis and/or treatment. For example, if Jeff comes in to see Dr. Feelgood because he has a severe pain in the upper right quadrant of his abdomen, Dr. Feelgood may do a hands-on examination and then order an ultrasound of the gall bladder to see if Jeff has gall stones in his gall bladder. Another example is when Tina comes in to the office and has a severe sore throat and a fever, then Dr. Feelgood may order a Strep test to see if Tina has strep throat.

- *Reviewing test results for abnormal findings.* When Dr. Feelgood gets the results for Jeff's gall bladder ultrasound, Dr. Feelgood can then determine whether or not Jeff has gall stones and will know whether to refer Jeff to a surgeon or perform further tests.

- *Recommending and design a plan of treatment.* Once Dr. Feelgood received the results of Tina's Strep test, he then knew whether or not to prescribe certain antibiotics, to have a culture done of a swab of her throat, or to order more tests. Physicians see patients and make diagnosis based on signs (what people can see) and symptoms (what people feel) and the physician's knowledge of those. They then can customize a treatment plan for each patient. Tina's Strep test may be positive but that does not mean that every time Tina has a sore throat it is the result of a Strep infection as it could be caused by a virus, sinus drainage or other condition.

- *Addressing concerns or answer questions that patients have about their health and the health of their families.* Often patients see physicians because of specific health concerns. They may want to know what caused their condition, what they can do to avoid it in the future, or the different methods available for treatment. For example, Mary asked Dr. Feelgood what her risk for getting diabetes was. Her sister and mother both have type II diabetes and she wants to know if she has it or if there is a higher chance she will have it.

- *Helping patients take care of their health by talking about lifestyle choices such as diet and exercise.* In the first part of the book you learned about health promotion and why people adopt certain health behaviors. Physicians use health promotion when working with their patients. This is the time that Dr. Feelgood will talk with Mary about losing weight, eating properly, and getting some physical activity in order to prevent the onset of type II diabetes.

Physician Specialties

Physicians work in one or more specialties. Some of them are very specific to a certain population. For example, a pediatric gastroenterologist with work with infants to older adolescents about gastrointestinal issues. Some examples of specialists are:

- *Anesthesiologists.* Anesthesiologists usually focus on two areas of care: surgical patients and pain management. They evaluate and treat patients and direct the efforts of their staffs to anesthetize a patient and then to continually monitor and assess that patient. Immediately before, during and after surgery, they are responsible for maintaining their patient's vital life functions, such as their heart rate, blood pressure, respirations (breathing) and body temperature. They will also provide pain relief in the Intensive Care Unit (ICU) and for those during labor and delivery. In the last twenty years, anesthesiologists have begun treating patients with chronic pain and helping those patients manage their pain. Many pain management specialists have private offices and see patients on a regular basis.

- *Family Practice Specialists.* The family practice physician took the place of the old family doctor or generalists. Family practice specialists are often called primary care providers because they are the first point of contact when a patient seeks care and they coordinate a patient's health care. Most family practice physicians have regular, long-term patents and they see patients of all ages ("from the cradle to the grave"). They may deliver a baby in the morning and go back to their clinic and take care of a 93 year old woman. Family practices doctors also diagnose a variety of conditions, everything from a sinus infection to an in-grown toenail. They may suture an 18-month-old's head and then cast a broken wrist. If there is something beyond their expertise, they will then refer their patient to the proper specialist

- *General Internists.* General internists (commonly called internists or internal medicine) diagnose and provide nonsurgical treatment to adults for a many issues that affect internal organ systems, such as the kidneys, liver, stomach, and digestive tract. They use different diagnostics tests and treatments and many treat patients through medications or through hospitalizations. For many adults, an internist is their primary care physician.

- *General Pediatrician.* A physician who specializes in general pediatrics is called a pediatrician and is often a primary care physician for infants, children, teenagers, and young adults (this includes college aged patients). Most pediatricians treat common everyday illnesses, minor injuries, and infectious diseases. Since they are primary care providers, pediatricians are actively involved in administering vaccinations. Some pediatricians become pediatric specialists such as pediatric surgeons (perform surgery on children), neonatologist (work on infants in the womb or newborns), pediatric rheumatologists (work with children with autoimmune disorders or transplant patients), pediatric orthopedists (take care of pediatric musculoskeletal problems like club feet or badly broken bones), pediatric cancer specialists, pediatric nephrologists (specializing in pediatric kidney disorders), and pediatric neurologists (takes care of pediatric brain and neurological disorders).

- *Obstetrics and Gynecology (OB/GYNs).* OB/GYNs specialize in women's health. They provide specialty care regarding pregnancy, childbirth, and the female reproductive system. They treat and counsel women throughout their pregnancy and deliver babies. They also diagnose and treat health issues specific to women such as cervical cancer, hormonal disorders, and symptoms related to menopause.

- *Psychiatrists.* Psychiatrists are primary mental health physicians. To be called a psychiatrists, one must possess an MD or DO. They diagnose and treat mental illnesses through a variety of methods such as counseling, hospitalization and medication. Since psychiatrists are MDs or DOs, they are allowed to prescribe medication to correct chemical imbalances that may cause mental illnesses. A psychologist who is not an MD or DO cannot prescribe medication.

- *Surgeons.* Surgeons are MDs or DOS who specialize in treating injuries, diseases and deformities through operations. They use many different surgical tools and today many are certified to perform robotic surgery by guiding specialized machines to perform incisions and treatments to correct physical deformities (such as cleft palate), repair bone and tissue after an injury, or preventive or elective surgeries on patients. Some surgeons are called general surgeons but many surgeons have chosen to specialize in specific areas. Those specialties include orthopedic surgery (the surgical treatment of the musculoskeletal system), neurological surgery (surgical treatment of the brain and nervous system, cardiovascular surgery (surgical treatment of the heart and cardiovascular system), and plastic or reconstructive surgery (surgical treatment for aesthetic reasons or to correct some deformity such as cleft palate). Like all other physicians, surgeons must examine patients, perform and interpret diagnostic tests, and counsel patients on preventive healthcare. Some specialist physicians also perform surgery.

- *Other physicians.* There are many types of physicians and to name them all would describe everything they do would make this book too long and boring. The following is a list of examples of other types of physicians:

  ○ *Allergists.* Allergists are specialists in diagnosing and treating allergies.

  ○ *Cardiologists.* Cardiologists are heart specialists. There are many different branches of cardiologists and subspecialties.

  ○ *Dermatologists.* Dermatologists are skin specialists

  ○ *Gastroenterologists.* These are digestive system specialists.

  ○ *Hospitalists.* Hospitalists specialize in the care of hospital patients. Often the primary care physician will transfer care to a hospitalist once the patient is admitted to a hospital. This is becoming increasingly more common.

  ○ *Ophthalmologists.* Ophthalmologists are MDs who specialize and diagnosing and treating disorders of the eye.

  ○ *Pathologists.* Pathologists are specialists who study body tissue to see if it is normal or abnormal. Some supervise pathology laboratories who conduct tests on body products such as blood and urine to determine diseases. Forensic pathologists conduct autopsies.

  ○ *Radiologists.* Radiologists review and interpret x-rays and other images and deliver radiation treatments for cancer and other illnesses.

Worksites and Conditions

In 2014 there were about 708,300 physician and surgeon working in the United States. Physicians and surgeons work in a variety of setting and a variety of conditions. Private offices or clinics, called private practice, are where many physicians and surgeons work. They often have a very small staff of nurses and administrative personnel. About one out of ten physicians was self-employed in 2014. Gradually, more and more physicians are working in group practices (working with other physicians),, healthcare organizations, or hospitals, where they can share a large number of patients with other doctors. This cuts down on administrative costs, gives them more time off, and lets them coordinate care for their patients. The down side to this is it gives them less independence than practicing alone so they have less autonomy over their practice. Surgeons and anesthesiologists often work in operating rooms in which the environment is sterile and cold and they may stand for long periods of time.

Most physicians work full time and often the hours are long and irregular. It is not uncommon for a physician to work overnight at the hospital if he or she has a very sick patient in need of their care. While on call, a physician may need to address a patient's concerns over the phone or make an emergency visit to a hospital or nursing home. Many physicians will share call duties. For example, instead of staying by the phone for the weekend, a physician take turns with another physician to be available for patient care. The patient will contact the on call physician for their concerns. While on call, the physician will deal with many different issues over the phone and make emergency visits to the hospital or nursing homes.

Educational Requirements

Becoming an MD or DO requires four years of college, four years of medical school, and three to eight years of an internship and residency depending on the specialty. Some medical schools offer combined college and medical education that may last six or seven years instead of the usual eight and some medical schools will accept an exceptional student after only three years of college if he or she completes all of the prerequisites. The undergraduate requirements for medical or DO school are very stringent and only the best students will gain admittance. If you decide to apply for medical or DO school you will be required to take courses in physics, mathematics, chemistry, biology, English, humanities, and social sciences, but you can major in any discipline. Most applicants are required to have a bachelor degree and many have advanced degrees. Often, you will be required to do some type of volunteer work or have some type of practical experience.

Students spend the first two years of medical school in laboratories and classrooms learning about anatomy, biochemistry, pharmacology, psychology, medical ethics, and laws pertaining to medicine. They also practice working with patients to gains communication skills and learn to take medical histories, examine patients, and diagnose illnesses and injuries. They last two years of medical school has students working with patients under the supervision of experienced physicians, called preceptors, in hospitals and clinics. They spend time rotating through different areas of medicine including internal medicine, family practice, obstetrics and gynecology, pediatrics, psychiatry, and surgery and they gain experience in diagnosing and treating illnesses in a variety of areas. Often these rotations will serve as the inspiration for choosing their future specialty.

After medical or DO school, almost all graduates enter a residency program in their specialty of interest. Residencies usually occur inside of a large hospital although some of the subspecialties, such as rheumatology, may occur in private clinics. All residencies are supervised by an experienced specialist in that field and will last from three to four years depending on the field of specialization.

Licensure

All states require physicians and surgeons to be licensed and requirements vary by State. You can find information about the Texas Medical Board here: http://www.tmb.state.tx.us/. Texas has a two-step licensure: screening and licensing. To qualify for a license, a person has to have successfully graduated an accredited medical or DO school, and complete a residency in their specialty. They then must pass a standardized national licensure exam. MDs take the U.S. Medical Licensing Examination (USMLE) and DOs take the Comprehensive Osteopathic Medical Licensing Examination (COMLEX-USA).

Certifications

Physicians and surgeons are not required to have certifications but many do. Certification may increase their employment opportunities. MDs and DOs seeking board certification are required to successfully complete a residency and then take a certification exam administered by either the American Board of Medical Specialties, the American Osteopathic Association (AOA), or the American Board of Physician Specialties (ABPS).

Important Qualities

Physicians and surgeons need to possess several different qualities. A few of those qualities are as follows:

- *Communication skills.* Physicians and surgeons must be able to communicate clearly and effectively with patient and other healthcare providers and staff. Often patients' lives may depend upon excellent communication.

- *Compassion.* Often when a physician or surgeon sees a patient, the patient is sick, injured, or in pain or distress. They must be able to treat their patients with empathy and understanding in order to correctly diagnose and effectively treat a patient.

- *Detail oriented.* MDs and DOs must ensure that their patients receive appropriate treatment and medications. There could be life-saving difference between .1 and .01 ml. Physicians and surgeons must also accurately record and monitor various information related to patient care.

- *Dexterity.* MDs and DOs must be good at working with their hands. Fine motor skills could make a difference when working with human bodies. Accidently nicking the Aorta during a procedure could easily cause a catastrophic even for the patient.

- *Leadership skills.* If physicians have their own practice, they need to be effective leaders. Often they will depend on a clinic manager but overall, the management of their practice is their responsibility.

- *Organization skills.* Good recordkeeping is critical when it comes to patient care in both medical and business settings.

- *Patience.* Physicians and surgeons often work for long periods of time with patients who need special attention. DOs and MDs may have to shore more forbearance with patients who are fearful of medical situations or have poor health literacy.

- *Physical stamina.* Physicians and surgeons work long, hard, irregular hours and surgeons often stand over patients for long periods of time during surgery. They also should be able to lift and turn patients when needed.

- *Problem*-solving skills. MDs and DOs need the ability to evaluate patients and administer the appropriate treatments. Some may need to do this quickly if a patient's life is at stake. In addition, often patients will go to see their physicians with puzzling symptoms that may not fit what is considered a normal pattern. Physicians and surgeons must be able put everything together to determine appropriate treatments for those patients.

Pay

Wages for physicians and surgeons are among the highest for any profession. The median total compensation for physician wages varies with their type of practice and specialty. In 2014, physicians practicing primary care received a total median income of $241,273 and specialists received a total median annual income of $411,852. Physician and surgeon incomes vary according to where they live, how long they have been in practice, how many hours they work, how skilled they are in certain areas, their personality and their professional reputation.

Job Outlook

With the aging of the baby boomers and the growing population over 65, there is a greater need for physicians and that is a trend that will continue. The U.S. Bureau of Labor Statistics predicts a growth of 14% between 2014 and 2024. Although the demand will continue to grow, some factors will likely deter that growth. Physician Assistants and Nurse Practitioners are starting to fill some roles traditionally played by physicians and surgeons. They are cheaper to employ than physicians thereby allowing people and insurance companies to save money on care. New technologies will allow MDs and DOs to treat more patients in the same amount of time, resulting in a decreased need for physician services. Demand for physician and services is also based on changes in healthcare reimbursement policies. For example, Medicare will only reimburse a hospital a set amount of money depending on the diagnosis. Patients may begin to quell their use of physicians if their out of pocket pay continues to rise. However, with the Affordable Care Act, more consumers than ever before are expected to have health insurance and that will increase demand for physicians and surgeons.

There will always be jobs for physicians and surgeons in underserved areas such as low-income areas, rural areas, and public supported hospitals. Those areas have challenges recruiting physicians to serve their populations because they are not popular places to live and because they tend to not pay as much as other places. Physicians who specialize in health issues that affect baby boomers or those over 65 years of age have excellent job prospects as there will be more age related maladies such as cancer and heart disease.

Conclusion

There will be a growing need for physicians and surgeons but becoming one is not easy. There are certain qualities and education requirements one must surpass. Also, many people do not like to work the long hard hours required of this profession.

Discussion

Do you think more students entering medical or DO school because they think it will make them rich, they want to help people, or they are interested in the science of the human body?

Why do physicians specialize? Do you think we will need more specialists in the future or more primary care providers? Why?

How do physicians use health promotion? Is it essential for them learn about health promotion in school or does it come to them naturally? Why do you think that?

Physician Assistants

Physician assistants, commonly called PAs, practice medicine under the supervision of a physician or surgeon. They can examine, diagnose, treat patients, and prescribe some medications. Each state has its own laws regulating supervision of PAs and what PAs can and cannot do.

Duties

PAs practice medicine much like physicians. They often work on teams with physicians or surgeons and other healthcare providers.[1] Their duties are much the same as a physician but they do not have the autonomy a physician has as PAs must be supervised by a licensed physician. The following duties are some of the regular duties of many PAs:

- *Take or review patients' medical histories

- Examine patients

- Order and interpret diagnostic tests, such as x-rays or blood tests

- Diagnose a patient's illness and injury[2]

- Give treatments such as setting broken bones and immunizations

- Use health promotion techniques when educating and counseling patients and their families about health concerns

- Prescribe medication (regulations vary by state as to which medicines they can and cannot prescribe
- Assess and record a patient's progress[3]
- Keep up with the latest treatments to ensure the quality of patient care
- Conduct or participate in outreach programs; talking to groups about managing diseases and promoting wellness[4]

PAs work in all specialties in medicine including primary care, emergency medicine, surgery, pediatrics, and psychiatry.[5] The scope of their work depends on where they work and what their specialty is. For example, a PA working for an orthopedic surgeon may see patients, assist in surgery, and oversee post-operative care. A PA working for a family practice clinic may see patients with routine illnesses such as ear infections or sore throats. PAs are especially welcome in rural areas and underserved areas where it is hard to recruit physicians. They may be the only primary care providers at clinics where a physician is only present a couple of days a week. Some physician assistants make house calls or visit nursing homes to treat patients.

Work Environment

PAs held about 94,400 jobs in 2014. More than half of all PAs were employed in physician offices. Other common employers of PAs are hospitals, outpatient care centers, the government, and educational services. Often PAs spend much of their time on their feet, making rounds and examining patients and the work can be emotionally draining. Physician assistants who work with surgeons often stand for long periods of time. A PAs schedule is much the same as a physician or surgeon. Most PAs work full time as only about 20% work part time. In hospitals, PAs may work nights, weekends or holidays. Also, they may be on call when they have to quickly respond to a work request with little notice.

Education

Most applicants to PA schools have very high grade point averages with a bachelor degree and some healthcare related work experience. Admission requirements vary from program to program but most programs require a bachelor degree with two to four years of undergraduate coursework with a focus in science. Many applicants have experience as registered nurses or EMTs and paramedics before they apply to a physician assistant program. PA programs usually take at least 2 years of full-time study and most programs offer a master degree.

PA school includes classroom and laboratory education in subjects such as pathology, human anatomy, physiology, clinical medicine, pharmacology, physical diagnosis, and medical ethics. These programs include supervised clinical training in several areas, including family medicine, internal medicine, emergency medicine and pediatrics.[6] Often students do clinical rotations and are supervised by physicians who want to hire a PA. Because of this, clinical rotations may lead to permanent employment.

Licenses, Certifications and Registrations

All states and the District of Columbia require physician assistants to be licensed. To become licensed, they must pass the Physician Assistant National Certifying Examination from the National Commission on Certification of Physician Assistants. A physician assistant who passes the exam can use the professional title, Physician Assistant-Certified (PA-C).[7] Every state has its own laws and regulations for PAs. State licensure laws require a PA to hold an agreement with a supervising physician. Even though the supervising physician does not have to be onsite at all times, collaboration between physicians and physician assistants is required for practice. The Texas Medical Board licensing information for physician assistants can be here at http://www.tmb.state.tx.us/page/licensing-physician-assistants.

Important Qualities

Like physicians, PAs need to exhibit certain important qualities. Some of those qualities include the following:

- *Communication skills
- Compassion
- Detail oriented
- Emotional stability.[8] PAs who work in surgery or emergency rooms are under a large amount of pressure and have to remain calm in stressful situations in order to provide quality care.
- Problem-solving skills[9]

Pay

In May 2015, the median annual wage for physician assistants was $98,180. The lowest 10% earned less than $62,760 and the highest 10% earned more than $139,540. The highest paying industries for PAs are outpatient care centers and hospitals. The lowest paying industry for PAs is the government, including the federal, state, and local government.

Job Outlook

Physician assistants are expected to have a larger role in routine healthcare because they are more cost effective than physicians, but they must be able to provide the same care as physicians. The U.S. Bureau of Labor

Statistics expects more PAs to take on the role of primary care providers. As states continue to allow PAs to perform more procedures, insurance companies expand their coverage to physician assistants, and as team-based models of care become more widely used, the role of PAs is expected to expand so the demand for their services will increase.

Conclusion

PAs practice medicine under the supervision of a licensed caregiver and are becoming more common in most healthcare settings. They are in great demand in rural and other underserved areas and are more cost effective than hiring more physicians in others. For more information about a career as a PA go to the American Academy of Physician Assistants at https://www.aapa.org/.

Discussion

What would be the benefit of going to physician assistant school over medical school?

Should physician assistants be able to deliver the same type of care as physicians? Why or why not?

Would you rather see a physician assistant or a physician? Why?

If you are the administrator of a large hospital, would you rather hire physician assistants or physicians to work in the ER?

Nursing

When one thinks about caregivers, often the first person who comes to mind is a nurse. There are different types of nurses. The common types of nursing in Texas are registered nurse (RN), clinical nurse specialist, nurse practitioner (CRNP), nurse midwife, licensed vocational nurse (LVN), nursing assistant or home health aide (CNA), and a nurse anesthetist (CRNA). In this portion we will discuss the several types of nurses and what they do.

Registered Nurses (RNs)

Registered nurses provide and coordinate caring for patients, use health promotion to educate patients and the public about various health topics and provide advice and emotional support for patients and families. Most RNs work as part of a team with physicians and other healthcare specialists. Some may have supervisory duties and manage LVNs, CNAs, and medical assistants. Their duties and their titles often depend on the type of work they do and in what setting they work. An example is a psychiatric nurse who works with patients with mental health challenges. There are many different types of specific patient groups with which a nurse can work. Example are addiction nurses who care for patients who need help to overcome their addictions, critical care nurses who work in intensive care units in hospitals, neonatology nurses who take care of newborn babies and nephrology nurses who care for patients who have kidney-related disorders.

Some nurses work in health promotion to educate the public about warning signs and symptoms of diseases or managing chronic health conditions. These nurses may also run health screenings for high blood pressure or diabetes, conduct immunization clinics, blood drives, or other community outreach programs. Some nurses staff clinics in schools and are called school nurses. Even though most nurses start out as care givers, some nurses with active registered nursing licenses do not work directly with patients. These nurses may work in healthcare administration, public policy advisors, nurse educators, researchers, medical writers and editors and pharmaceutical salespeople.

Duties

RNs perform many different caregiving functions depending on the setting in which they work and the population with which they work. The following are examples of some of their duties:

- Take and record a patient's medical history and symptoms

- Administer patient medication and treatments

- Create plans for patients' care or add to existing plans

- Observe patients and record the observations

- Collaborate and consult with doctors and other healthcare professionals

- Operate and monitor medical equipment

- Help perform diagnostic tests and analyze the results

- Patient and family education concerning illness or injury management

- Instruct and explain treatments and what happens after treatments[10]

Work Environments

RNs are considered the largest healthcare occupation in the US. In 2014, there were about 2.8 million jobs for registered nurses. Hospitals employed about 61% of them and they make up the largest amount of staff at hospitals. Other businesses that employ the most registered nurses in the US are nursing and resident care services, physician offices, home health-care, and governments (this includes the military). Registered nurses can be found throughout the United States and internationally. Some nurses work for philanthropic or government organizations providing healthcare and education to remote parts of the world.

One of the biggest challenges that nurses face is their vulnerability to back injuries. Lifting a 250 pound person is difficult, especially if that person is fighting back or is totally paralyzed. They must also move patients from one bed to another or to a wheelchair and then back to bed. This is usually done in pairs, but sometimes, it is difficult to find someone to help, especially if the other nurses are busy with their patients.

Another challenge for nurses is they are often exposed to serious or potentially serious infectious diseases or harmful substances. Remember the Ebola outbreak of 2014–2015? Two nurses in the US who worked with Ebola patients actually contracted the serious, often deadly disease. One way nurses protect themselves is to use protective equipment and follow strict protocols. If you see a nurse wearing gloves, it is to not only protect them from something you may have, but to protect you from something they may have or with something with which they may have come into contact. If a patient has a known infectious disease such as methicillin resistant staph aureus (MRSA), the nurses (and everyone else) entering that room will wear a protective gown, a mask, a hair covering and gloves. The gloves will cover the lower portion of their sleeves to protect their wrists. As soon as they leave the room, they will remove the protective gear and place it into a container to be destroyed and then they will wash their hands before they touch anything else.

Many nurses spend a large proportion of their time on their feet and if they work in a hospital or nursing care setting, they may work long shifts (including nights), holidays and weekends. If they work in offices or schools who do not provide round the clock care then they usually work regular business hours and some work on Saturdays. School nurses usually work on school days and most are off during summer vacations.

How to Become a RN

There are several different paths to becoming a registered nurse. Nursing students need to attend a state-approved educational program. In Texas, that is involves receiving either an associate degree or a bachelor degree. Before one is admitted to the program, they must complete certain prerequisites that usually consist of general education and science classes such as microbiology and biology. Associate degree programs are usually found at community or junior colleges and those nurses are said to have an Associate degree in nursing (ADN). Many ADNs go on to complete a bachelor degree in programs called bridging programs or RN-to-BSN programs. Many major universities that have BSN programs also offer a master's degree program and some offer a bachelor to master degree for those who already have a bachelor degree in something else. There are doctoral degree programs for nursing, especially for those who want to teach in a nursing school.

All of the states in the US require a RN to be licensed. In order to obtain one's license, a person must graduate from a state-approved nursing school and pass the National Council licensure Examination (NCLEX-RN). Information about the program in Texas can be found at the Texas Board of Nursing website. Its address is http://www.bne.state.tx.us/. The Texas Board of Nursing (BON) approves schools of nursing, issues licenses, enforces the

Nursing Practice Act and BON rules and regulations and provides information about nursing in Texas.

Certification is for nurses who want to specialize in specific areas such as ambulatory care, gerontology, and pediatrics. To obtain certification in certain areas, nurses must work through professional organizations and pass their standards. Certification is strictly voluntary, but many employers require it for positions in their organizations.

Important Qualities

The following are important qualities for registered nurses to possess:

- Critical-thinking skills
- Communication skills
- Compassion
- Detail oriented
- Emotional stability
- Organizational skills
- Physical stamina[11]

Advancement

Most RNs begin as staff nurses in hospitals and with experience, good performance and continuing education, they can move to other settings or be promoted to positions with more responsibility. Often management personnel are comprised of BSNs who have advanced in their organization. However, it is becoming more common to see graduate degrees in nursing or health administration in management positions. There are many nurses who decide to leave patient care and enter the business side of healthcare. Nursing expertise is needed in home health agencies, ambulatory care, chronic care businesses, insurance companies, pharmaceutical manufacturers and managed care organizations. In these types of occupations, nurses are needed for healthcare policy, planning and development, marketing, consulting, and quality assurance.

Some RNs study further to become nurse anesthetists, nurse midwives, or nurse practitioners. These are considered Advanced Practice Registered Nurses (APRNs). APRNs are usually much more cost effective than hiring more physicians and are becoming increasingly popular. In Texas, APRNs must be under the supervision of a physician much the same as a physician assistant.

Job Outlook

Registered nurses is the largest healthcare occupation in the US and in 2014, there were about 2.7 million jobs in the US and the US Bureau of Labor Statistics predicts this field to grow by 16% from 2014–2024. The vast majority of RNs were employed by hospitals. Like the previous mentioned healthcare occupations, healthcare nursing jobs are expected to grow because of the graying of the baby boomers (aging of the population) and the demand for more healthcare. Also factored into that growth is the Affordable Care Act in which all Americans are required to have health insurance thereby increasing demands on the system. Because of Medicare financial restrictions of keeping patients in hospitals for shorter periods of time, rapid growth is expected in residential facilities, home health care, rehabilitation centers, and Alzheimer's disease units.

References

http://www.bls.gov/ooh/healthcare/registered-nurses.htm

http://www.bon.texas.gov/index.asp

Licensed Vocational Nurses (LVN)

In Texas, a step under the registered nurse is the licensed vocational nurse or LVN. According to the Texas Board of Nursing, the has a focus on patient safety and is responsible for providing safe, compassionate, and focused nursing care to assigned patients with predictable health care needs. They must work under the supervision of a registered nurse, advanced practice registered nurse, physician assistant, physician, dentist, or podiatrist. In other states they are often referred to as licensed practical nurse or LPN.

What an LVN Does

The duties of a LVN depends on state regulations and in what setting. For example, in Texas they can administer certain medications but cannot administer others. There are some duties that LVNs can perform in all states. Those include:

- Monitor a patient's vital signs (blood pressure, temperature, and pulse rate)

- Report those vital signs to their supervisors and/or physicians

- Administer basic patient care such as changing bandages

- Tell their patients about the type of care they provide and listen to their patients concerns

- Maintain record keeping for their patients' health

- Do routine laboratory tests such as taking blood sugars readings

- Collect samples for testing

- Feed patients who need feeding

- Turn and move patients safely

Work Environment

In the US in 2014 there were about 720,000 LVNs and LPNs and about 38% of them were employed by nursing and residential care facilities. Many nurses work on their feet most of the day and often have to lift heavy patients who cannot stand on their own. Often the work environment is very stressful, especially when working with ill and injured people.

Most LVNs and LPNs work full time. Many, depending on where they are employed, work shifts including nights, weekends and holidays. Some employers require LVNs and LPNs to work longer than 8 hour shifts, but they do not work as many days in the week.

How to Become One

Most LVN programs in Texas are through community colleges and technical schools. These programs often award a certificate and most programs usually take about 1 year to complete. These programs often combine classroom learning in subjects like biology and nursing. All programs require supervised clinical experience in a wide variety of circumstances.

Upon finishing a state-approved educational program, graduates are required to pass the National Council on Licensure Examination (NCLEX-PN) in order to get a license. You can find more information on the examination by looking on this site: https://www.ncsbn.org/index.htm. Some LVNs continue their education and become certified by professional associations in specialty areas such as gerontology or pediatrics.

Important Qualities

LVNs often have direct patient contact and in some situations they are the only healthcare provider the patients sees regularly. It is imperative that they possess the following qualities:

- Compassion
- Detail oriented
- Interpersonal skills
- Patience
- Physical stamina
- Speaking skills[12]

Advancement and Job Outlook

Since the LVN has no college diploma (associate or bachelor degree), there are few management positions available for them. Depending on the organization, some may advance to supervisory positions and supervise other LVNs and Nurses' Aids but they will often be passed over for higher management positions. Some LVNs will enroll in a bridging program and can study and take the examination to become a RN. There are more supervisory positions open for RNs than LVNs. In addition, RNs earn a much higher salary than LVNs as LVNs must be supervised by a RN or physician. You can find out about their pay and other dimensions of their jobs at http://www.bls.gov/ooh/healthcare/licensed-practical-and-licensed-vocational-nurses.htm.

The job market for LVNs is projected to grow 16% from 2014 to 2024, but in some states, LVNs and LPNs are being phased out in preference to RNs. The reason for the job growth is the same for all of the healthcare professions. As the baby boomers age, there will be a higher need for healthcare, especially in residential care facilities and home health environments.

Advanced Practice Registered Nurses (APRNs)

Advanced practice registered nurses are nurses who have gone further in completing their education and taken examinations in order to do special jobs. Three types of APRNs are nurse anesthetists, nurse midwives, and nurse practitioners. All of these coordinate some type of patient care and they may provide primary (nurse practitioners) or specialty care (nurse midwives and nurse anesthetists). Each state varies in what duties an APRN can perform and you can find Texas rules and regulations at the State Board of Nursing Website. All APRNs in Texas must be under the supervision of a physician.

What an APRN Does

The duties of an APRN are determined by the type of APRN and the organization for which he or she works and include many of the duties performed by registered nurses. Some of the common duties of APRNs are included in the following list:

- *Take and record patients' medical histories and symptoms
- Perform physical exams and evaluate patients
- Create care plans for patients and/or contribute to existing plans
- Perform and order diagnostic tests and interpret those tests
- Operate and monitor medical equipment
- Diagnose various health problems
- Analyze test results or changes in a patient's condition, and alter treatment plans, as needed[13]
- Administer medications and treatments and evaluate patient responses to those treatments
- Consult with physicians and other healthcare professionals as needed
- Use health promotion when working with patients

In Texas, nurse practitioners are limited to which kinds of medicine they can prescribe and all work must be done under the supervision of a physician. APRNs focus on patient-centered care, meaning they understand a patient's concerns and lifestyles before choosing a course of action. Many nurse practitioners specialize in primary care, care of all age groups called "from the cradle to the grave" or patients with mental health disorders, but they can specialize in other areas including allergy, rheumatology, pediatrics, and neurology.

Types of APRNs

The first type of APRN that we will address is the certified registered nurse anesthetists or CRNAs. CRNAs provide care for surgery patients and pain management for those with chronic or acute pain. Many of these are employed by hospitals and surgical centers. Their duties are to provide anesthesia and related care before, during and after surgical, therapeutic, diagnostic and obstetrical procedures. They meet with the patient before a procedure and take a medical history along with asking about any allergies or underlying illnesses a patient may have. Then they will anesthetize (put to sleep) the patient and care for him or her during the procedure monitoring vital signs and adjusting the anesthesia as necessary. Then will then monitor the patient in recovery. If the patient requires pain control, the CRNA will prescribe whatever pain control is necessary including doing epidurals and IV self-administered pain medication. Some CRNAs work with pain management physician specialists in pain management clinics providing pain control for those with chronic pain issues.

The second type of common APRN is the certified nurse midwife or CNM. CNMs provide care for women's health issues, including gynecological exams, family planning services, prenatal care, childbirth, and newborn care. They are best known for prenatal care and labor and delivery. Some CNMs may provide assistance to physicians during cesarean births (a surgical incision by which the baby is removed). CNMs are known for health promotion especially during pregnancy and postpartum care. Some CNMs provide primary care for their women and newborns and some may provide care to the partners of their patients for sexual or reproductive health issues.

The third type of APRN that we will study is the nurse practitioner or the NP. The vast majority of these work in physician offices or clinics and provide primary care to their patients. Typically, NPs will care for a certain population of people such as geriatric health for adults over 65 or psychiatric and mental health. Some NPs may specialize in areas such as pediatrics, pain management, neurology, and rheumatology. One very popular NP in central Texas specializes in migraine headaches in women. She is so popular that it is often difficult to get an appointment with her. She attended advanced classes and education and spent hours working toward her neurology specialty. In Texas, there are certain medications that NPs cannot prescribe. If they believe that their patients need that particular drug, they will often approach their supervising physician to write the prescription for them.

Work Environment

In the US in 2014, there were approximately 170,400 jobs for APRNs. Their work environment depends on the type of work they do and where they are employed. For example a CRNA may work weekends and shift work or may be on call for surgeries if employed in a hospital or surgical setting. APRNs who work in clinics or physician offices or schools may work during normal business hours and share call with the other healthcare professionals. CNMs will deliver babies and their schedule is often very hectic with long hours, nights, weekends and holidays. Babies do not wait until 8 – 5 for delivery!

Some APRNs may be exposed to infectious diseases, especially those who work in primary care. Using the same techniques as the RN, they will use personalized protective equipment to avoid diseases or other dangerous substances such as accidental needles sticks or coming into contact with someone's bodily fluids.

How to Become One

All APRNs have a master's degree in their specialty roles from an accredited program. These programs include supervised patient contact as well as classroom experience. Before they are admitted to the program, they must possess a RN license, a bachelor degree, and a strong background in science is helpful. Most APRN programs only admit students with a BSN. Although a master's degree is the most common, some APRNs continue their education to earn a Doctor of Nursing Practice or a Ph.D. In order for a person to be admitted to a CRNA program, candidates must have at least one year of clinical experience especially in critical care areas and acute care settings.

Licenses and Certifications

Almost all of the states recognize all of the APRN roles, including Texas. Texas will recognize all of the roles if an APRN has a registered nursing license, completes an accredited graduate-level program, and passes a national certification exam. You can find information about licensing requirements at the Texas Board of Nursing website.

Texas requires certification to use an APRN title. In order to obtain certification, you will need to pass an exam given by the national board for that specialty. For example, the National Board of Certification and Recertification for Nurse Anesthetists gives an examination and requires recertification every two years and 40 hours of continuing medical education. The American Midwifery Certification Board offers the Certified Nurse-Midwife and CNMs must recertify every 5 years. Different professional organizations offer exams for nurse practitioners. Two of the more common ones are American Nurses Credentialing Center and the Pediatric Nursing Certification Board.

Important Qualities

Like the other nursing medical professions, APRNs need to exhibit certain characteristics that are important to patient care. Those qualities include the following:

- Communication skills
- Critical-thinking skills
- Compassion
- Detail oriented
- Interpersonal skills
- Leadership skills
- Resourcefulness[14]

Advancement

The APRN is considered a terminal degree, meaning that many APRNs continue to fulfill the role for which they studied and entered throughout their career. Many, however, decide to go into healthcare administration or academia, teaching at nursing schools. APRNs who complete a doctorate may conduct research studies or work in an inter-professional team. For information about the pay for APRNs go to the US Department of Labor Bureau of Labor Statistics at http://www.bls.gov/ooh/healthcare/nurse-anesthetists-nurse-midwives-and-nurse-practitioners.htm.

Job Projections

Employment for APRNs is expected to grow by 31% from 2014–2024 in the US. As the baby boom population ages, there will be a greater demand on the healthcare system as well as more people having health insurance because of the Affordable Care Act. The rise in chronic diseases and the rise in inactivity are contributing to more chronic diseases than ever before. Another factor for the growth is that APRNs save healthcare organizations money. It is much more cost effective to hire an APRN than to hire a physician. As states begin to accept the APRN widening role, APRNs will be allowed to perform more services thereby increasing the demand for their services.

Advanced practice registered nurses hold a vital role in the healthcare industry. Many act as primary care providers but others specialize in much needed areas. The growth of the healthcare industry due to consumer demand will continue to influence job projections for APRNs and at the time of the writing of this book, APRNs will enjoy job security for years to come.

Optometrists

Optometrists are also known as doctors of optometry or ODs and are the main provider of vision care. An optometrist is a health care practitioner trained to diagnose signs of ocular, neurological and systemic health problems and treat vision disorders. A therapeutic optometrist may also treat eye diseases and injuries, prescribe medicine and perform other procedures such as eye foreign body removal. An optometric glaucoma specialist may also treat glaucoma as authorized by the Texas Optometry Act and prescribe oral prescription drugs listed in the Texas Optometry Act.

Most optometrists work in their own offices (about 17% in the US are self-employed) but a few work in doctors' offices (such as ophthalmologists) and optical goods (eyeglasses and contact lenses) stores or optical chains or franchises. Some work evenings and weekends and most of them work full-time. In the US in 2014, there were about 40,600 optometrists working in the field.

How to Become One

In order to become a Doctor of Optometry, a person must possess a bachelor degree and take certain prerequisites like biology and chemistry courses. They will then apply and take the Optometry Admission Test, a computerized exam that assess competencies in four subject areas, science, reading comprehension, physics, and quantitative reasoning. After applying to OD school, upon acceptance, they will attend a four year program at an accredited school of optometry. In 2015, there were 23 accredited programs in the US; one of these programs is in Houston and another is in San Antonio. After OD school, graduates must complete a 1 year residency program to get clinical training. Some ODs specialize at this time and do their residency in a specialty like low vision rehabilitation, pediatric or geriatric optometry, or optometric glaucoma specialist (in Texas).

Licensures

All states in the US, including Texas, require that all optometrists be licensed. In order to get one's license, a person has to graduate from an accredited school and pass a written national board examination and a state clinical examination. To keep your license you must take 16 hours of continuing education classes yearly and renew it yearly. To find out the state of Texas' requirements go to the Texas Optometry Board website at http://www.tob.state.tx.us/.

Important Qualities

- Business oriented and self-disciplined
- Tactful to deal with problem patients

- Detail oriented

- Possess manual dexterity

- Good decision making skills

- Communication skills

Job Outlook

Employment of optometrists is projected to grow 27% between 2014 and 2024. One of the reasons for this is the aging baby boomer population. As people age, their vision changes and they require more services. They may also be susceptible to diseases and conditions of the eye such as cataracts and macular degeneration. Another reason for the projected growth is that as there are more diabetes cases, there will be more problems with the eye as diabetes affects blood vessels in the eye.

Reference

http://www.bls.gov/ooh/healthcare/optometrists.htm

Opticians

Once a person receives a prescription for eyeglasses, he or she takes the prescription to an optician to be filled. They are trained to measure the distance between the two pupils and look at customers' eyes and faces. They help customers choose eyeglass frames and lenses, such as sport lenses, lenses with tints or anti-glare coating. They then create work orders for ophthalmic laboratories to make the lenses. They then fit the new eyeglasses to the customer's face and educate the customer about how to care for the new lenses. They may also order contact lenses and show customers how to put in and care for contact lenses. Most opticians also repair or replace broken eyeglass frames and maintain sales records and inventory.

Work Environment

Dispensing opticians spend most of their time working indoors, mainly in optometry or ophthalmology offices, optical stores, or in large department stores or club stores. Opticians who work in small shops or prepare custom orders may cut lenses and insert them into frames. Although most work during regular business hours, those working in retail stores may work evenings or weekends. Most opticians work full time but there are some part-time positions available.

How to Become an Optician

Learning to become an optician only requires a high school diploma and some on-the-job training. Some opticians enter the professions with an associate's degree or a certificate from a community college or technical school. Training requires technical instruction on how to measure the distance between eyes, sales and office management practices, types of lenses, and care of lenses. Some offices require an optician to complete an apprenticeship before officially earning the title of optician.

In 2015, there were 22 programs in 14 states accredited by the Commission on Opticianry Accreditation. Training at these schools involves classroom instruction and clinical experience. Coursework includes optics, eye physiology, math and business management. Some programs have distance learning options.

Licensure

About half of the states in the US require licensure for opticians. As of 2015, Texas no longer requires an optician to be licensed. To receive a license in another state, a person must complete a formal education program or apprenticeship and pass one or more exams: either the National Contact Lens Examiners or the national certification examination offered by the American Board of Opticianry. For more information about the American Board of Opticianry, you can visit their website at http://www.abo-ncle.org/.

Important Qualities

- Business skills
- Communication skills
- Decision making skills
- Customer service skills
- Dexterity[15]

Job Outlook

In the US, there were about 75,200 jobs in 2014 and is expected to grow by 24% from 2014–2024. Just like all of the other healthcare jobs, we discussed, the graying of the population will lead to greater demand for eye care services. More and more physician offices such as ophthalmologists and optometrists are offering retail glasses and contact lenses as a way to expand their business and revenue. For earnings of opticians, please see the US Bureau of Labor Statistics at http://www.bls.gov/ooh/healthcare/opticians-dispensing.htm.

Physical Therapy

Physical Therapist (PT)

Physical therapy is a form of health care that prevents, identifies, corrects, or alleviates acute or prolonged movement dysfunction or pain of anatomic or physiologic origin, usually due to illness or injury. The practice of physical therapy includes but is not limited to:

- Measurement or testing of the function of the musculoskeletal, neurological, pulmonary, or cardiovascular system;

- Rehabilitative treatment concerned with restoring function or preventing disability caused by illness, injury, or birth defect;

- Treatment, consultative, educational, or advisory services to reduce the incidence or severity of disability or pain to enable, train, or retrain a person to perform the independent skills and activities of daily living; and

- Delegation of selective forms of treatment to support personnel while a physical therapist retains the responsibility for caring for the patient and directing and supervising the support personnel.

Work Environment

In the US, PTs held about 210,900 jobs in 2014. PTs usually work in private offices and clinics, hospitals, and nursing home. About 33% of all PTs in the US work in offices and about 28% work in hospitals in 2014. Because their work is so physically involved by moving patients and patients' limbs and bodies, it can be physically exhausting and they spend most of their time standing up. If PTs are not careful and lift patients properly, they may receive back and musculoskeletal injuries. Most PTs work full time, but in 2015 about 20% worked part time. The majority of PTs work normal business hours, but some may work evenings and/or weekends.

How to Become a PT

In the past, a PT needed to obtain a master's degree from an accredited physical therapy school, but those are slowly being phased out for the Doctor of Physical Therapy degree. Most DPT programs last 3 years and include both classroom and clinical experience. Most programs require a bachelor's degree for admission as well as specific prerequisites in courses such as biology, anatomy, physiology, and physics. Most DPT programs require applicants to apply for their programs through the Physical Therapist Centralized Application Service. You can find out about that service at their website: http://www.ptcas.org/home.aspx. There are 14 physical therapy schools in Texas. After graduation from the program, some PTs complete a residency in a specialization. Getting extra training and clinical experience in a specific area of care.

Licensure, Certifications, and Registrations

All states in the US require PTs to be licensed. While licensing requirements may vary state-by-state, all require passing the National Physical Therapy Examinations administered by the Federation of State Boards of Physical Therapy. Several states require a law exam and a criminal background check.

Only physical therapists (PTs) and physical therapist assistants (PTAs) licensed by the Texas Board of Physical Therapy Examiners can provide physical therapy in Texas. A PTA can provide physical therapy services only under the direction and supervision of a PT. A physical therapy aide or technician is a person not licensed by this Board who has on-the-job training and aids in the provision of physical therapy services only with onsite supervision of a PT or PTA. As of December 31, 2015, there were 16,239 actively licensed PTs in Texas. You can find information by the Texas Board of Physical Therapy Examiners here: http://www.ptot.texas.gov/page/home.

Important Qualities

As with all health professions, being a PT requires certain character traits. Some of those traits include:

- Communication skills

- Compassion

- Detail oriented

- Dexterity

- Interpersonal skills

- Physical stamina

- Resourcefulness[16]

Job Outlook

Job opportunities for physical therapists is expected to grow by 34% from 2014 to 2024. A large reason for this growth is for the same reason healthcare jobs will continue to increase – the added demand on the healthcare system due to the aging of the baby boomers. Older adults are more likely to suffer strokes, falls, and other mobility-related injuries than younger adults, thereby needing more rehabilitation. Further, chronic diseases are becoming more prevalent and those will demand more physical therapy. In addition, advances in medical technology allows us to treat more injuries and illnesses than ever before such as trauma inflicted injuries and birth defects. This will also create demand for rehabilitative care.

As you can see, physical therapy is a growing field and the demand for physical therapists is also growing. Most PTs work in offices along with occupational therapists and other healthcare professionals. They can make the difference in someone's life with whether or not they will walk again or be wheel-chair bound.

References

http://www.bls.gov/ooh/healthcare/physical-therapists.htm
http://www.ptot.texas.gov/page/home

Physical Therapy Assistants

Physical therapy assistants are often called PTAs and their job is do work under the direction of supervision of licensed physical therapists. PTAs are directly involved in patient care and work alongside PTs in helping people recover from injuries or illnesses and improve their movement.

Duties

Often a PT will evaluate a patient and work out a patient care plan for that patient. Then the PT will turn the patient over to the PTA to work through the exercises or activities in the care plan. They may give therapy through exercising, massage, balance training and teaching to walk and may use different types of equipment to help their patients heal or improve. They then record what the patient did and report directly to the physical therapist. Many times, they are involved with health promotion when working with patients to improve to the best of their ability.

Work Environment

In 2014, there were about 79,000 PTA in the US and as of December 31, 2015, there were 8,457 actively licensed PTAs in Texas. Almost half of all PTAs (43%) worked in offices and most work full time. Depending on the organization for which they worked, they may be required to work nights and weekends. PTAs are on their feet much of the day and must help move patients and set up special equipment. This requires using techniques to decrease the incidence of back and spinal injuries.

How to Become a PTA

Most states, including Texas, require PTAs to have an associate's degree from an accredited program and this program usually lasts about two years. In 2014 there were 298 accredited associate's degrees for PTAs in the

United States, 27 of those are in Texas. Training involves both classroom and clinical experience. You can learn about PTA schools in Texas at the Texas Physical Therapy Association at http://www.tpta.org/?page=PTASchools.

Licensure

All states except Hawaii require PTAs to be licensed or certified. In order to gain one's license, they must graduate from an accredited school and pass the National Physical Therapy Exam administered by the Federation of State Boards of Physical Therapy. Texas requires a criminal background check in addition to the exam. You can find out more about licensure at the Texas Board of Physical Therapy Examiners at http://www.ptot.texas.gov/page/home.

Important Qualities

Like physical therapists and other healthcare providers, physical therapy assistants need to exhibit certain character traits. Some of those qualities include:

- Compassion
- Detail oriented
- Dexterity
- Interpersonal skills
- Physical stamina[17]

Job Outlook

The US Bureau of Labor Statistics predicts that the employment of physical therapy assistants is projected to grow by 41% from 2014 to 2024. The reason for the increase in demand is the same for all other healthcare jobs and for physical therapists. The baby boomers are becoming older adults and will therefore will need more medical care. In addition, modern technological developments will increase the demand. Another reason for their rise in popularity is they will be cheaper to hire than PTs. An office can hire two PTAs for much less money than two PTs.

As one can see, physical therapy is a growing field with the demand rising quickly. Physical therapists and physical therapy assistants help people recover from injuries and diseases and improve their movement or mobility. Become a PT requires seven years of schooling and becoming a PTA requires two years of schooling beyond high school. Both are worthy professions.

Occupational Therapy

Occupational Therapists (OTs)

The practice of occupational therapy means the therapeutic use of everyday life activities (occupations) with individuals or groups for the purpose of participation in roles and situations in home, school, workplace, community, and other settings. Occupational therapy services are provided to those who have or are at risk for developing an illness, injury, disease, disorder, condition, impairment, disability, activity limitation, or participation restriction. Occupational therapy addresses the physical, cognitive, psychosocial, sensory, and other aspects of performance in a variety of contexts to support engagement in everyday life activities that affect health, wellbeing, and quality of life.

Occupational therapy allows patients to resume their activities of daily living (ADLs) and to resume work. They teach people skills like how to button their clothes, tie their shoes, brush their teeth and wash dishes either by hands or with assistive devices and they teach older adults how to make their living areas safer. These skills allow patients to live more independently. They also work with children and some work in educational settings. They evaluate children's disabilities and help teachers adapt their lessons and equipment to accommodate theirs students' disabilities.

Occupational therapists also work in mental health settings helping patients to cope with anger, developmental disabilities, mental illness or emotional problems. They may also work with patients who suffer from drug addictions, alcoholism, and depression. They teach skills such as time management and hobbies to help patients cope.

Duties

- Observe and evaluate patients doing tasks

- Evaluate patient's condition and needs

- Develop a treatment plan for patients, laying out the types of activities and specific goals to be accomplished

- Help people with various disabilities with different tasks, such as leading an autistic child in play activities

- Demonstrate exercises that can relieve pain for people with chronic pain

- Educate a patient's family and employer about how to accommodate and care for the patient

- Recommend special equipment like wheelchairs hearing aids and teach patients and families how to use the equipment

- Assess and record patients' progress and activities

- Report assessments and evaluations to physicians

- Utilize health promotion to help patients and their families live healthier lives

Work Environment

In 2014, there were about 114,600 jobs for occupational therapists. About 28% of them worked in hospitals and another 22% worked in offices. OTs spend quite a bit of time standing and often are required to lift patients and wheelchairs and other heavy equipment. Many work in more than one facility and must travel. Only about 25% of them work part time and depending on where they work, they may be required to work nights and weekends to accommodate patients' schedules.

How to Become an OT

Most OTs enter an accredited master degree program in occupational therapy having a bachelor degree in some type of health or science. Most OT schools have certain prerequisites and require a student to volunteer in a healthcare setting. In March 2013 there were 149 OT master degree programs in the US, with nine of those in Texas. These programs typically take about 3 years and include classroom and clinical experience. There are some programs that are dual degree where a student earns a bachelor and a master degree usually in about five or six years. Some OTs attend a Doctor of Occupational Therapy program and that usually takes about four years. All programs require at least 24 weeks of supervised clinical work where they gain experience. There are twelve doctor of occupational therapy schools in the US, none of which are in Texas.

Licensing

Only occupational therapists and occupational therapy assistants licensed by the Texas Board of Occupational Therapy Examiners (TBOTE) can provide occupational therapy in Texas. Approximately 9,525 occupational therapists are currently licensed by TBOTE. To obtain one's license a graduate from an accredited must pass the national examination administered by the National Board for Certification in Occupational Therapy. Occupational therapists can further their education and specialize in specific population groups or conditions. To learn about licensing in Texas, go to the Executive Council of Physical Therapy and Occupational Therapy Examiners website at http://www.ptot.texas.gov/page/home or the Texas Occupational Therapy Association website at http://www.tota.org/.

Important Qualities

- As with all healthcare occupations, OTs must possess certain personal characteristics. Those traits include the following:

- Communication skills

- Compassion

- Flexibility

- Interpersonal skills

- Patience

- Writing skills[18]

Job Outlook

The US Bureau of Labor Statistics expects the employment of occupational therapists to grow at least 27% between 2014 and 2024. The reason for this growth is much the same as for the other healthcare occupations studied thus far. The US has a large aging population that will need more therapeutic services and the population with chronic diseases is growing. Also, as more children are diagnosed with disabilities, occupational therapists will be needed to assist those children in learning ADLs. Lastly, as more people have health insurance, partly due to the Affordable Care Act, there will be a greater demand for healthcare services, occupational therapy included.

References

http://www.bls.gov/ooh/healthcare/occupational-therapists.htm

http://www.ptot.texas.gov/page/home

Occupational Therapy Assistant

Certified occupational therapy assistants (COTAs) assist OTs in their work. Most have direct patient contact and they help patients develop, recover, and improve ADLs and are directly involved in providing therapy to patients. Occupational therapy assistants work under the supervision of an occupational therapist.

Duties

While COTAs work under the supervision of an OT, they often perform much of the hands-on therapy and have a plethora of duties. Some of those duties include:

- Help patients do therapeutic activities, such as stretches and other exercises

- Lead children who have developmental disabilities in play activities that promote coordination and socialization

- Teach patients how to use special equipment; for example, showing a patient with Parkinson's disease how to use devices that make eating easier

- Record patients' progress, report to occupational therapists, and do other administrative tasks

- Prepare treatment areas, such as setting up therapy equipment

- Transport patients

- Clean treatment areas and equipment

- Help patients with billing and insurance forms

- Perform clerical tasks, including scheduling appointments and answering telephones[19]

Work Environment

In 2014, the US Bureau of Labor Statistics estimated there about 33,000 occupational therapy assistant jobs in the US and in December of 2015 there were 5,125 occupational therapy assistants in Texas. About 40% of those worked in offices and about 18% worked in skilled nursing facilities. COTAs spend most of their time on their feet working with patients and often lift heavy equipment and move patients. Most COTAs work full time and some may need to work evenings and weekends depending on the organization for which they work.

How to Become One

If you are interested in becoming a COTA, then you will need to take some prerequisite classes and volunteer or work in a healthcare setting, preferable for a physical therapist or an occupational therapist. Occupational therapists need an associate's degree from an accredited program. Most occupational therapy assistant programs can be found in community colleges or technical schools. In March 2013, there were 162 programs in the US accredited by the Accreditation Council for Occupational Therapy

Education; 13 of those schools were in Texas. Most programs usually require two years of full-time study and in addition to classroom work, students must complete 16 weeks of clinical experience.

Important Qualities

Much the same as the other healthcare providers studied thus far, occupational therapy assistants should possess key characteristics. Some of those qualities include the following:

- Compassion
- Detail oriented
- Flexibility
- Interpersonal skills
- Physical strength[20]

Licenses and Certifications

Almost all states require occupational therapy assistants to be licensed and Texas is one of those. To obtain one's license, a student must graduate from an accredited program, complete the fieldwork or clinical experience requirements and must pass the National Board for Certification in Occupational Therapy exam, thereby making them eligible to use the title "Certified Occupational Therapy Aide" (COTA).

Job Outlook

Employment of COTAs is projected by the US Bureau of Labor Statistics to grow by 43% from 2014 to 2024. Demand for this profession is caused by the demand for the other professions such as more people having health insurance, the aging of the population, new technology, and help for children with disabilities. COTAs with experience working in an occupational therapy office or other healthcare setting should have the best job opportunities.

As you can see, occupational therapy is a growing field and the need for occupational therapists and certified occupational therapy assistants is expected to grow exponentially in the next ten years. Becoming an OT requires at least six years of schooling and becoming a COTA requires about two to three after high school. As the older population grows, the demand for these professions will grow. Often hiring COTAs is very cost effective as compared to hiring an OT. It will be interesting in the coming years to see all of the many different ways occupational therapy will be used.

Pharmacy Occupations

Pharmacists

The practice of pharmacy is more than just counting out the right amount of a drug for a prescription. There is much more involved in the occupation and the Texas Pharmacy Act governs the practice of pharmacy in Texas and defines it as:

- Providing an act or service necessary to provide pharmaceutical care;

- Interpreting or evaluating a prescription drug order or medication order;

- Participating in drug or device selection as authorized by law, and participating in drug administration, drug regimen review, or drug or drug-related research

- Providing patient counseling;

- Being responsible for:
  - Dispensing a prescription drug order or distributing a medication order;
  - Compounding or labeling a drug and device other than by a manufacturer, repackager, or distributor of a nonprescription drug or commercially packaged prescription;
  - Properly and safely storing a drug or device; or
  - Maintaining proper records for a drug or device;
  - Performing for a patient a specific act of drug therapy management delegated to a pharmacist by a written protocol from a physician licensed in Texas; or
  - Administering an immunization or vaccination under a physician's written protocol.

Pharmacists also check medications so see if there are any negative interactions between them when given together. Many are available to answer phone calls a patient may have about a certain medication regarding side effects or over the counter drugs. Pharmacists also advise patients about general health topics such as diet, exercise and managing common every day illnesses and help patients select the best equipment or supplies to best treat a health problem. Further, pharmacists must maintain paperwork and oversee pharmacy technicians and pharmacists in training. Often physicians will consult with pharmacists before prescribing certain medication therapies.

Pharmacist Specialties

Pharmacists can specialize much the same as other healthcare providers. Often this comes with more education and experience in the field. Some of the pharmacist specialties include:

- Community pharmacists. Community pharmacists work in retail or chain drug stores or in independently owned pharmacies. They dispense medicines to patients and answer patients questions about medications and/or other health concerns. These pharmacists also give immunizations such as the shingles shot or flu shots.

- Clinical pharmacists. These pharmacists work in hospitals, clinics, and other healthcare settings. The direct medication dispensing to pharmacy technicians and are often involved in direct patient care. They may work with a team of physicians and nurses and give advice on certain medication dosages or administration and some conduct medical tests and advise patients.

- Consultant pharmacists. Consultant pharmacists advise healthcare facilities or insurance providers on patient medication or improving pharmacy services. Some may give advice to patients.

- Pharmaceutical industry pharmacists. These pharmacists work in areas such as marketing, sales, and research and development. They may design and conduct clinical drug trials for new drugs or help to develop new drugs. Pharmaceutical industry pharmacists may also help establish safety regulations and ensure quality control for drugs.

- College professors. Some pharmacists may teach pharmacy or medical students or conduct research.[21]

Work Environment

In the US in 2014, there were about 297,100 pharmacist jobs. Pharmacies and drug stores provided almost half of those jobs. Most pharmacists work in pharmacies, including those in grocery and drug stores. They spend quite a bit of time standing up and most work full time. Depending on the organization for which a pharmacist works, he or she may have to work some nights, weekends, or holidays.

How to Become a Pharmacist

In Texas, a person must graduate from a college of pharmacy with an accredited Bachelor of Science in Pharmacy or Doctor of Pharmacy degree (Pharm. D). It is important to note that it takes a minimum of five years to receive the BS degree and usually six years for the Pharm. D. Graduates of a foreign college of pharmacy must show that their pharmacy education meets US standards by passing the pharmacy graduate exam. To apply for the Doctor of Pharmacy degree, schools require certain science prerequisites and competition for acceptance is often stiff. In addition to graduation, a person must complete an internship of 1,500 hours and be at least 18 years of age and of good moral character.

R.Ph is an abbreviation for registered pharmacist and means that the person is registered or licensed by the Texas State Board of Pharmacy and is authorized to practice pharmacy in Texas. The pharmacist must be currently registered by the Texas State Board of Pharmacy to practice pharmacy in the state of Texas. A pharmacist in Texas must complete 30 hours of continuing education every two years in order to renew his or her pharmacist license.

Some pharmacists, especially those who own their own pharmacy, may get further education by getting a master of business administration (MBA) in addition to the Pharm D. degree while others may get Master of Public Health degree.

Licenses

All states license pharmacists. After they finish the Pharm D. program, they must pass two exams to get their license. The North American Pharmacist Licensure Exam tests pharmacy skill and knowledge. The Multistate Pharmacy Jurisprudence Exam or a state specific test on pharmacy law is also required. In order to be licensed in the state of Texas one must successfully complete and graduate from an accredited pharmacy school, complete an internship of 1,500 hours and pass a licensure examination given by the Texas State Board of Pharmacy which includes the subjects of chemistry, mathematics, pharmacy, pharmacology, practice of pharmacy and pharmacy law. A pharmacist is required to complete 30 hours of continuing education every two years in order to keep his or her license.

If a pharmacist moves to Texas and wants to practice pharmacy, the pharmacist must first obtain a license to practice pharmacy in Texas. Pharmacists may transfer their license from another state to Texas through a process called reciprocity. In order to use the title R.PH, a pharmacist must be registered or licensed by the Texas State Board of Pharmacy and authorized to practice pharmacy in Texas. The pharmacist must be currently registered by the Texas State Board of Pharmacy to practice pharmacy in the state of Texas. For information about pharmacists in Texas go to the Texas State Board of Pharmacy at http://www.pharmacy.texas.gov/index.asp.

Important Qualities

Much like the other healthcare professions, pharmacists are required to have certain personal characteristics. Some of those characteristics are as follows:

- Analytical skills
- Communication skills
- Computer skills
- Detail oriented
- Managerial skills[22]

Job Outlook

Employment of pharmacists is projected to grow by only 3% from 201.4 to 2024. While the aging population will require more medications, many will begin to use mail order pharmacies that employ many pharmacy technicians and fewer pharmacists. Still, demand is projected to increase in other healthcare settings such as hospitals and clinics. These pharmacists will be more directly involved in patient care.

The number of pharmacy schools has expanded recently. This creates more pharmacists and more competition for jobs. With the growth in the population and as it ages, though, there will always be a need for pharmacists. Pharmacists are well-respected members of the community and studies show they are one of the most trusted healthcare providers.

Pharmacy Technicians

A pharmacy technician is a person trained to assist pharmacists. Under the direction of licensed pharmacists, they can dispense prescription medication and usually work in retail pharmacies and hospitals. In Texas they can compound or mix certain medications and call physicians for prescription refill authorizations. They are the people in the pharmacy that create the prescription labels and packaging for patient medications. Often, they are responsible for inventorying medications and supplies and most accept payment and process insurance claims. They can also operate dispensing equipment when filling prescription orders. In hospitals, their jobs may require patient contact by giving medications to patients both intravenous medications and oral medications. To see the duty chart in the state of Texas, go to the Texas State Board of Pharmacy pharmacy technician page at http://www.pharmacy.texas.gov/techduties.asp. It differentiates between pharmacy technicians working in drug stores and those working in hospitals.

Work Environment

Most pharmacy technicians work in pharmacies and drug stores including chain stores. In the US in 2014, there were more than 297,000 pharmacy technician jobs in the US. More than half of those technicians worked in pharmacies and drug stores and this profession requires long hours of standing. Most pharmacy technicians work full time and because many pharmacies are open long hours a pharmacy tech may be required to work nights, weekends, and holidays.

How to Become a Pharmacy Technician

To work in a pharmacy as a pharmacy technician or pharmacy technician trainee, individuals must be registered with the Texas State Board of Pharmacy (TSBP). After TSBP notifies an individual of registration, the individual may work in a pharmacy. Texas requires every pharmacy to provide pharmacy technicians/trainees initial on-the-job training. All pharmacy technicians/trainees are required to complete the initial training when beginning employment in a pharmacy. The rules are very specific as to the areas that must be covered in on-the-job training programs. On-the-job training is the only training required for pharmacy technicians/trainees. Currently, there is not a requirement for a pharmacy technician/trainee to attend a formal education program. However, TSBP is aware that many pharmacy technicians are choosing to complete formal training programs in local community colleges or technical schools. The TSBP recognizes the importance and value of completing a formal education program and encourages pharmacy technicians/trainees to consider these programs. It should be noted that the curriculum and the costs of attending a formal program varies greatly. Individuals considering formal pharmacy technician education programs should consider the following:

- Is the pharmacy technician program accredited by the American Society of Health-System Pharmacists (ASHP)? TSBP has designated as "Board Approved Programs" any program that is currently accredited by ASHP.

- How long is the program and how much does the program cost? Length of and cost of programs may vary but must include at least 600 hours of instruction over a minimum of 15 weeks.

- Most programs include an externship during allowing the student to work in a pharmacy as part of the program. Individuals must be registered with TSBP as a pharmacy technician or pharmacy technician trainee before starting an externship in a pharmacy.

Licensure and Registration

Most states regulate pharmacy technicians. Usually they will include a criminal background check, high school diploma or GED, formal education or training program (this can be on the job training), an exam, fees, and continuing education hours. In Texas, when pharmacy trainees complete their training, they must take and pass a national certification examination through the Pharmacy Technician Certification Board. They will then be fingerprinted and go through a background check. There is a fee for becoming a registered pharmacy technician in Texas. For more information go to the Texas State Board of Pharmacy website and see the pharmacy technician registration information at http://www.pharmacy.texas.gov/Upgradetech.asp.

Important Qualities

Pharmacy technicians must possess certain character traits much the same as other professions. Some of those traits are included in the following:

- Customer-service skills

- Detail oriented

- Listening skills

- Math skills

- Organizational skills[23]

Job Outlook

Employment of pharmacy technicians is expected to grow by 9% from 2014 to 2024. The same factors that leads to the increase of available healthcare jobs contribute to this projection. The population is aging and therefore more there will be more chronic diseases requiring more medications as well as more people have access to health insurance and that will place a demand on the system. Another reason is that as the scope of practice for a pharmacist enlarges (giving immunizations and such), pharmacy techs are needed to fill in the gaps. It is also less expensive to employers to hire pharmacy technicians with a 2015 median salary of $30,100 compared to the 2015 median pay of a pharmacist at $121,500.

Even though growth in the pharmacy industry is slower than other healthcare fields, it is still expected to grow. Pharmacy is one of the most respected and trusted profession in the country. While some may prefer to go to pharmacy school, others may want to become pharmacy technicians with much less responsibility. For more information check out the US Bureau of Labor Statistics at http://www.bls.gov/ooh/healthcare/home.htm and the Texas State Board of Pharmacy at http://www.pharmacy.texas.gov/index.asp.

Dentistry

Dentists diagnose and treat problems with their patients' teeth, gums, and parts of the mouth. They use health promotion to provide advice on how to take care of their teeth and gums and how foods affect their oral health. Most dentists are general practitioners, although some may specialize in certain areas.

Duties

A Dentist has several duties and if one is in private practice, he or she may also be responsible for clinic management and bookkeeping. Some of those duties include the following:

- Remove cavities (decay) from teeth and fill in the cavity

- Repair cracked or broken teeth and remove teeth

- Straighten teeth to straighten the bite.

- Place sealants on teeth to protect from decay

- Use whitening agents to whiten teeth

- Administer numbing medications to prevent pain during procedures

- Examine x-rays of teeth, gums, the jaw and other nearby structures to detect decay and diseases

- Make models and measurements for dental appliances to fit patients

- Use health promotion techniques to teach patients about diet, fluoride use, flossing and other dental care

Dental Specialties

Some dentists want to further their education and specialize in an area. This usually requires more schooling and clinical experience under the supervision of licensed specialists. Some of the more popular dental specialties are:

- Dental public health specialists. These dentists work with special communities to promote dental health and prevent dental diseases.

- Endodontists. These dentists work with root canal therapy, where they remove the nerve and blood supply of injured or infected teeth.

- Oral and maxillofacial surgeons. These specialists perform surgery on the mouth, such as bumps or ulcers, and oral diseases such as cancer. They will often remove teeth, especially wisdom teeth, when the patient prefers to be anesthetized for the tooth extraction.

- Oral pathologists. These dentists diagnose conditions in the mouth such as ulcers, infections, and cancer.

- Orthodontists. These specialists straighten teeth by using braces or other appliances.

- Pediatric dentists. These dentists specialize in dentistry for children and adolescents.

- Periodontists. These specialists treat gums diseases and bones that support teeth.

- Prosthodontists. Prosthodontists replace missing teeth with permanent fixtures such as implants or crowns or bridges. They also work with dentures.[24]

Work Environment

In 2015, there were about 151,500 dentist jobs in the US. Some dentists own their businesses or clinics and work alone with a small staff including dental hygienists and dental assistants. Some dentists form partnerships with other dentists and have larger offices and share call. Most dentists work full time and some may work in the evenings and weekends. Most dentists continue to work past the usual retirement age of 65.

How to Become a Dentist

Most dental schools require a bachelor degree with certain science courses such as chemistry and biology as prerequisites, but each school varies in their requirements. College undergraduates who want to apply to dental school must take the Dental Acceptance Test (DAT) their junior year and admission to dental school is often very competitive. Dental schools look at the DAT, grade point averages, and recommendations very closely before they accept a student.

There are 65 dental schools in 36 states in the US, three of which are in Texas. Dental schools require students to take subjects like local anesthesia, anatomy, periodontology, and radiology. All dental schools include clinical experience where students work with patients in a clinical setting under the supervision of a licensed dentist. Some of the clinics are free or low cost clinics serving the community.

All nine specialties require extra training and practicing in their specialty and often require a one or two year residency. General dentists do not require any additional training after dental school. Dentists who want to teach at a dental school or do research must do even more advanced dental training for two to five years. Some dentists also teach part-time, including supervising students in dental school clinics.

Licensure

All states require dentists to obtain a license and the requirements for license vary by state but most require passing an examination. To get a license in Texas, an applicant must be 21 years old and of good moral character. They also must have graduated from an accredited dental school and pass an examination that includes everything from anatomy to jurisprudence to periodontia. Upon passing the exam, applying for a license in Texas, and paying the licensing fees, licensed dentists must complete 12 hours of continuing education yearly to renew their license. They also must complete and pass a healthcare provider cardiopulmonary resuscitation class.

If a dentist wants to specialize, then he or she must complete further schooling and at least two years of clinical residency before becoming eligible to apply for a specialty license. Information about licensing can be found at the Texas State Board of Dental Examiners at http://www.tsbde.texas.gov/index.html.

Important Qualities

As with all healthcare occupations, dentists are no different when it comes to needing to possess certain qualities. Some of those qualities include:

- Business management, leadership and organizational skills
- Communication skills
- Detail oriented
- Dexterity
- Patience
- Physical stamina
- Problem-solving skills[25]

Job Outlook

The growth of dentist jobs in the US is expected to grow by 18% from 2014–2024. The reason for this growth is much the same as for other health-care fields. As members of the baby boom generation age, they will probably need complicated dental work, such as root canals, bridges, crowns, and dentures. As people know more today about basic tooth care (brushing and flossing) more people are keeping their teeth and will need more dental care. Dentists will continue to use health promotion to help patients keep their teeth in good condition rather than just filling cavities.

Job Prospects

The US Bureau of Labor and Statistics projects that the employment of dentists will not keep up with the demand. There are still many areas of the country, especially rural and inner city that do not have access to dental care and experience maldistribution. For those with access to dentists, cosmetic dentistry involving procedures such as teeth whitening is becoming more popular. This trend is expected to continue to grow as new methods and technology will create less invasive and faster procedures.

Dental Assistants

Dental assistants work under the supervision of licensed dentists and often help dentists complete tasks during procedures, record keeping, making casts of a patient's teeth and prepare materials for use in treating patients. Depending on the state, dental assistant duties vary widely. In Texas if they make x-rays, monitor nitrous oxide conscious sedation, apply pit and fissure sealants or perform coronal polishing they are required to register with the Texas State Board of Dental Examiners. There are three types of dental assistants recognized by the TSBDE. Those three are called qualified dental assistants, registered dental assistants, and certified dental assistants. We will discuss how they got their titles later in the chapter

What Dental Assistants Do

Dental assistants work under the supervision of licensed dentists and many have the same job descriptions and duties. Some of those duties are as follows:

- Work with patients to make them comfortable in the dental chair and to prepare them for treatments and procedures

- Sterilize dental instruments

- Prepare the work area for patient treatment by setting out instruments and materials

- Help dentists by handing them instruments during procedures

- Keep patients' mouths dry by using suction hoses and other equipment

- Instruct patients in proper dental hygiene

- Process x-rays and complete lab tasks, under the direction of a dentist

- Keep records of dental treatments

- Schedule patient appointments

- Work with patients on billing and payment

Work Environment

In 2014 in the US there were about 318,800 dental assistant jobs. Most work in private dentist offices and always work under the supervision of a dentist. Many work closely with dental hygienists in day-to-day activities. They often wear safety glasses or shields, surgical masks, protective clothing and gloves to protect themselves and patients from infectious diseases. They also wear protective clothing when working with x-ray machines. Most dental assistants work part time, but about a third of them worked part time in 2014.

How to Become a Dental Assistant

Many community colleges and technical schools offer courses in dental assistants. In 2015, there were about 300 programs offered in the US. Some community colleges offer associate's degrees in dental assistantship. Texas has three levels of dental assistants. The levels depend on training and completing programs. Those levels are the following:

- A **Qualified Dental Assistant** is a dental assistant who has received on-the-job training or instruction through a dental assisting school or has been employed and trained by a licensed dentist. The TSBDE does not issue a certificate for this level of training or instruction. If a qualified dental assistant wants to make x-rays in Texas they must complete a TSBDE-approved Registered Dental Assistant (RDA) Course.

- A Registered Dental Assistant is a dental assistant who has successfully completed the state-level registration process with the TSBDE to hold a Texas RDA Certificate which will legally permit the assistant to make x-rays in Texas. Dental Assistants who successfully register with the TSBDE and hold the Texas RDA Certificate may use the credential "Registered Dental Assistant" or "RDA". An RDA Certificate must be displayed where x-rays are made.

- A Certified Dental Assistant is a dental assistant who meets the education and/or experience requirements established by the Dental Assistant National Board (DANB). This requires an assistant to take a course and pass the DANB Certified Dental Assistant (CDA) Examination (including Radiation Health and Safety (RSH), Infection Control (ICE) and national-level General Chairside (GC) component(s). The assistant must also hold a current CPR Card. Holding this certification requires a yearly renewal fee and continuing education. Dental Assistants who hold a CDA Card issued by DANB may use the "Certified Dental Assistant" or "CDA" credential behind their name.

Important Qualities

Similar to other healthcare professions, there are certain important characteristics a dental assistant must possess. Some of those qualities include:

- Detail oriented
- Interpersonal skills
- Listening skills
- Organizational skills[26]

Licensing, Certification, and Registration

Some states require dental assistants to be certified, licensed, or registered with the Dental Assisting National Board. To receive this certification, dental assistants must pass the Certified Dental Assistant Exam. The Texas State Board of Dental Examiners webpage for dental assistants can be found at http://www.tsbde.texas.gov/node/33.html.

Job Outlook

Employment of dental assistants is projected to grow 18% from 2014 to 2024. There is so much research linking good dental health to overall good health including heart health and pulmonary health, that the demand for these services will likely increase. When dentist hire dental assistants to perform routine tasks it gives them more time to devote to patient care. In addition, this field will grow because the baby boom population is aging and older adults need more dental care.

Dental Hygienists

Dental hygienists clean teeth, examine patients for signs of oral diseases and provide preventative care. They also employ health promotion techniques to teach people how to take care of their teeth. They use many different types of tool and perform x-rays on patients.

What Dental Hygienists Do

Dental hygienists often work with patients in a preventative setting. Most dental hygienists do some of the following:

- Remove tartar, stains, and plaque from teeth
- Apply sealants and fluorides to help protect teeth
- Take and develop dental x-rays
- Keep track of patient care and treatment plans
- Teach patients oral hygiene techniques, such as how to brush and floss correctly[27]

Work Environment

In 2015 there were about 200,500 dental hygienists employed in the US. Most dental hygienists work in dentists' offices and they work closely with dentists and dental assistants. In order to protect themselves from infectious diseases, they wear personal protective equipment much the same as dental assistants. They wear safety glasses or shields, surgical masks, and gloves. When they take x-rays, they follow strict procedures in order to protect themselves and their patients from unnecessary radiation. They often spend long periods of time bent over their patients. About half of all dental hygienists worked part time in 2014. That may be because many dentists take off one day a week.

How to Become a Dental Hygienist

Most dental hygienist enter the field by obtaining an associate degree in dental hygiene although bachelor degrees in dental hygiene are available in some states. In order to teach dental hygiene, a bachelor degree is required. Some programs require prerequisites in order to apply for the program and some require at least 30 hours of college, but each school has its own set of requirements. Dental hygiene school requires both classroom and clinical instruction. Hygienists study anatomy, physiology, nutrition, radiography, and periodontology (study of gum disease). Texas has 26 schools for dental hygiene. Most are community colleges or technical schools.

Licensing

Every state requires dental hygienists to be licensed and requirements for each state vary. Most states, including Texas, require a degree from an accredited dental hygiene program and passing grades on both written and clinical exams. Texas requires the exam to cover subjects and operations relating to dentistry and dental hygiene and include anatomy, pharmacology, x-ray, ethics, jurisprudence, hygiene, dental hygiene treatment planning, dental materials, physiology, pathology, microbiology and any other subject regularly taught in reputable schools that the board may require. Texas performs a criminal background check and an applicant has to be at least 18 years old and of good moral character. The rules and regulations about applying for a dental hygiene license can be found at the Texas State Board of Dental Examiners website at http://www.tsbde.texas.gov/documents/laws-rules/2014%20DPA.pdf. In Texas, licenses are renewed annually.

Important Qualities

There are many different character traits that are helpful for dental hygienists. Some of the more important ones include the following:

- Compassion
- Detail oriented
- Dexterity
- Interpersonal skills
- Physical stamina[28]

Job Outlook

Much like other healthcare professions, the demand for dental hygiene is expected to grow over the next ten years. The US Bureau of Labor Statistics projects a 19% growth from 2014-2024. The reason for this growth is the same as it is for other areas in dentistry: the aging of the population, the higher demand for services, and more insurance to cover preventative dental care.

Reference

http://www.bls.gov/ooh/healthcare/dental-assistants.htm

http://www.tsbde.texas.gov/node/32.html

As one can see, the field of dentistry is growing and is projected to grow faster than other non-healthcare professions in the next ten years. Texas requires formal education for dentists and dental hygienists but dental assistants can receive on-the-job training. With all of the new information we are learning about health and the correlation between dental health and personal health, it is becoming more important to maintain one's dental health. The general public realized this and thus the demand will be there for years to come.

Endnotes

*Denotes the beginning of a multiple-item reference.

1. http://www.bls.gov/ooh/healthcare/physician-assistants.htm#tab-2
2. Ibid
3. Ibid
4. Ibid
5. Ibid
6. http://www.bls.gov/ooh/healthcare/physician-assistants.htm#tab-4
7. Ibid
8. Ibid
9. Ibid
10. http://www.bls.gov/ooh/healthcare/registered-nurses.htm#tab-2
11. http://www.bls.gov/ooh/healthcare/registered-nurses.htm#tab-4
12. http://www.bls.gov/ooh/healthcare/licensed-practical-and-licensed-vocational-nurses.htm#tab-4
13. http://www.bls.gov/ooh/healthcare/nurse-anesthetists-nurse-midwives-and-nurse-practitioners.htm#tab-2
14. http://www.bls.gov/ooh/healthcare/nurse-anesthetists-nurse-midwives-and-nurse-practitioners.htm#tab-4
15. http://www.bls.gov/ooh/healthcare/opticians-dispensing.htm#tab-4
16. http://www.bls.gov/ooh/healthcare/physical-therapists.htm#tab-4
17. http://www.bls.gov/ooh/healthcare/physical-therapist-assistants-and-aides.htm#tab-4
18. http://www.bls.gov/ooh/healthcare/occupational-therapists.htm#tab-4

19. http://www.bls.gov/ooh/healthcare/occupational-therapy-assistants-and-aides.htm#tab-2

20. http://www.bls.gov/ooh/healthcare/occupational-therapy-assistants-and-aides.htm#tab-4

21. http://www.bls.gov/ooh/healthcare/pharmacists.htm#tab-2

22. http://www.bls.gov/ooh/healthcare/pharmacists.htm#tab-4

23. http://www.bls.gov/ooh/healthcare/pharmacy-technicians.htm#tab-4

24. http://www.bls.gov/ooh/healthcare/dentists.htm#tab-2

25. http://www.bls.gov/ooh/healthcare/dentists.htm#tab-4

26. http://www.bls.gov/ooh/healthcare/dental-assistants.htm#tab-4

27. http://www.bls.gov/ooh/healthcare/dental-hygienists.htm#tab-2

28. http://www.bls.gov/ooh/healthcare/dental-hygienists.htm#tab-4

Chapter 8

Allied Health Professions

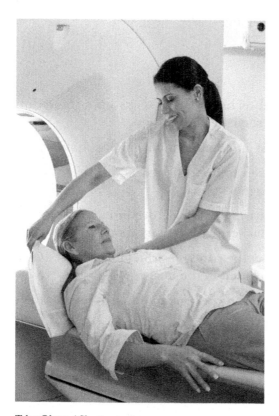

Tyler Olson / Shutterstock.com

Imaging

Radiologic and MRI Technologists

Healthcare professionals often use different types of imaging equipment when making diagnoses. Radiologic technicians (rad techs) are known as radiographers and perform diagnostic imaging examinations. They specialize in x-ray and computed tomography (CT scan or CAT scan) on patients. Some rad techs prepare medications for patients to take before the exams that allows soft tissue to be viewed more easily. Some rad techs may specialize in mammography. Mammographers use lose dose x-rays to produce images of the breast tissue to check for diseases like cancer. Many rad techs are certified in several different types of specialties and are flexible in their jobs.

Magnetic resonance imaging (MRI) technicians, known as MRI techs, use scanners to create diagnostic images of the insides of patients. They inject dyes into their patients that help certain images show up better on the scanner. The scanners use magnetic fields combined with the contrasting agents (usually some type of non-dangerous radioactive isotope) to produce images that help physicians make diagnoses.

Duties

Both rad techs and MRI techs have some duties in common. The following are some of their duties:

- Adjust and maintain imaging equipment

- Precisely follow orders from physicians on what areas of the body to image

- Prepare patients for procedures, including taking a medical history and answering questions about the procedure

- Protect the patient by shielding exposed areas that do not need to be included in the images

- Position the patient and the equipment to get the correct image

- Operate the computerized equipment to take the images

- Work with physicians to evaluate the images and to determine whether images need to be taken

- Keep detailed patient records.[1]

Work Environment

Rad techs held about 197,000 jobs in 2014 and MRI techs held about 33,600 jobs in the US. Rad techs and MRI techs work in healthcare facilities and are often on their feet for long periods of time. They must also be able to lift and/or turn heavy patients or patients who are disabled. Most rad techs and MRI techs work full time, and dependent on where they work, they may have to work nights, weekends, and holidays.[2]

How to Become One

Most MRI techs start out as rad techs and then return to school to specialize. Becoming a rad tech involves getting an associate degree in radiography. Most of these programs can be found at community colleges or technical institutes. This type of education involves both classroom work and clinical work. The Joint Review Committee on Education in Radiologic Technology accredits radiographic programs in the US and in Texas you must complete one of the programs to be licensed.

Licenses and Certifications

As of October 2015, Rad techs and MRI techs in Texas are licensed by the Texas Medical Board. To receive your license you must pass a certification exam from the American registry of Radiologic Technologists, submit fingerprints and pass a criminal background check, submit all transcripts and verification of education and exams, and pay an eighty dollar fee. You can find out more about the Texas Medical Board licensing rad techs here; http://www.tmb.state.tx.us/page/licensing-full-medical-radiologic-technologist.

MRI techs are first licensed rad techs who have a certain amount of work experience with MRIs to meet certification criteria. MRI techs must complete a certain number of documented imaging examinations and 16 hours of formal education to be certified. MRI tech certification is done through the American Registry of Radiologic Technologists (ARRT) and you can find information about this profession on their website at https://www.arrt.org/. Texas accepts certification from the ARRT.

Important Qualities

Just as other healthcare providers need to have certain personal characteristics, rad techs and MRI techs are no different. Some of the most important traits for them to have include the following:

- Detail oriented
- Interpersonal skills
- Math skills
- Physical stamina
- Technical skills[3]

Job Outlook

The employment of rad techs is expected to grow by more than 9% from 2014 to 2024 and the employment of MRI techs is projected to grow by 10% during that same time period. Reasons for growth are the same as all of the other healthcare professions we covered thus far. As the population ages, they will need more imaging examinations because they are at higher risk of cancer, heart disease, Alzheimer's and breaking bones. Rad techs and MRI techs are needed to take these images. Another reason for growth is that there will be a higher demand due to the increase in number of the people who have health insurance.

Radiation Therapists

Radiation therapists operate machines called linear accelerators used to deliver radiation therapy. Linear accelerators deliver high-energy x-rays at specific cancer cells in a patient's body, thereby shrinking them or removing them. Radiation therapists are part of an oncology team that treat cancer patients and they often work with radiation oncologists, oncology nurses, and medical physicists.

Duties

Radiation therapists have certain job oriented tasks. Some of those include the following:

- Explain treatments to patients and answer questions
- Follow safety procedures to protect patients and themselves from unnecessary radiation exposure
- Make sure the machines are in proper working order
- X-ray the patient to determine the exact location of the area needing treatment
- Adjust the machine to deliver the correct dosage of radiation to the patient
- Operate the linear accelerator
- Monitor the patient to check for unusual reactions to the treatment
- Keep detailed records and report back to the physician

Work Environment

In 2014, there were about 16,000 radiation therapists' jobs in the US. Most worked in hospitals, doctors' offices, and outpatient centers. Radiation therapists often stand on their feet for long periods of time and may need to lift or turn patients. Because of their continuous work with radiation, they must take proper precautions to protect themselves from exposure to radiation. Usually, radiation therapists will stand in a different lead lined room while the patient undergoes the radiation. Most radiation therapists work full time and most work regular business hours.

How to Become a Radiation Therapist

Most radiation therapists have either an associate degree or a bachelor degree in radiation therapy. In some states, radiation techs can complete a certificate program that usually is a twelve month program. In 2014, there were 120 accredited schools recognized by the American Registry of Radiation Technologists (ARRT) and there are six radiation therapy schools in Texas. You can find a listing of those schools at https://www.arrt.org/Education/Educational-Programs.

Important Qualities

Since radiation therapists work mainly with people who are sick or have cancer, there are certain personal traits they must possess. Some of those traits include the following:

- Detail oriented
- Interpersonal skills
- Physical stamina
- Technical skills[4]

Licenses

In most states, radiation therapists must be certified and this includes Texas. In order to be licensed, a candidate must have successfully completed an accredited program, passed a background check, pass the ARRT certification exam, and pay a licensing fee. The exam covers radiation protection, quality assurance, clinical concepts, treatment planning and delivery, and patient care and education. In Texas, licenses are provided by the Texas Department of State Health Services and you can find that information on their website at http://dshs.texas.gov/radiation/.

Job Outlook

Radiation therapists will see a 14% growth in jobs from 2014 to 2024. Since it is such a small occupation and is so very specialized, this will only add about 2,300 new jobs over the ten year period. As people age, their risk of cancer increases and continued advancement in the early detection of some cancers will create the demand for radiation therapists. As science develops new treatments, there may be an even greater demand for their services.

Diagnostic Medical Sonographers and Cardiovascular Technologists and Technicians, including Vascular Technologists

Diagnostic medical sonographers and cardiovascular technologists and technicians operate special imaging equipment to create images or conduct tests.[5] These images help physicians diagnose and assess medical conditions. Sometimes, technologists assists physicians and surgeons during procedures. For example, a sonographer may use an ultrasound machine to show a physician exactly where to place a needle to deliver an injection.

Duties

Diagnostic medical sonographers and cardiovascular technologists and technicians, including vascular technicians usually do the following duties:

- Prepare patients for procedures and answer any questions about the procedure

- *Prepare and maintain diagnostic imaging equipment

- Operate equipment to obtain diagnostic images or to conduct tests

- Review images or test results to check for quality and adequate coverage of the areas needed for diagnoses

- Recognize the difference between normal and abnormal images and other diagnostic information

- Analyze diagnostic information to provide a summary of findings for physicians

- Record findings and keep track of patients' records[6]

Diagnostic Medical Sonographers

Using ultrasound or sonograms, a diagnostic medical sonographer creates images of the body's organs and tissues or of unborn babies. Because of the low exposure to radiation and the low cost, sonogram is often the first imaging test physicians order when a person is suspected of having certain conditions. For example, if a physician expects a patient to have gall stones or gall bladder disease, he or she will order a sonogram of the gall bladder to see if there are any stones or if it looks okay.

Diagnostic sonography uses high-frequency sound waves to produce images of the inside of the body. It is much like radar. The sonographer uses an instrument called an ultrasound transducer on the patient's body where it will be examined. The transducer emits sound waves that bounce back causing echoes. The ultrasound machine then processes those echoes into an image and displays it for the sonographer and physician to see.

Sonogram is often used to determine the sex, gestational age, weight, and length of unborn babies.

There are different types of diagnostic medical sonographers. Here are some examples:

- Abdominal sonographer. Abdominal sonographer specializes in patients' abdominal cavity and nearby organs like the kidney, liver, gallbladder, pancreas, or spleen.[7] If biopsies require ultrasound guidance, the abdominal sonographer will often assist with the procedure.

- Breast sonographer. Breast sonographers specialize in breast tissues. Often when a cyst or tumor is detected with mammography, a breast sonographer can confirm the growth and can help guide physicians for a needle biopsy.

- Musculoskeletal sonographers. These sonographers specialize in imaging muscles, ligaments, tendons, and joints.[8] They often assist with guiding injections or with surgical procedures to guide medication or treatment directly to the affected area.

- Pediatric sonographers. Pediatric sonographers specialize in imaging child and infant patients.[9] Since many of the medical conditions they image are associated with premature births or birth defects, pediatric sonographers often work closely with physicians and other healthcare professionals.

- Obstetric and gynecological sonographers. These sonographers specialize in imaging female reproductive organs. When a patient presents with pelvic pain, often her physician will order a pelvic sonogram to detect any abnormal cysts or tissue. Many of these are done in the physician's office.

Cardiovascular Technologists and Technicians

Cardiovascular technologists and technician create images, conduct tests, or assist with surgical procedures involving the heart. The following are examples of cardiovascular technologists and technicians[10]:

- Cardiac sonographers (echocardiographers). Cardiac sonographers specialize in imaging a patient's heart using ultrasound equipment. They are able to examine the heart's chambers, valves, and vessels. The images are called echocardiograms or cardiac echoes for short. The echocardiogram can be done while the patient is resting or after being physically active.[11] An interesting point about cardiac sonographers is that they can take pictures of the fetal heart so physicians can diagnose cardiac conditions in babies before they are born. Sometimes, physicians are then able to surgically correct those abnormalities while the baby is still in the uterus.

- Cardiovascular invasive specialists or cardiac catheterization technologists, also known as cardiovascular technologists. Cardiovascular technologists monitor patients' heart rates and help physicians diagnose and treat problems with patients' hearts. They assist with cardiac catheterization involving a thin tube through a patient's artery up to the coronary arteries.[12] They then will inject dye and take images to see if there is any blockages in the coronary arteries (the arteries that feed the heart muscle). Cardiovascular techs also prepare patients before and during open heart surgery and when inserting pacemakers and stents.

- Cardiographic electrocardiogram (EKG) technician (EKG tech). EKG techs specialize in administering EKG testing. EKG monitor patients' heart through electrodes attached to the patient's chest, arms, and legs.[13] EKG testing can be done while the patient is at rest or is active. For stress tests, patients are hooked up to an EKG machine and walk on a treadmill until they get their heart rate up. The technician gradually increases the speed to observe the effect on the heart of increased exertion.

Vascular Technologists (Vascular Sonographers)

Vascular techs are closely related to cardiovascular techs and their duties are very similar. They create images of the blood vessels and collect data that help doctors diagnose disorders affecting blood flow. Often they will measure patients' blood pressure and the volume of blood in their arms, legs, fingers, and toes to evaluate blood flow and identify blocked arteries. They use ultrasound equipment blood pressure cuffs and oximeters to check the amount of oxygen saturation in the blood and to detect the presence of blood clots.

Work Environment

There were about 112,700 jobs in 2014 for diagnostic sonographers and cardiovascular technicians and technologists, including vascular technologists. Many of them work in hospitals (68%) and outpatient centers and often stand up for long periods of time. Often they work in dimly lit rooms, but they may also perform procedures at patients' bedsides. Most diagnostic imaging workers work full time and depending on what they do and where they work, many will work nights, weekends, and holidays.

How to Become One

Colleges and universities offer both associate and bachelor degree programs in sonography and cardiovascular and vascular technology. One year certificate programs are also available from colleges and/or hospitals. Education in this field requires both classroom work and clinical work and courses include anatomy, physiology, medical terminology, and applied sciences. Most sonography programs are divided into specialized fields that correspond to relevant certification exams.

Most employers prefer to hire diagnostic imaging workers with professional certification. Many insurance companies and Medicare will only pay for procedures performed by a certified sonographer or technologist. Certification is available from the American Registry for Diagnostic Medical Sonographers) http://www.ardms.org/Pages/default.aspx) and Cardiovascular Credentialing International (http://www.cci-online.org/).

Licenses and/or Certification

Diagnostic imaging workers can earn certification by graduating from an accredited program and passing an exam. Most of the certifications are for specialties in diagnostic imaging such as abdominal sonography. Few states require diagnostic medical sonographers to be licensed. Texas does not require licensing at this time but they prefer certification.

Important Qualities

There are certain personal qualities that a person needs to be in this specialty area. Because of their direct patient contact and the technicality of the job, some of those qualities include the following:

- Detail oriented
- Hand-eye coordination
- Interpersonal skills
- Physical stamina
- Technical skills

Job Outlook

*Employment of diagnostic medical sonographers is projected to grow 26 percent from 2014 to 2024, much faster than the average for all occupations. Employment of cardiovascular technologists and technicians, including vascular technologists, is projected to grow 22 percent from 2014 to 2024, much faster than the average for all occupations.

As imaging technology evolves, medical facilities will continue to use ultrasound to replace more invasive, costly procedures. Ultrasound is often less expensive than other imaging technologies and is often used as a first-line tool for diagnosis. Third-party payers encourage the use of these noninvasive measures over invasive ones in order to save on costs. Diagnostic medical sonographers, cardiovascular technologists and technicians, and vascular technologists will continue to be needed in healthcare settings to provide an alternative to imaging techniques that involve radiation.

In addition, growth in the industry will continue due to the aging of the baby boom population and the increased demand for healthcare services. Heart disease is the number one cause of death in the US and we will need more workers who can help diagnose and treat this issue.[14]

Nuclear Medicine Technologists

Nuclear medicine technologists operate equipment that creates images of areas of a patient's body. They prepare and inject radioactive drugs into the patient and then take images of their body. The radioactive drugs cause abnormal areas "light up" and to appear differently than normal areas.

Duties

Nuclear medicine technologists have very specialized jobs but almost all perform the same duties. Those duties include:

- Explaining the procedures to the patient and answer questions

- Follow safety procedures to protect themselves and the patient from unnecessary radiation exposure

- Examine machines to ensure that they work correctly

- Prepare radioactive drugs and administer them to the patient

- Monitor the patient to check for unusual reactions to the drugs

- Operate equipment that creates images of areas in the body, such as images of organs

- Keep detailed records of procedures

Radiopharmaceuticals are radioactive drugs that give off radiation that allow special scanners to monitor tissue and organ functions. Abnormal areas will either absorb more of the drug and therefore show up more brightly or absorb less of the drug and show up more darkly than normal tissue. Physicians and surgeons can then interpret the images and make diagnoses based on those.

Work Environment

Nuclear medicine technologists held about 20,700 jobs in 2014. Hospitals employed about 69% of them. Most technologists spend quite a bit of time on their feet and have to be able to physically lift or turn disabled patients. Most of these techs work full time and depending on where they are employed, they may be expected to work nights, weekends and holidays.

There are some hazards associated with this occupation, but they are minimized by the use of gloves and other shielding devices. Nuclear medicine techs wear radiation badges that measure the amount of radiation to which they are exposed. Instruments monitor their radiation exposure and keep detailed records of how much radiation they get. When preparing the radioactive drugs, they use safety procedures to minimize their exposure. Life other healthcare professionals, they are often exposed to infectious diseases and so take personal protection very seriously.

How to Become a Nuclear Medicine Technologist

Usually, nuclear medicine technologists earn an associate degree in nuclear medicine technology but bachelor degrees are also common. Some technologist earn a bachelor degree in a related field such as physiology, chemistry radioactive drugs, or biology and then complete a one year certificate program. The Joint Review Committee on Educational Programs in Nuclear Medicine Technology accredits nuclear medicine programs. You can find information about them at their website at http://jrcnmt.org/.

Licenses and Certifications

As of 2015, about half of all states required nuclear medicine technologists to be licensed. Requirements vary by state and Texas licenses go through the Texas Department of State Health Services. In order to be licensed, they must be certified through the American Registry of Radiologic Technologists and/or the Nuclear Medicine Technology Certification Board (NMTCB). Once a person is certified, then they are usually qualified for licensing in any state.

Technologists can earn specialty certifications that show proficiency in specific procedures or on certain equipment. Specialty areas include positron emission tomography (PET scans), nuclear cardiology (NCT), or computed tomography (CT). The NMTCB offers certification for all of these specialties.

Important Qualities

Just as other healthcare professionals have to possess certain traits, nuclear medicine technologists must possess certain qualities. Those qualities include the following:

- Ability to use technology
- Analytical skills
- Compassion

- Detail oriented
- Interpersonal skills
- Physical stamina

Job Outlook

Nuclear medicine techs is projected to grow about 2% from 2014 to 2024. This is one of the slowest growing fields of all of the healthcare professions. Although, more people will need this type of medicine as the population ages, insurance companies and Medicare encourage the use of less costly tests such as ultrasound and noninvasive imaging techniques.

As you can see, imaging has many different occupational paths that one might take. Some take more schooling and training than others but all of these paths are projected to increase in the number of available jobs in the next ten years or so. You can find links to all of these occupations at the US Bureau of Labor Statistics at http://www.bls.gov/ooh/healthcare/home.htm.

Respiratory Technology

Respiratory Therapists

Respiratory Therapists (RTs) take care of people who have breathing problems such as pneumonia, emphysema or asthma. They have patients in all age ranges from premature babies to older adults. Many RTs also provide patient to care from people who drowned, had a heart attack, experienced some type of traumatic injury or are in shock.

Duties

Respiratory therapists work with patients to improve the levels of oxygen and their blood and help them breathe more easily. The following are some of their duties:

- Interview and examine patients with breathing or cardiopulmonary disorders
- Consult with physicians to develop patient plans for treatment
- Perform diagnostic tests, such as measuring lung capacity and blood oxygen and carbon dioxide levels
- Treat patients by using a variety of methods, including chest physiotherapy and aerosol medications (medications entering the body through breathing)
- Remove mucus from patients' lungs to help them breathe easier

- Insert a tube in patients' windpipes and attach those patients to ventilators

- Monitor and record patients' progress

- Teach patients how to use treatments and equipment, such as ventilators

Work Environment

About four out of five RTs work in hospitals and others work in nursing facilities and physicians' offices. They may stand for long periods of time and they have to be able to lift or turn patients who cannot do so on their own. RTs work closely with a medical team to deliver care to patients and most work full time. Because the majority of them work in hospital or nursing facilities, they may be required to work evenings, weekends, and holidays.

How to Become One

In most states, including Texas, completion of a program that is accredited by the Commission on Accreditation for Respiratory Care is required. RTs need at least an associate's degree in respiratory care but some employers prefer applicants who have a bachelor degree. Respiratory therapy programs are offered by colleges and universities, vocational-technical institutes, and the Armed Forces. RT school usually requires courses in human anatomy and physiology, chemistry, physics, math, microbiology and pharmacology. They also study treatments, making diagnoses, equipment, and cardiopulmonary resuscitation. In addition, they must complete clinical components of the program to give them practical experience.

Licensing

In Texas, The Texas Medical Board issues all licensing and licensure is required to practice respiratory therapy. In order to become licensed, an applicant must pass a national exam, pass a background check, submit all necessary documents and transcripts and pay a fee.

The National Board for Respiratory Care is the main certifying body for respiratory therapists and offers two levels of certification: Certified Respiratory Therapist (CRT) and Registered Respiratory Therapist (RRT). CRT is the first-level of certification and required applicants to have completed a program from an accredited school (at least an associate degree) and pass an exam. RRT applicants must have a CRT certification, meet additional education requirement and experience requirements and pass an exam.

Important Qualities

Respiratory therapists work directly with patients, families, and medical staff and must possess certain personal characteristics. The following are some of the important characteristics.

- Compassion
- Detail oriented
- Interpersonal skills
- Patience
- Problem-solving skills
- Science and math skills

Job Outlook

Employment of respiratory therapists is projected to grow at least 12% from 2014 to 2024 for the same reasons as other healthcare professions. The aging of the population will lead to more respiratory conditions such as pneumonia, chronic obstructive pulmonary disease (COPD), chronic bronchitis and other lung disorders or dysfunctions. Because there is a growing emphasis on reducing hospital readmissions, there may be more opportunities for respiratory therapists in offices of physicians and other outpatient services. In addition, with the increase of medical technology and the development of new treatments, there will be an increase in demand for these services.

Dietetics

Dietitians and Nutritionists

Often people who have certain chronic diseases or other issues will need to work with someone who specializes in the use of food and nutrition. Those specialists are called dietitians and nutritionists. They are the specialists who advise people on what to eat in order to lead a healthy lifestyle or achieve a specific health-related goal.

Duties

The profession of dietetics includes six primary areas of expertise: clinical, educational, management, consultation, community and research, and includes without limitation the development, management, and provision of nutrition services. Some of their duties include:

- Assess patients' and clients' nutritional and health needs
- Counsel patients on nutrition issues and healthy eating habits

- Develop meal plans, taking both cost and clients' preferences into account

- Evaluate the effects of meal plans and change the plans as needed

- Promote better health by speaking to groups about diet, nutrition, and the relationship between good eating habits and preventing or managing specific diseases

- Keep up with or contribute to the latest food and nutritional science research

- Write reports to document patients' progress

- Dietitians and nutritionists evaluate the health of their clients. Based on their findings, dietitians and nutritionists advise clients on which foods to eat—and which to avoid—to improve their health.

- Many dietitians and nutritionists provide customized information for specific individuals. For example, a dietitian or nutritionist might teach a client with diabetes how to plan meals to balance the client's blood sugar. Others work with groups of people who have similar needs. For example, a dietitian or nutritionist might plan a diet with healthy fat and limited sugar to help clients who are at risk for heart disease. They may work with other healthcare professionals to coordinate patient care.

- Dietitians and nutritionists who are self-employed may meet with patients, or they may work as consultants for a variety of organizations. They may need to spend time on marketing and other business-related tasks, such as scheduling appointments, keeping records, and preparing educational programs or informational materials for clients.

Types of Dietitians and Nutritionists

There are three major types of dietitians and nutritionists in the US. Often, they have different levels of education and clinical practices. Those three types are:

- *Clinical dietitians and clinical nutritionists* provide medical nutrition therapy. They work in hospitals, long-term care facilities, clinics, private practice, and other institutions. They create nutritional programs based on the health needs of patients or residents and counsel patients on how to improve their health through nutrition. Clinical dietitians and clinical nutritionists may further specialize, such as by working only with patients with kidney diseases or those with diabetes.

- *Community dietitians and community nutritionists* develop programs and counsel the public on topics related to food, health, and nutrition. They often work with specific groups of people, such as adolescents or the elderly. They work in public health clinics, government and nonprofit agencies, health maintenance organizations (HMOs), and other settings.

- *Management dietitians* plan food programs. They work in food service settings such as cafeterias, hospitals, prisons, and schools. They may be responsible for buying food and for carrying out other business-related tasks, such as budgeting. Management dietitians may oversee kitchen staff or other dietitians.

Work Environment

Dietitians and nutritionists held about 66,700 jobs in 2014 in the US. About 30% of those were employed by hospitals, the government employed about 14%, nursing and residential care facilities employed about 19%, outpatient care centers employed about 8% and accommodation and food services employed about 5%. They often visit directly with clients and most of their work is done in an office setting. Most work regular business hours but may be called in on weekends if they work at an in-care facility.

How to Become One

Most dietitians and nutritionists have a bachelor degree in dietetics, foods and nutrition, clinical nutrition, public health nutrition, or a related area. Many have advanced degrees such as a master degree or a Ph.D. Dietitians and nutritionists must have several hundred hours of clinical supervised training in different settings as required by the degree. Some programs, especially advanced degreed programs, include the clinical training with the degree requirements.

Licensure

Most states require dietitians and nutritionists to be licensed in order to practice, but some only require registration or certification to use certain titles. The requirements differ state by state but must include at least having a bachelor degree, clinical experience and passing an exam. Many choose to earn the Registered Dietitian Nutritionist (RDN) credential. Although the RDN is not always required, the qualifications are often the same as those necessary for becoming a licensed dietitian in states that require a license. Many employers prefer or require the RDN that is administered by the Commission on Dietetic Registration, the credentialing agency for the Academy of Nutrition and Dietetics.

Texas requires licensure to practice and at the time of this writing, licensing is granted by the Department of State Health Services. However, in 2017, licensing will be regulated by the Texas Department of Licensing and Regulation. In order to apply for a license in Texas, one must possess a bachelor degree or higher degree with a major course of study in human nutrition, food and nutrition, nutrition education dietetics or food systems management, served an internship that was completed within three years of graduation, pass an examination within three years of applying for the license, pass a background check, submit all official documents and pay a licensing fee. More about licensing in Texas can be found at http://dshs. texas.gov/dietitian/dt_rules.shtm.

Important Qualities

Nutrition is a vital part of health and proper nutrition can sometimes mean the difference between life and death and definitely impacts the quality of life a person has. Because of the important role they play, here are some of the personal characteristics nutritionists and dietitians must possess:

- Analytical skills
- Compassion
- Listening skills
- Organizational skills
- Problem-solving skills
- Speaking skills

Job Outlook

Employment of dietitians and nutritionists is projected to grow 16% from 2014 to 2024. One of the reasons for this is that knowledge of the role food plays in health has increased and more people are aware of the part in plays in preventative care and treatment. According to the Centers for Disease Control and Prevention (CDC), more than 33% of the adults in the US are obese. Obesity affects all body systems and major organs and many serious and dangerous conditions are associated with obesity. As the population's weight grows, there will be more health problems resulting in the need for more dietitians and nutritionists. Also, as the population ages, there will be more chronic diseases that require certain nutrient based treatments and prevention, thereby increasing the need for their services.

Emergency Medical Technicians (EMT) and Paramedics

EMTs and paramedics deliver care for the critically sick or injured population when they respond to an emergency call. Often a person's life depends on the quick reaction and competent care provided by these workers. They are usually involved in on-the-scene care and transporting the patient to a medical facility. In the US, people in emergency situations call 911 on their telephones. The 911 operator then dispatches the type(s) of responder those people need. If it is a medical emergency, the operator will dispatch emergency medical services made of EMTs and paramedics.

Duties

- Respond to 911 calls for emergency medical assistance, such as cardiopulmonary resuscitation (CPR) or bandaging a wound

- Assess a patient's condition and determine a course of treatment

- Provide first-aid treatment or life support care to sick or injured patients

- Transport patients safely in an ambulance

- Transfer patients to the emergency department of a hospital or other healthcare facility

- Report their observations and treatment to physicians, nurses, or other healthcare facility staff

- Document medical care given to patients

- Inventory, replace, and clean supplies and equipment after use

- When transporting a patient in an ambulance, one EMT or paramedic may drive the ambulance while another monitors the patient's vital signs and gives additional care. If it is a heart attack victim, then it often requires 2 responders in the back of the ambulance with the patient so often a fire truck or another ambulance will show up to the scene. Some paramedics work as part of a helicopter's or an airplane's flight crew to transport critically ill or injured patients to a hospital

- EMTs and paramedics also transport patients from one medical facility to another. Some patients may need to be transferred to a hospital that specializes in treating their particular injury or illness or to a facility that provides long-term care, such as a nursing home

- If a patient has a contagious disease, EMTs and paramedics decontaminate the interior of the ambulance and may need to report the case to the proper authorities

How to Become One

Becoming an EMT or paramedic requires both classroom and clinical experience. Often these programs are provided by community colleges or technical institutions. Some universities offer certifications for EMTs and paramedics. Many students studying to be healthcare providers become EMTs when they are in college to give them hands-on patient experience.

Educational and Legal Requirements in Texas (From the Texas Department of State Health Services)

- You must be at least 18 years old

- Have a high school diploma or GED certificate

- Successfully complete a DSHS approved EMS training course

- Submit a completed EMS Personnel Certification application and fee

- Pass the National Registry exam

- Submit fingerprints for Texas/FBI criminal history check

- Paramedic licensure applicants are required to follow the steps above and submit proof of either a two-year EMS degree or a 4 year degree in any field.

Levels of Certification

The specific responsibilities of EMTs and paramedics depend on their level of certification and the state in which they work. The National Registry of Emergency Medical Technicians provides national certification of EMTs and paramedics at three levels: EMT, Advanced EMT, and Paramedic. Some states have their own certification programs and use similar titles.

Texas has five levels of certification for emergency responders. You can find out more about the requirements for each level in Texas at the Texas Department of State Health Services website at http://www.dshs. texas.gov/emstraumasystems/CertInfo.shtm. Those levels of certification are (highest to lowest):

- Licensed Paramedic

- EMT-Paramedic

- EMT-Intermediate

- EMT-Basic

- Emergency Care Attendant (ECA)

Work Environment

EMTs and paramedics work indoors and out in all types of weather and terrain. Their job can be physically strenuous and often requires kneeling, heaving lifting, and bending. It can be stressful work as often it may involve life or death situations and exposure to injuries and infections. Back injuries are common and so is exposure to human body tissues and fluids. Even though an EMT or paramedic may take extreme measures to prevent back injuries or exposure, sometimes, the situation is often hectic and accidents happen.

In 2014 there were 241,200 jobs in the US for EMTs and paramedics. Most EMTs and Paramedics work full time and in 2014, about one in three worked more than 40 hours per week. Because they work emergencies, they may work overnight, weekends, and holidays and many work 12 to 14 hours shifts. Some EMTs and paramedics are employed by hospital emergency rooms and utilized often for their expertise.

Important Qualities

Because EMTs and Paramedics often work in stressful and life threatening conditions and because they are also healthcare providers they must possess certain personal characteristics. Some of those characteristics include:

- Compassion
- Interpersonal skills
- Listening skills
- Physical strength
- Problem-solving skills

Job Outlook

In the US, the employment of EMTS and paramedics is expected to grow by 24% from 2014 to 2024. Emergencies, such as car crashes, natural disasters, and acts of violence will continue to create demand for EMTs and paramedics. Also as the population ages, there will be more emergencies such as heart attacks and strokes that will require emergency medical care.

Athletic Trainers and Exercise Physiologists

Athletic Trainers

Athletic trainers specialize in preventing, diagnosing and treating injuries and disorders of the musculoskeletal system. You have probably seen many of them on the sidelines of athletic events or treating injuries at athletic events.

Duties

Athletic Trainers are hands-on practitioners that care for people of all ages and skill levels. They are usually one of the first providers on the scene when injuries occur. Because of this, many of the procedures they perform at those sites are first responder treatments. Some of their duties consist of the following:

- Applying protective or injury-preventive devices, such as tape, bandages or braces

- Recognize and evaluate injuries

- Provide first aid or emergency care

- Develop and carry out rehabilitation programs for injured athletes (much the same as physical therapy)

- Plan and implement comprehensive programs to prevent injury and illness among athletes

- Perform administrative tasks such as record keeping and writing reports on injuries and treatment programs

Work Environment

In 2014, there were about 25,400 athletic training jobs in the US. Educational institution employed about 37% of them, about 26% were employed by ambulatory healthcare services, and about 13% were employed by hospitals. Fitness and recreational sports centers employed about 11% of athletic trainers and only about 5% of athletic trainers in the US were employed by spectator sports teams and settings. Many athletic trainers spend quite a bit of their time working outdoors on sports fields in all types of weathers. Most athletic trainers work full time but some work on a contract basis. Athletic trainers who work with sports teams may work nights, weekends and holidays and this type of work may require travel.

How to Become an Athletic Trainer

Athletic trainers need at least a bachelor degree in athletic training rom an accredited college or university. Many have a master degree. Classroom components include courses in the sciences, math and health-related sciences. For a full list of required courses in Texas you can find those on the Texas Department of State Health Services under the Texas Administrative Code at http://texreg.sos.state.tx.us/public/readtac$ext.TacPage?sl=R&app=9&p_dir=&p_rloc=&p_tloc=&p_ploc=&pg=1&p_tac=&ti=22&pt=40&ch=871&rl=7.

Licensing

Nearly all states require athletic trainers to obtain certification, including Texas. The Board of Certification for Athletic Trainer offers the standard certification examination that most states use for licensing athletic training. Once successfully completing an accredited program, athletic trainers must complete an 1800 hour apprenticeship and pass an exam. Applicants must also have successfully completed a healthcare provider cardiopulmonary resuscitation course including defibrillation and have current certification for emergency medical services. For all of the requirements in Texas regarding athletic trainers, go to the Texas Administrative Code webpage for athletic training at http://texreg.sos.state.tx.us/public/readtac$ext. ViewTAC?tac_view=5&ti=22&pt=40&ch=871&sch=A&rl=Y.

Important Qualities

Because athletic training sometimes working in stressful situations (trauma and emergency) and because they may work with physical rehabilitation, there are different important qualities they must possess. Some of those qualities are:

- Compassion
- Decision-making skills
- Detail oriented
- Interpersonal skills

Job Outlook

In 2014, there were about 25,400 athletic trainers in the US and that number is projected to grow by the US Bureau of Labor Statistics by 21% from 2014 to 2024. However, unlike the other healthcare professions, the reason does not heavily rely on the aging of the population. Yes, as the population ages there will be more sport injuries because older adults today are more active than older adults in the past and that will undoubtedly lead to more sports-related injuries. One of the largest reasons for the increase is recent research revealing how the effects of concussions on children can be particularly severe and have a profound effect on brain health and permanent complications. Most states require or are beginning to require secondary schools to employ athletic trainers as part of their sports programs and require them to be onsite with athletes at practices and sporting events. Athletic trainers are trained to recognize injuries (including brain injuries) and how to select and use protective equipment. Depending on the state, some insurance companies recognize athletic trainers as a reimbursable healthcare provider and will thereby pay for treatment given by an athletic trainer.

Exercise Physiologists

Exercise physiologists assess, plan, design or implement fitness programs that include exercise or physical activities such as those designed to improve cardiorespiratory function, body composition, muscular strength, muscular endurance, or flexibility.

Duties

Exercise physiologists usually have certain duties and responsibilities. Those include:

- Analyze a patient's medical history to determine the best possible exercise and fitness regimen for the patient

- Perform fitness and stress tests with medical equipment and analyze the resulting patient data

- Measure blood pressure, oxygen usage, heart rhythm, and other key patient health indicators

- Develop exercise programs to improve patient health

- Supervise clinical tests to ensure patient safety

- Exercise physiologists, sometimes called *kinesiotherapists*, work to improve overall patient health. Many of their patients suffer from health problems such as cardiovascular disease or pulmonary (lung) disease. Exercise physiologists provide health education and exercise plans to improve key health indicators.

- Some physiologists work closely with primary care physicians, who may prescribe exercise regiments for their patients and refer them to exercise physiologists. The physiologists then work with patients to develop individualized treatment plans that will help the patients meet their health and fitness goals.

- Exercise physiologists should not be confused with fitness trainers and instructors (including personal trainers) or athletic trainers.

Work Environment

In 2014, there were about 14,500 jobs for exercise physiologists in the US. About 27% of them worked in hospitals and about 10 worked in ambulatory care services. Almost half of all exercise physiologists are self-employed and most work full time.

How to Become One

Exercise physiologists usually have a bachelor degree in exercise physiology and some have a master degree. Both programs include science, health, kinesiology, and nutrition courses as well as clinical work. In 2015 there were about 50 exercise programs accredited by the Commission on Accreditation of Allied Health Education Programs.

Licenses, Certifications, and Registrations

At the time of the writing of this book, Louisiana is the only state that requires exercise physiologists to be licensed, although many states have pending legislation to create formal licensure requirements. Texas does not have any legislation pending at this time.

The American Society of Exercise Physiologists (ASEP) offers the Exercise Physiologist Certified (EPC) certification, which physiologists can use to demonstrate their qualifications. Certification requires graduation with a relevant bachelor's degree and coursework, completing the ASEP exam, and taking continuing education courses every 5 years.

The American College of Sports Medicine (ACSM) also offers certifications for exercise physiologists: the Certified Clinical Exercise Physiologist (CEP) credential for candidates with a bachelor's degree and the Registered Clinical Exercise Physiologist® (RCEP) for candidates with a master's degree. Candidates also must have at least 400 or 600 hours of supervised clinical experience for the CEP and RCEP credential, respectively, and pass an exam.

Important Qualities

Because of the hands-on patient care, exercise physiologists must possess certain important personal characteristics. Those characteristics include:

- Compassion
- Decision-making skills
- Detail oriented
- Interpersonal skills
- Problem-solving skills

Job Outlook

Employment of exercise physiologists is projected to grow 11 percent from 2014 to 2024, faster than the average for all occupations. Demand may rise as hospitals emphasize exercise and preventive care as part of their treatment and long-term rehabilitation from chronic diseases, such as cardiovascular and pulmonary diseases.

However, because this is a small occupation in terms of employment, competition for available positions is expected to remain high. Additionally, because licensure for exercise physiologists is not common, there are few recognized standards of practice for these workers.

Psychologists

Psychologists study cognitive, emotional, and social processes and behavior by observing, analyzing, interpreting, and recording how people relate to one another and their environments.

Duties

Since psychologists work with people and their behavior, they have several duties they must perform in order to successfully carry out their role. Some of those duties include:

- Conduct scientific studies of behavior and brain function

- Collect information through observations, interviews, surveys, and other methods

- Identify psychological, emotional, behavioral, or organizational issues and diagnose disorders, using information obtained from their research

- Research and identify behavioral or emotional patterns

- Test for patterns that will help them better understand and predict behavior

- Discuss the treatment of problems with their clients

- Write articles, research papers, and reports to share findings and educate others

- Psychologists seek to understand and explain thoughts, emotions, feelings, and behavior. Psychologists use techniques such as observation, assessment, and experimentation to develop theories about the beliefs and feelings that influence a person.

Psychologists often gather information and evaluate behavior through controlled laboratory experiments, psychoanalysis, or psychotherapy. They also may administer personality, performance, aptitude, or intelligence tests. They look for patterns of behavior or relationships between events, and use this information when testing theories in their research or treating patients.

Types of Psychologists

There are several different types of psychologists and all require advanced training. Some of those psychologists include the following:

- *Clinical psychologists* assess, diagnose, and treat mental, emotional, and behavioral disorders. Clinical psychologists help people deal with problems ranging from short-term personal issues to severe, chronic conditions.

- Clinical psychologists are trained to use a variety of approaches to help individuals. Although strategies generally differ by specialty, clinical psychologists often interview patients, give diagnostic tests, and provide individual, family, or group psychotherapy. They also design behavior modification programs and help patients implement their particular program.

- Some clinical psychologists focus on certain populations, such as children or the elderly, or certain specialties, such as the following:

  ○ *Health psychologists* study how psychological and behavioral factors interact with health and illness. They educate both patients and medical staff on psychological issues and promote healthy-living strategies. They also investigate and develop programs to address common health-related behaviors, such as smoking, poor diet, and sedentary behavior.

  ○ *Neuropsychologists* study the effects of brain injuries, brain disease, developmental disorders, or mental health conditions on behavior and thinking. They test patients affected by known or suspected brain conditions to determine impacts on thinking and to direct patients' treatment.

- Clinical psychologists often consult with other health professionals regarding the best treatment for patients, especially treatment that includes medication. Currently, Illinois, Louisiana, and New Mexico allow clinical psychologists to prescribe medication to patients. Most states, however, do not allow psychologists to prescribe medication for treatment.

- *Counseling psychologists* help patients deal with and understand problems, including issues at home, at the workplace, or in their community. Through counseling, they work with patients to identify their strengths or resources they can use to manage problems. For information on other counseling occupations, see the profiles on mental health counselors and marriage and family therapists, substance abuse and behavioral disorder counselors, and social workers.

- *Developmental psychologists* study the psychological progress and development that take place throughout life. Many developmental psychologists focus on children and adolescents, but they also may study aging and problems facing older adults.

- *Forensic psychologists* use psychological principles in the legal and criminal justice system to help judges, attorneys, and other legal specialists understand the psychological aspects of a particular case. They often testify in court as expert witnesses. They typically specialize in family, civil, or criminal case work.

- *Industrial-organizational psychologists* apply psychology to the workplace by using psychological principles and research methods to solve problems and improve the quality of work life. They study issues such as workplace productivity, management or employee working styles, and employee morale. They also work with management on matters such as policy planning, employee screening or training, and organizational development.

- *School psychologists* apply psychological principles and techniques to education and developmental disorders. They may address student learning and behavioral problems; design and implement performance plans, and evaluate performances; and counsel students and families. They also may consult with other school-based professionals to suggest improvements to teaching, learning, and administrative strategies.

- *Social psychologists* study how people's mindsets and behavior are shaped by social interactions. They examine both individual and group interactions and may investigate ways to improve interactions.

- Some psychologists become postsecondary teachers or high school teachers.

Work Environment

There were about 173,900 jobs for psychologists in the US in 2014. Elementary and secondary schools employed about 25% of those psychologists and the government employed about 10%. Nearly 1 in 3 psychologists were self-employed in 2014.

Dependent on the type of psychologist a person is the work environment in which he or she works. For example industrial-organizational psychologists work in a business setting or can sometimes be found in human resource offices. Many clinical and counseling psychologists work in private practices and see patients in their offices. Most psychologists work full time and if in private practice, they may set their own schedules.

How to Become a Psychologist

Most clinical, counseling and research psychologists need a doctoral degree: either a Ph.D. in psychology or a Doctor of Psychology (Psy.D.). A Ph.D. is usually considered a research or an academic degree and is usually obtained after taking coursework, taking a comprehensive exam and writing a dissertation based on original research. A Psy.D. is considered a practical degree and is often based on clinical practice (including at least a one year internship) and exams rather than research. School psychologists must have an advanced degree, usually in education, and certification and a license to work. Some school psychologists have a doctoral or master degree in school psychology. Most graduate schools do not require an undergraduate degree in psychology but do require introductory coursework in psychology and experimental psychology. Most graduates with a bachelor degree in psychology find work in other fields such as education, business, or sales.

Licenses, Certifications, and Registrations

In most states, including Texas, practicing psychology or using the title of "psychologist" requires licensure. In all states and the District of Columbia, psychologists who practice independently must be licensed where they work.

Licensing laws vary by state and type of position. Most clinical and counseling psychologists need a doctorate in psychology, an internship, at least 1 to 2 years of supervised professional experience, and to pass the Examination for Professional Practice in Psychology. Information on specific state requirements can be obtained from the Association of State and Provincial Psychology Boards. In many states, licensed psychologists must complete continuing education courses to keep their licenses.

The American Board of Professional Psychology awards specialty certification in 15 areas of psychology, such as clinical health, couple and family, or rehabilitation. The American Board of Professional Neuropsychology offers certification in neuropsychology. Board certification can demonstrate professional expertise in a specialty area. Certification is not required for most psychologists, but some hospitals and clinics do require certification. In those cases, candidates must have a doctoral degree in psychology, state license or certification, and any additional criteria of the specialty field.

The Texas Department of State Health Services oversees all licensing in Texas. In addition to education, clinical experience and examinations, licensing in Texas requires a criminal background check and paying a fee. How many hours of continuing education and licensing renewal depends on what type of psychologist a person is. You can learn more about the licensing requirements in the state of Texas at http://dshs.texas.gov/plc/TDLR/.

Important Qualities

As one can imagine, working with people's behavior requires a unique set of personal characteristics and traits. Some of those traits are:

- Analytical skills
- Communication skills
- Observational skills
- Patience
- People skills
- Problem-solving skills
- Trustworthiness

Job Outlook

The overall employment of psychologist is projected to grow 19% from 2014 to 2024 in the US. Job prospects and competition for psychologists depend on the type of psychologist. The demand for clinical and counseling psychologists will increase as people turn to them more for help with their personal problems. The number of school psychologists will grow as the population grows and more children are in school and the US Bureau of Labor Statistics predicts the number of industrial-organizational psychologists will grow by 19%, even though it is a very small field and that number will only increase by about 400 jobs.

Psychologists with graduate degrees are more likely to find a job related to their field of study than those with bachelor degrees. Competition for admittance to graduate programs is often very stiff and the few who are admitted will have good job prospects upon finishing their degree and becoming licensed.

Social Work

Social workers help people solve and cope with problems related to their everyday lives such as housing needs, medical treatment, and clinical social workers help people with mental, behavioral, and emotional issues.

Duties

The scope of their work in Texas depends on what type of social worker they are. Almost all social workers share the same duties. Some of those duties include the following:

- Identify people and communities in need of help

- Assess clients' needs, situations, strengths, and support networks to determine their goals

- Help clients adjust to changes and challenges in their lives, such as illness, divorce, or unemployment

- Research, refer, and advocate for community resources, such as food stamps, childcare, and healthcare to assist and improve a client's well-being

- Respond to crisis situations such as child abuse and mental health emergencies

- Follow up with clients to ensure that their situations have improved

- Evaluate services provided to ensure that they are effective

- Develop and evaluate programs and services to ensure that basic client needs are met

- Provide psychotherapy services

Types of Social Workers

There are several different types of social workers in the United States. They help with many different problems. To learn about the classifications and scope of work of social workers in Texas visit the Texas Department of State Health Services website at http://www.dshs.texas.gov/socialwork/sw_scope.shtm. Some of the most popular social workers are the following:

- *Child and family social workers* protect vulnerable children and help families in need of assistance. They help families find housing or services, such as childcare, or apply for benefits, such as food stamps. They intervene when children are in danger of neglect or abuse. Some help arrange adoptions, locate foster families, or work to reunite families.

- *Clinical social workers*—also called *licensed clinical social workers*—diagnose and treat mental, behavioral, and emotional disorders, including anxiety and depression. They provide individual, group, family, and couples therapy; they work with clients to develop strategies to change behavior or cope with difficult situations; and they refer clients to other resources or services, such as support groups or other mental health professionals. Clinical social workers can develop treatment plans with the client, doctors, and other healthcare professionals and may adjust the treatment plan if necessary based on their client's progress. They may also provide mental healthcare to help children and families cope with changes in their lives, such as divorce or other family problems. Many clinical social workers work in private practice. In these settings, clinical social workers also perform administrative and recordkeeping tasks, such as working with insurance companies in order to receive payment for their services. Some work in a group practice with other social workers or mental health professionals.

- *School social workers* work with teachers, parents, and school administrators to develop plans and strategies to improve students' academic performance and social development. Students and their families are often referred to social workers to deal with problems such as aggressive behavior, bullying, or frequent absences from school.

- *Healthcare social workers* help patients understand their diagnosis and make the necessary adjustments to their lifestyle, housing, or healthcare. For example, they may help people make the transition from the hospital back to their homes and communities. In addition, they may provide information on services, such as home healthcare or support groups, to help patients manage their illness or disease. Social workers help doctors and other healthcare professionals understand the effects that diseases and illnesses have on patients' mental and emotional health.

- Some healthcare social workers specialize in geriatric social work, hospice and palliative care, or medical social work:

  ○ *Geriatric social workers* help senior citizens and their families. They help clients find services, such as programs that provide older adults with meals or with home healthcare. They may provide information about assisted living facilities or nursing homes, or work with older adults in those settings. They help clients and their families make plans for possible health complications or for where clients will live if they can no longer care for themselves.

  ○ *Hospice and palliative care social workers* help patients adjust to serious, chronic, or terminal illnesses. Palliative care focuses on relieving or preventing pain and other symptoms associated with serious illness. Hospice is a type of palliative care for people who are dying. Social workers in this setting provide and find services, such as support groups or grief counselors, to help patients and their families cope with the illness or disease.

  ○ *Medical social workers* in hospitals help patients and their families by linking patients with resources in the hospital and in their own community. They may work with medical staff to create discharge plans, make referrals to community agencies, facilitate support groups, or conduct follow-up visits with patients once they have been discharged.

- *Mental health and substance abuse social workers* help clients with mental illnesses or addictions. They provide information on services, such as support groups and 12-step programs, to help clients cope with their illness. Many clinical social workers function in these roles as well.

Work Environment

In the US in 2014 there were about 649,300 jobs in the US. Government was the largest employer employing about 29% of all social workers. Most work full-time in offices but may travel and visit clients or patients. Sometimes they work evening, weekends, and holidays, depending on where they work or what the scope of their work entails.

How to Become a Social Worker

Most social workers have a bachelor degree in social work (BSW), but clinical social workers must have a master degree and two years of post-master's experience in a clinical setting. A BSW prepares students for direct-service positions such as caseworker or mental health assistant. These programs teach students about diverse populations, human behavior, social welfare policy, and ethics in social work. All programs require students to complete supervised fieldwork or an internship. Clinical social workers must also be licensed in the state in which they practice. A bachelor degree in social work is not required to enter into a master degree program (MSW) but is usually preferred or in a related field such as psychology or sociology. A MSW program usually takes about two years to complete and requires students to complete a supervised practicum or internship. In 2015 there were more than 500 bachelor degree programs and more than 200 master degree programs accredited by the Council of Social Work Education.

Licenses

Most states have licensure or certification requirements for nonclinical social workers and they vary by state. The Texas State Board of Social Worker Examiners issues three licenses and several specialty recognitions. The three licenses include: Licensed Baccalaureate Social Worker (LBSW), Licensed Master Social Worker (LMSW), and Licensed Clinical Social Worker (LCSW).

Recognition for independent practice (Independent Practice Recognition or IPR) of non-clinical social work is available to LMSWs and LBSWs who meet the requirements. Additionally, LMSWs who meet certain requirements may receive recognition as an "Advanced Practitioner" of non-clinical social work services.

The board may also grant board-approved supervisor status to a qualified licensee. A board-approved supervisor may supervise other licensees in certain board-approved roles supervisor.

Persons who hold social worker licenses in other states or jurisdictions who wish to practice in the state of Texas must apply for a Texas licenses and meet all of the Texas requirements. The board does not issue licenses by reciprocity. Under certain circumstances, the board may accept satisfaction of some minimum requirements for Texas licensure which were obtained while holding a social work license in another state or jurisdiction and which meet the Texas requirements through a process of endorsement. Endorsement is determined on a case-by-case basis. Licensure in Texas requires proof of a degree fitting the title wanted, taking a couple of exams (including a law exam), a criminal background check and at this writing paying a $91.00 fee. To learn about the requirements more in depth, go to the Texas State Board of Social Worker Examiners home page and click on licensing. You can find the page at http://www.dshs.texas.gov/socialwork/sw_lbsw-lmsw.shtm.

Important Qualities

The important qualities for social workers are as follows:

- Communication skills

- Empathy

- Interpersonal skills

- Organizational skills
- Problem-solving skills
- Time-management skills

Job Outlook

The US Bureau of Labor Statistics projects the field of social work to grow by 12% from 2014 to 2024. This growth will be fueled by the increased demand for healthcare services and social services, but will vary according to social worker specialty.

The employment of healthcare social workers is expected to grow by 19% from 2014 to 2024 because of the aging population and their families will need to adjust to new treatments, medications, and lifestyles. Employment of mental health and substance abuse social workers is projected to grow 19% during that same time period. Employment will grow as more people seek treatment for mental health and substance abuse issues. In contrast, the employment of child, family, and school social workers is expected to only grow about 6% during that same time period. This particular field may be limited by federal, state, and local budget restraints.

Audiology

Audiologists diagnose, manage, and treat patients' hearing, balance, and/or ear problems.

Duties

- Audiologists use audiometers, computers, and other devices to test patients' hearing ability and balance. They work to determine the extent of hearing damage and identify the underlying cause. Audiologists measure the loudness at which a person begins to hear sounds and the person's ability to distinguish between sounds and understand speech.

- Before determining treatment options, audiologists evaluate psychological information to measure the impact of hearing loss on a patient. Treatment may include cleaning wax out of ear canals, fitting and checking hearing aids, or fitting the patient with cochlear implants to improve hearing. Cochlear implants are tiny devices that are placed under the skin near the ear and deliver electrical impulses directly to the auditory nerve in the brain. This allows a person with certain types of deafness to be able to hear.

- Audiologists also counsel patients on other ways to cope with profound hearing loss, such as by learning to lip read or by using technology.

- Audiologists can help a patient suffering from vertigo or other balance problems. They work with patients and provide them with exercises involving head movement or positioning that might relieve some of their symptoms.

- Some audiologists specialize in working with the elderly or with children. Others educate the public on hearing loss prevention. Audiologists may design products to help protect the hearing of workers on the job. Audiologists who are self-employed hire employees, keep records, order equipment and supplies, and complete other tasks related to running a business.[15]

Work Environment

In 2014, there were about 13,200 jobs for audiologists in the US. Most audiologists work in healthcare facilities, such as hospitals, physicians' offices and audiology clinics. Some work in school districts and travel between facilities. Others work in health and personal care stores such as retail establishments that sell hearing aids.

Most audiologists work full time, but about one third of the ones in the US work part time. There may be travel required for some audiologists, especially those who work on a contract basis for companies or schools.

How to Become an Audiologist

To become an audiologist, one must obtain a doctor degree in audiology (Au.D.). This is a graduate degree that typically takes four years to complete and includes both coursework and clinical experience. Graduation from the Council on Academic Accreditation is required to acquire a license in most states. There are currently 73 accredited programs at universities in the United States.

Licenses

All states require audiologists to be licensed. Texas audiologists were licensed by the Texas Department of State Health Services but that will transition to the Texas Department of Licensing and Regulation by August 2017. For information about the program in Texas go to the State Board of Examiners for Speech-Language Pathology and Audiology home page at http://www.dshs.texas.gov/speech/.

Audiologists can earn the Certificate of Clinical Competence in Audiology (CCC-A), offered by the American Speech-Language-Hearing Association. They also may be credentialed through the American Board of Audiology. Certification can be earned by graduating from an accredited doctoral program and passing a standardized exam. Certification may be required by some states or employers. Some states may allow certification in place of some education or training requirements needed for licensure.

Important Qualities

Audiologists deliver a very specialized health care and require certain characteristics and skills. Some of those are:

- Communication skills

- Compassion

- Critical-thinking skills

- Patience

- Problem-solving skills[16]

Job Outlook

The US Bureau of Labor Statistics expects the employment of audiologists to grown by 29% from 2014 to 2024, resulting in an additional 3,800 new jobs over the ten year period. As the baby boomers age, they will experience more hearing loss and balance disorders thereby increasing the demand for audiologists. With the invention of new technology that decreases the size for hearing aids, the popularity of these devices increases. Also, the early identification of hearing disorders in infants will also influence the growth in this field. In Texas, babies are screened as newborns before they leave the hospital for hearing disorders.

Health Educators and Community Health Workers

Health educators teach people about behaviors that promote wellness. They develop and implement programs to improve the health of individuals and communities. Community health workers provide a link between the community, health educators, and other healthcare and social service professionals. They collect data and discuss health concerns with members of specific populations or communities.

Duties

Although the two occupations often work together on projects and programs, their responsibilities are often very different and distinct. The following are responsibilities of health educators:

- The duties of health educators, also known as *health education specialists,* vary with their work settings. Most work in healthcare facilities, colleges, public health departments, nonprofits, and private businesses. Those who teach health classes in middle and high schools are considered teachers. For more information, see the profiles on middle school teachers and high school teachers.

- In *healthcare facilities*, health educators may work one-on-one with patients or with their families. They teach patients about their diagnoses and about any necessary treatments or procedures. They may be called *patient navigators* because they help consumers find out about their health insurance options and direct people to outside resources, such as support groups or home health agencies. They lead hospital efforts in developing and administering surveys to identify major health issues and concerns of the surrounding communities and developing programs to meet those needs. Health educators also help organize health screenings, such as blood pressure checks, and health classes on topics such as installing a car seat correctly. They also create programs to train medical staff to interact more effectively with patients. For example, they may teach doctors how to explain complicated procedures to patients in simple language.

- In *colleges*, health educators create programs and materials on topics that affect young adults, such as smoking and alcohol use. They may train students to be peer educators and supervise the students' delivery of health information in person or through social media. Health educators also advocate for campus-wide policies to promote health.

- In *public health departments*, health educators administer public health campaigns on topics such as emergency preparedness, immunizations, proper nutrition, or stress management. They develop materials to be used by other public health officials. During emergencies, they may provide safety information to the public and the media. Some health educators work with other professionals to create public policies that support healthy behaviors and environments. They may also oversee grants and grant-funded programs to improve the health of the public. Some participate in statewide and local committees dealing with topics such as aging.

- In *nonprofits* (including community health organizations), health educators create programs and materials about health issues faced by the community that they serve. They help organizations obtain funding and other resources. They may educate policymakers about ways to improve public health and work on securing grant funding for programs to promote health and disease awareness. Many nonprofits focus on a particular disease or audience, so health educators in these organizations limit programs to that specific topic or audience. For example, a health educator may design a program to teach people with diabetes how to better manage their condition or a program for teen mothers on how to care for their newborns.

- In *private businesses*, health educators identify common health problems among employees and create programs to improve health. They work with management to develop incentives for employees to adopt healthy behaviors, such as losing weight or controlling cholesterol. Health educators recommend changes in the workplace to improve employee health, such as creating smoke-free areas.

Community health workers often work under the direction of health educators or other public health officials. They are people who are embedded in the community already and know the community well. The responsibilities of community health workers include the following:

- Community health workers have an in-depth knowledge of the communities they serve. Within their community, they identify health-related issues, collect data, and discuss health concerns with the people they serve. For example, they may help eligible residents of a neighborhood enroll in programs such as Medicaid or Medicare and explain the benefits that these programs offer. Community health workers address any barriers to care and provide referrals for such needs as food, housing, education, and mental health services

- Community health workers share information with health educators and healthcare providers so that health educators can create new programs or adjust existing programs or events to better suit the needs of the community. Community health workers also advocate for the health needs of community members. In addition, they conduct outreach to engage community residents, assist residents with health system navigation, and to improve care coordination.

Work Environment

In 2014, health educators held about 61,400 jobs and there were about 54,300 community health workers. Most health educators spend the majority of their time in an office but may spend some time working in the field to carry out programs or attend meetings. Community health workers spend the majority of their time out in the communities they serve, communicating with community members, holding events, and collecting data. Most people in these two professions work full time.

How to Become a Health Educator or Community Health Worker

Health Educators

- Health educators need at least a bachelor's degree in health education or health promotion. Students learn theories and methods of health behavior and health education and gain the knowledge and skills they will need to develop health education materials and programs. Most programs include an internship.

- Some health educator positions require a master's or doctoral degree. Graduate programs are commonly in community health education, school health education, public health education, or health promotion. A variety of undergraduate majors may be acceptable for entry to a master's degree program.

- Community health workers typically have a high school diploma, although some jobs may require postsecondary education. Education programs may lead to a 1-year certificate or a 2-year associate's degree and cover topics such as wellness, ethics, and cultural awareness, among others.

Community Health Workers

- Community health workers typically have a high school diploma, although some jobs may require postsecondary education. Education programs may lead to a 1-year certificate or a 2-year associate's degree and cover topics such as wellness, ethics, and cultural awareness, among others.

- Community health workers typically complete a brief period of on-the-job training. Training often covers core competencies, such as communication or outreach skills, and information about the specific health topics that they will be focusing on. For example, community health workers who work with Alzheimer's patients may learn about how to communicate effectively with patients dealing with dementia.

Licenses, Certifications, and Registrations

States do not require licensure for either of these professions although some employers may require certifications. Some employers require health educators to obtain the Certified Health Education Specialist (CHES) certification that is offered by the National Commission for Health Education Credentialing, Inc. To obtain certification, candidates must have a bachelor degree in health education and pass an exam aimed at entry-level health educators. To maintain their certification, they must take 75 hours of continuing education every five years. There is also the Master Certified Health Education Specialist (MCHES) for health educators with advanced education and experience.

Even though most states do not require community health workers to be certified, voluntary certification exists or is being considered or developed in a number of states. Texas is not one at this time. Requirements vary but may include competing an approved training program.

Important Qualities

Health educators and community health workers are usually people who enjoy working with other people and should possess certain characteristics. Some of those qualities include:

- Analytical skills
- Communication skills
- Instructional skills
- Interpersonal skills
- Problem-solving skills
- Writing skills

Job Outlook

With all of the emphasis being placed on lifestyle factors and chronic disease prevention, employment of health educators and community health workers is expected to grow by 13% between 2014 and 2024. Also fueling its growth will be insurance companies, employers, and governments trying to find ways to improve the quality of care and health outcomes while reducing costs. Health educators and community health workers are uniquely qualified to complete this task. Also as the population ages and there are more cases of chronic diseases, cancer, and other serious health issues, health educators focus on prevention thereby improving the quality of life and saving healthcare costs. In addition, more health educators and community health workers are needed to assist people in enrolling in insurance plans and teaching them how to access health services.

Health educators and community health workers are frontline workers in health prevention and improving the quality of life. They work in many different settings and with many different populations. They are considered essential to the healthcare community

Orientation and Mobility Specialists

Orientation and mobility specialists teach individuals with visual impairments how to get around safely and to live independent lives. They work with people of all ages and some of their duties include the following:

- Teach how to walk across the street and planning routes to where a person needs to go
- Teach how to remember how to get places
- Work with all ages: infants to older adults
- Encourages those who have impaired vision to be independent

- Teaches balance, posture and how to use assistive devices such as a cane

- Teaches how to develop the sensory perception of the remaining senses such as hearing at a street crossing or smelling when cooking

- Teaches how to find things a person drops

- Teaches body image and how to position things in the environment

- Teach how to navigate streets, buildings and neighborhoods

- How to fold their money so they can recognize the value by the way it is folded

- Assess people's needs who have visual impairments and plan a program to address those needs

Work Environment

Orientation and mobility specialists work in all environments. They often teach clients how to get from one place to another and this requires extensive walking and repetition on finding places. This may require them to work in all types of weather and while working with their clients, they are responsible for their clients' safety and well-being. Traveling to another town to work with clients is not uncommon and their schedules must be flexible.

Most orientation specialists work for schools, government agencies and the US Veterans Administration. Some work for private individuals, guide dog schools, camps for people with disabilities and on a contract/self-employment basis.

How to Become an Orientation and Mobility Specialist

In order to become an orientation and mobility specialist a person must graduate with a bachelor degree from an accredited university with a degree in orientation and mobility. Their degree requires a supervised internship and includes classes in detailing orientation and mobility responsibilities and how to plan and fulfill them. There are 12 universities in the US with these programs, two of those are in Texas.

Certification

Most states require orientation and mobility specialists to pass a national exam given by the Academy for Certification of Vision Rehabilitation and Education Professionals. This requires a bachelor degree from an accredited school in orientation and mobility and passing a national exam. For more information about this process go to the Academy for Certification of Vision Rehabilitation and Education Professionals' website at https://www.acvrep.org/index.

Genetic Counselors

Genetic counselors assess individual or family risk for a variety of inherited conditions, such as genetic disorders and birth defects. They provide information and support to other healthcare providers, or to individuals and families concerned with the risk of inherited conditions.

Duties

Working with individuals or families to see their risk for inherited conditions, genetic counselors have a variety of duties. Those job responsibilities include the following:

- Genetic counselors identify specific genetic disorders or risks through the study of genetics. A genetic disorder or syndrome is inherited. For parents who are expecting children, counselors use genetics to predict whether a baby is likely to have hereditary disorders, such as Down syndrome and cystic fibrosis, among others. Genetic counselors also assess the risk for an adult to develop diseases with a genetic component, such as certain forms of cancer.

- Counselors identify these conditions by studying patients' genes through DNA testing. Medical laboratory technologists perform lab tests, which genetic counselors then evaluate and use for counseling patients and their families. They share this information with other health professionals, such as physicians. For more information, see the profiles on medical and clinical laboratory technologists and technicians and physicians and surgeons.

- According to a 2014 survey from the National Society of Genetic Counselors, approximately three-fourths of genetic counselors work in traditional areas of genetic counseling: prenatal, cancer, and pediatric. The survey noted that the number of specialized fields for genetic counselors has increased. More genetic counselors are specializing in fields such as cardiovascular health, genomic medicine, neurogenetics, and psychiatry.

Work Environment

In 2014 there were about 2,400 jobs for genetic counselors in the US. Hospitals employed about 39% of those, physician offices employed about 20%, and about 12% were employed by colleges and universities. Most genetic counselors work full time and work regular business hours. Genetic counselors who are also physicians may work a physician's schedule.

How to Become a Genetic Counselor

Genetic counselors need a master degree in genetics counseling or genetics. Their coursework will include public health, epidemiology, psychology, and developmental biology. Students must also complete clinical rotations during which they work directly with patients and clients. Clinical rotations provide supervised experience for students, allowing them to work in different work environments such as prenatal diagnostics, pediatric hospitals, or cancer centers. In 2014, there were 31 master degree programs in the US that were accredited by the Accreditation Council for Genetic Counseling.

Licenses and Certifications

The American Board of Genetic Counseling provides certification for genetic counselors. To become certified, a student must complete an accredited master degree program and pass an exam. Counselors must complete continuing education courses to maintain their board certification. In 2015, twenty states required genetic counselors to be licensed, and other states have pending legislation for licensure. Certification is required to practice in Texas. At the time of writing this book, there are over 150 board certified genetic professionals in Texas working in about 70 clinics and hospitals. For more information about genetic counseling in Texas go to the Texas Department of State Health Services Genetics website at http://www.dshs. texas.gov/genetics/default.shtm.

Important Qualities

Genetic counseling requires a strong science background but there are other important characteristics that the field requires. Some of those qualities include the following:

- Compassion
- Critical-thinking skills
- Decision-making skills
- Speaking skills

Job Outlook

Employment of genetic counselors is projected to grow 29% from 2014 to 2024. Because the profession is so small that is just an increase of about 700 new jobs over the ten year period. Ongoing technological discoveries, including laboratory tests and equipment and developments in genomics are giving counselors the opportunities to conduct more types of analyses than ever before. Cancer genomics, for example, can determine a patient's risk for specific types of cancer. There has been a large increase of the number and types of genetics that can be conducted over the last few years and that lead to a larger demand for counselors. In addition, many health insurance plans now cover genetic tests.

Massage Therapists

Massage therapists treat clients and patients by using touch to manipulate the muscles and other soft tissues of the body. Using their hands, therapists relieve pain, heal injuries, relieve stress, improve circulation, increase relaxation, and aid in the general wellness of clients.

Massage therapy means the manipulation of soft tissue by hand or through a mechanical or electrical apparatus for the purpose of body massage and includes effleurage (stroking), petrissage (kneading), tapotement (percussion), compression, vibration, friction, nerve strokes, and Swedish gymnastics. The terms "massage," "therapeutic massage," "massage technology," myotherapy," "body massage," "body rub," or any derivation of those terms are synonyms for "massage therapy."

Duties

Massage therapist talk with their clients or with other healthcare providers who refer their clients to determine what their needs are and what type of massage to use. Some of their duties include the following:

- Massage therapists use touch to treat clients' injuries and to promote the clients' general wellness. They use their hands, fingers, forearms, elbows, and sometimes feet to knead muscles and soft tissues of the body.

- Massage therapists may use lotions and oils, and massage tables or chairs, when treating a client. A massage can be as short as 5–10 minutes or could last more than an hour.

- Therapists talk with clients about what they hope to achieve through massage. Massage therapists may suggest personalized treatment plans for their clients, including information about additional relaxation techniques to practice between sessions.

- Massage therapists can specialize in many different types of massage or modalities. Swedish massage, deep-tissue massage, and sports massage are just a few of the many modalities of massage therapy. Most massage therapists specialize in several modalities, which require different techniques.

- The type of massage given typically depends on the client's needs and physical condition. For example, therapists may use a special technique for elderly clients that they would not use for athletes.

Some forms of massage are given solely to one type of client; for example, prenatal massage is given only to pregnant women.

- Massage therapists who are self-employed may need to do business-related tasks such as marketing, booking appointments, and maintaining financial records. They may also have to buy supplies and do laundry.

Work Environment

In 2014 there were about 168,800 jobs for massage therapists in the USA. About half of all massage therapists are self-employed. They may work in a plethora of settings, including spas, franchised massage clinics, physician offices, fitness centers, hotels, and private offices. Some massage therapists may travel to clients' homes or offices to give a massage. Others work out of their own homes in a room set aside for massage. Because many massage therapists are self-employed, they must provide their own equipment such as their own table or chair, sheets, pillows, lotions, and/or oils.

Their working conditions depend on the venue in which the massage is performed and on what the client wants and needs. For example, if a client needs stress relief and to relax, the massage is performed in a dimly lit room that uses candles and aroma therapy with soft soothing music in the background. If a client needs a massage for rehabilitation purposes for an injury, the massage may be performed in a well-lit setting with several other receiving treatment in the same room as in a physical therapy clinic.

Massage therapy requires the therapists to be in good health and able to stand for long periods of time. It can be physically demanding and massage therapists can become injured if they use improper techniques and do not use good body mechanics, space their clients out so they can rest, and in many cases, receiving a massage themselves regularly.

About half of all massage therapists in the USA worked part time in 2014. Massage therapists work by appointment so their schedules often vary week to week and can be very flexible. Because of the physical endurance required to be a massage therapist, it is often difficult to work five eight-hour days per week. In addition to performing massages, self-employed therapists may spend time recording clients' notes, scheduling appointment, maintaining their equipment, washing linens and performing other general business tasks.

How to Become a Massage Therapist

Education requirements for massage therapists vary state to state. Massage therapy education programs are usually found in private or public post-secondary institutions. A high school diploma is all that is usually required to apply to a massage school. Most programs require at least 500 hours of study for their completion and some programs require 1,000 or more hours. Programs contain both classroom hours and clinical hours. Classroom hours typically study anatomy, body mechanics, pathology, ethics, business management, and physiology. Some programs concentrate on certain modalities or types of massage such as deep tissue massage or Rolfing.

In 2014, 45 states and the District of Columbia regulated massage therapy. Texas is one that does. To become licensed in Texas an applicant must have satisfactorily completed massage therapy studies in an accepted course of instruction, pass the examination administered by the Federation of State Massage Therapy Boards and pay a $200 dollar fee. The license will be good for two years and must be renewed before it expires to keep practicing. For more information about massage therapy licensing in Texas go to the Texas Department of State Health Services Massage Therapy Licensing Program Home Page at http://www.dshs.texas.gov/massage/default.shtm.

Important Qualities

Massage therapy requires a unique set of skills and character traits. Some of those qualities include:

- Communication skills
- Decision-making skills
- Empathy
- Integrity
- Physical stamina
- Physical strength and dexterity
- Time-management skills

Job Outlook

Employment of massage therapists is projected to grow 22 percent from 2014 to 2024, much faster than the average for all occupations. Continued growth in the demand for massage services will lead to new openings for massage therapists. As an increasing number of states adopt licensing requirements and standards for therapists, the practice of massage is likely to be respected and accepted by more people as a way to treat pain and to improve overall wellness.

Similarly, as more healthcare providers understand the benefits of massage, demand will likely increase as these services become part of treatment plans. However, demand in healthcare settings will be tempered by limited insurance coverage for massage services. Massage also offers specific benefits to particular groups of people whose continued demand for massage services will lead to overall growth for the occupation. For example, many sports teams hire massage therapists to help their athletes rehabilitate from injuries and to relieve or manage pain.

The number of massage clinic franchises has increased in recent years. Many franchised clinics offer more affordable massages than those provided at spas and resorts, making massage services available to a wider range of customers.

However, demand for massage services may be limited by the overall state of the economy. During tough economic times, both the number of people who seek massage therapy and the frequency of their massages may decline. Because referrals are an important source of work for massage therapists, marketing and networking may help increase the number of job opportunities. Joining a professional association also can help build strong contacts and further increase the likelihood of steady work. In addition, massage therapists may be able to attract a wider variety of clients by completing education programs in multiple modalities.

Speech Pathologist

Speech-language pathologists (sometimes called *speech therapists*) assess, diagnose, treat, and help to prevent communication and swallowing disorders in patients. Speech, language, and swallowing disorders result from a variety of causes, such as a stroke, brain injury, hearing loss, developmental delay, Parkinson's disease, a cleft palate, or autism.[17]

Duties

The duties of speech pathologists include the following:

- Counsel patients and families on how to cope with communication and swallowing disorders

- Speech-language pathologists work with patients who have problems with speech and language, including related cognitive or social communication problems. Their patients may be unable to speak at all, or they may speak with difficulty or have rhythm and fluency problems, such as stuttering. Speech-language pathologists may work with people who are unable to understand language or with those who have voice disorders, such as inappropriate pitch or a harsh voice.

- Speech-language pathologists also must complete administrative tasks, including keeping accurate records. They record their initial patient evaluations and diagnoses, track treatment progress, and note any changes in a patient's condition or treatment plan.

- Some speech-language pathologists specialize in working with specific age groups, such as children or the elderly. Others focus on treatment programs for specific communication or swallowing problems, such as those resulting from strokes or a cleft palate.

- In medical facilities, speech-language pathologists work with physicians and surgeons, social workers, psychologists, and other healthcare workers. In schools, they work with teachers, other school personnel, and parents to develop and carry out individual or group programs, provide counseling, and support classroom activities.[18]

Work Environment

In the USA in 2014, speech pathologists held about 135,400 jobs. Educational services employed 44% followed by offices of physical, occupational, and speech therapists, and audiologists employing 19% of speech pathologists. Most speech pathologists work full time and some may need to travel, especially those that work for schools and must move around to different schools. Few speech pathologists work nights, weekends, and holidays.

How to Become a Speech Pathologist

Speech-language pathologists typically require a master degree in speech-language pathology. Even though the master programs may not require a particular field for the bachelor degree, there are certain prerequisite courses a student must take to be accepted into the master degree program. Graduate programs often include courses in speech and language development, age-specific speech disorders, alternative communication methods (such as sign language), and swallowing disorders. These programs also require supervised clinical experience. The Council on Academic Accreditation, part of the American Speech-Language-Hearing Association, accredits education programs in speech-language pathology. Graduation from an accredited program is required for certification and usually is required for state licensure.

Licenses

Almost all states require speech-language pathologists to be licensed.[19] Licensing requires at least a master degree and supervised clinical experience, graduation from an accredited program and other requirements vary by state. In Texas, an applicant must also pass the PRAXIS exam in speech pathology and pass a criminal background check. You can find out more about licensing in Texas at the Texas Department of State Health Services website at http://dshs.texas.gov/speech/sp_req.shtm.

Important Qualities

Important qualities for speech-language pathologists include the following:

- Analytical skills
- Communication skills
- Compassion
- Critical thinking skills
- Detail oriented
- Listening skills
- Problem-solving skills[20]

Job Outlook

Employment of speech-language pathologists is projected to grow 21 percent from 2014 to 2024, much faster than the average for all occupations. As the large baby-boom population grows older, there will be more instances of health conditions, such as strokes and hearing loss that cause speech or language impairments. Speech-language pathologists will be needed to treat the increased number of speech and language disorders in the older population.

Increased awareness of speech and language disorders, such as stuttering, in younger children should lead to a need for more speech-language pathologists who specialize in treating that age group. Also, an increasing number of pathologists will be needed to work with children with autism to improve their ability to communicate and socialize effectively. In addition, medical advances are improving the survival rate of premature infants and victims of trauma and strokes, many of whom need help from speech-language pathologists.

Endnotes

*Denotes the beginning of a multiple-item reference.
1. http://www.bls.gov/ooh/healthcare/radiologic-technologists.htm#tab-2
2. Modified from http://www.bls.gov/ooh/healthcare/radiologic-technologists.htm#tab-2
3. http://www.bls.gov/ooh/healthcare/radiologic-technologists.htm#tab-2
4. http://www.bls.gov/ooh/healthcare/radiation-therapists.htm

5. http://www.bls.gov/ooh/healthcare/diagnostic-medical-sonographers.htm

6. Ibid

7. Ibid

8. Ibid

9. Ibid

10. http://www.bls.gov/ooh/healthcare/diagnostic-medical-sonographers.htm#tab-2

11. Ibid

12. Modified from http://www.bls.gov/ooh/healthcare/diagnostic-medical-sonographers.htm#tab-2

13. http://www.bls.gov/ooh/healthcare/diagnostic-medical-sonographers.htm#tab-2

14. http://www.bls.gov/ooh/healthcare/diagnostic-medical-sonographers.htm#tab-6

15. http://www.bls.gov/ooh/healthcare/mobile/audiologists.htm

16. Ibid

17. http://www.bls.gov/ooh/healthcare/mobile/speech-language-pathologists.htm

18. Ibid

19. Ibid

20. Ibid

Chapter 9

Health Professions without Patient Contact

Franck Boston / Shutterstock.com

Healthcare Administration

Medical and Health Services Managers

Medical and health services managers, also called healthcare executives or healthcare administrators, plan, direct, and coordinate medical and health services. They may manage an entire facility, a specific clinical area or department, or a medical practice for a[1] physician or group of physicians. Medical and health services must continue to adapt to new laws, technology, regulations, changes in staffing.

Duties

Healthcare administrators have many duties depending on where they work and what their job is. Some of their duties include the following:

- *Work to improve efficiency and quality in delivering healthcare services

- Develop departmental goals and objectives

- Ensure that the facility in which they work is up to date on and compliant with new laws and regulations

- Recruit, train, and supervise staff

- Manage the finances of the facility, such as patient fees and billing

- Create work schedules

- Prepare and monitor budgets and spending to ensure departments operate within allocated funds

- Represent the facility at investor meetings or on governing boards

- Keep and organize records of the facility's services, such as the number of inpatient beds used

- Communicate with members of the medical staff and department heads

- Medical and health services managers work closely with physicians and surgeons, registered nurses, medical and clinical laboratory technologists and technicians, and other healthcare workers. Others may interact with patients or insurance agents.

- Medical and health services managers' titles depend on the facility or area of expertise in which they work. The following are examples of types of medical and health services managers:

  o *Nursing home administrators* manage staff, admissions, finances, and care of the building, as well as care of the residents in nursing homes. All states require licensure for nursing home administrators; licensing requirements vary by state.

- *Clinical managers* oversee a specific department, such as nursing, surgery, or physical therapy, and have responsibilities based on that specialty. Clinical managers set and carry out policies, goals, and procedures for their departments; evaluate the quality of the staff's work; and develop reports and budgets.

- *Health information managers* are responsible for the maintenance and security of all patient records and data. They must stay up to date with evolving information technology, current or proposed laws about health information systems, and trends in managing large amounts of complex data. Health information managers must ensure that databases are complete, accurate, and accessible only to authorized personnel. They also may supervise the work of medical records and health information technicians.

- *Assistant administrators* work under the top administrator in larger facilities and often handle daily decisions. Assistants might direct activities in clinical areas, such as nursing, surgery, therapy, medical records, or health information. They also handle administrative tasks, such as ensuring that their department has the necessary supplies and that equipment is operational and up to date.[2]

Work Environment

There were about 333,000 jobs for medical and health services managers in 2014. Hospitals employed 36%, nursing and residential facilities employed 10%, offices of physicians employed 10%. The rest were employed by either the government or home healthcare services. Most healthcare administrators work in offices in healthcare facilities, including hospitals and nursing homes and group medical practices.

Most medical and health services managers work full time. About 1 in 3 managers worked more than 40 hours per week in 2014. Work during evenings or weekends may be required in healthcare settings that are open at all hours, such as hospitals and nursing homes. Medical and health services managers may need to be on call in case emergencies arise.[3]

How to Become a Medical or Health Services Manager

Medical and health services managers typically need at least a bachelor's degree to enter the occupation. However, master's degrees are common and sometimes preferred by employers. Graduate programs often last between 2 and 3 years and may include up to 1 year of supervised administrative experience in a hospital or healthcare consulting setting.

Prospective medical and health services managers typically have a degree in health administration, health management, nursing, public health administration, or business administration. Degrees that focus on both management and healthcare combine business-related courses with courses in medical terminology, hospital organization, and health information systems.

For example, a degree in health administration or health information management often includes courses in health services management, accounting and budgeting, human resources administration, strategic planning, law and ethics, health economics, and health information systems.

Many employers require prospective medical and health services managers to have some work experience in either an administrative or a clinical role in a hospital or other healthcare facility. For example, nursing home administrators usually have years of experience working as a registered nurse. Others may begin their careers as medical records and health information technicians, administrative assistants, or financial clerks within a healthcare office.[4]

Important Qualities

As with any profession, especially in those that deal with the health of individuals and communities, healthcare managers need to possess certain qualities. Some of those characteristics are as follows:

- Analytical skills

- Communication skills

- Detail oriented

- Interpersonal skills

- Leadership skills

- Technical skills[5]

Licenses

All states require licensure for nursing home administrators; requirements vary by state. In most states, these administrators must have a bachelor's degree, complete a state-approved training program, and pass a national licensing exam. Some states also require applicants to pass a state-specific exam; others may require applicants to have previous work experience in a healthcare facility. Some states also require licensure for administrators in assisted-living facilities. For information on specific state-by-state licensure requirements, visit the National Association of Long Term Care Administrator Boards at http://www.nabweb.org/nursing-home-administrators-licensure-requirements.[6] For information about certification in Texas, go to the Texas Department of Aging and Disabilities website at http://www.dads.state.tx.us/providers/NF/credentialing/nfa/index.html.

*A license is typically not required in other areas of medical and health services management. However, some positions may require applicants to have a registered nurse or social worker license.

Although certification is not required, some managers choose to become certified. Certification is available in many areas of practice. For example, the Professional Association of Health Care Office Management offers certification in medical management, the American Health Information Management Association offers health information management certification, and the American College of Health Care Administrators offers the Certified Nursing Home Administrator and Certified Assisted Living Administrator distinctions.

Medical and health services managers advance by moving into higher paying positions with more responsibility. Some health information managers, for example, can advance to become responsible for the entire hospital's information systems. Other managers may advance to top executive positions within the organization.[7]

Job Outlook

Employment of medical and health services managers is projected to grow by 17% from 2014 to 2024.[8] As the baby boomers age, called the *graying of a population*, there will be a higher demand on healthcare thereby leading to more healthcare facilities and practitioners. In addition, as widespread use of electronic medical records (EMRs) increases there will be a continue demand for managers with information about medical and health information technology and informatics systems.

Job prospects for medical and health services managers are likely to be favorable. In addition to rising employment demand, the need to replace managers who retire over the next decade will result in some openings. Candidates with a master's degree in health administration or a related field, as well as knowledge of healthcare IT systems, will likely have the best prospects.[9]

Medical Records and Health Information Technicians

Medical records and health information technicians, commonly referred to as *health information technicians*, organize and manage health information data. They ensure that the information maintains its quality, accuracy, accessibility, and security in both paper files and electronic systems. They use various classification systems to code and categorize patient information for insurance reimbursement purposes, for databases and registries, and to maintain patients' medical and treatment histories.[10]

Duties

The duties of medical records and health information technicians include the following:

- *Health information technicians document patients' health information, including their medical history, symptoms, examination and test results, treatments, and other information about healthcare services that are provided to patients. Their duties vary by employer and by the size of the facility in which they work.

- Although health information technicians do not provide direct patient care, they work regularly with registered nurses and other healthcare professionals. They meet with these workers to clarify diagnoses or to get additional information to make sure that records are complete and accurate.

- The increasing adaptation and use of electronic health records (EHRs) will continue to change the job responsibilities of health information technicians. Technicians will need to be familiar with, or be able to learn, EHR computer software, follow EHR security and privacy practices, and analyze electronic data to improve healthcare information, as more healthcare providers and hospitals adopt EHR systems.

- Health information technicians can specialize in many aspects of health information. Some work as *medical coders*, sometimes called *coding specialists*, or as *cancer registrars*.

  - Medical coders

    - Review patient information for preexisting conditions, such as diabetes

    - Assign appropriate diagnoses and procedure codes for patient care, population health statistics, and billing purposes

    - Work as a liaison between the health clinician and billing offices

  - Cancer registrars

    - Review patients' records and pathology reports to verify completeness and accuracy

    - Assign classification codes to represent the diagnosis and treatment of cancers and benign tumors

    - Conduct annual follow-ups to track treatment, survival, and recovery

    - Compile and analyze cancer patient information for research purposes

    - Maintain facility, regional, and national databases of cancer patients[11]

Work Environment

In 2014, there were about 188,600 medical records and health information technician jobs in the USA. Hospitals employed about 38% of them and another 21% were employed by physician offices. The rest were employed by nursing care facilities, administrative and support services, and professional, scientific, and technical services. They typically work in offices and may spend many hours inputting data into computers, although some technicians may work from home.

How to Become a Medical records or health information technician

A high school diploma and previous experiences are all that is needed in some places for these jobs, but most organizations require some college or certification programs. Postsecondary certificates and/or associate degrees in medical records or health information technology programs are usually offered in community colleges or technical schools. Those paths usually require courses in medical terminology, anatomy and physiology, health data requirements and standards, classification and coding systems, health-care reimbursement methods, healthcare statistics, and computer systems.

Licensing and Certification

Texas does not require any type of licensing for these position but *most employers prefer to hire health information technicians who have certification, or they may expect applicants to earn certification shortly after being hired. A health information technician can earn certification from several organizations. Certifications include the Registered Health Information Technician (RHIT) and the Certified Tumor Registrar (CTR), among others.

Some organizations base certification on passing an exam. Others require graduation from an accredited program. Many coding certifications also require coding experience in a work setting. Once certified, technicians typically must renew their certification regularly and take continuing education courses.[12]

Important Qualities

Medical records or health information technicians will need a specific set of skills and characteristics to be successful in this field. Some of those qualities include:

- Analytical skills
- Detail oriented
- Integrity
- Interpersonal skills
- Technical skills[13]

Job Outlook

From 2014 to 2024, employment of health information technicians is projected to grow by 15% in the USA. Again, the reasons for growth in the field are due to the aging of the baby boom population, more access to health insurance, and the increased demand for healthcare services. Additionally, as healthcare providers across the country move to electronic medical records (EMRs), more technicians will be needed to organize and manage the information in all areas of the healthcare industry.

Reference

http://www.bls.gov/ooh/healthcare/medical-records-and-health-information-technicians.htm

Occupational Health And Safety Specialists

Occupational health and safety specialists analyze many types of work environments and work procedures[14] to keep the workers safe and healthy. Specialists inspect workplaces and equipment for adherence to[15] rules, regulations, and laws on safety, health, and the environment. They also design and develop programs to prevent diseases or injuries to workers and to prevent environmental damage or hazards.

Duties

Occupational health and safety specialists perform many different duties. Some of those include the following:

- *Occupational health and safety specialists examine the workplace for environmental or physical factors that could affect employee health, safety, comfort, and performance. They may examine factors such as lighting, equipment, materials, and ventilation. Specialists seek to increase worker productivity by reducing absenteeism and equipment downtime. They also seek to save money by lowering insurance premiums and workers' compensation payments and by preventing government fines.

- Some specialists develop and conduct employee safety and training programs. These programs cover a range of topics, such as how to use safety equipment correctly and how to respond in an emergency.

- In addition to protecting workers, specialists work to prevent harm to property, the environment, and the public by inspecting workplaces for chemical, physical, radiological, and biological hazards. Specialists who work for governments conduct safety inspections and can impose fines.

- Occupational health and safety specialists work with engineers and physicians to control or fix hazardous conditions or equipment. They also work closely with occupational health and safety technicians to collect and analyze data in the workplace.

- The tasks of occupational health and safety specialists vary by industry, workplace, and types of hazards affecting employees. The following are examples of types of occupational health and safety specialists:

- *Ergonomists* consider the design of industrial, office, and other equipment to maximize workers' comfort, safety, and productivity.

- *Industrial or occupational hygienists* identify workplace health hazards, such as lead, asbestos, noise, pesticides, and communicable diseases.[16]

Work Environment

In 2014, there were approximately 70,300 jobs for occupational health and safety specialists in the USA. *About 29 percent of occupational health and safety specialists worked for federal, state, and local governments in 2014. In the federal government, specialists are employed by various agencies, including the Centers for Disease Control and Prevention's National Institute for Occupational Safety and Health (NIOSH) and the Occupational Safety and Health Administration (OSHA). Most large government agencies employ specialists to protect agency employees. In addition to working for governments, occupational health and safety specialists worked in management, scientific, and technical consulting services; education services; hospitals; and manufacturing.

Occupational health and safety specialists work in a variety of settings, such as offices, factories, and mines. Their jobs often involve considerable fieldwork and travel. They may be exposed to strenuous, dangerous, or stressful conditions. Specialists use gloves, helmets, respirators, and other personal protective and safety equipment to minimize the risk of illness and injury.[17]

How to Become an Occupational Health and Safety Specialist

Most jobs for occupational health and safety specialists require a bachelor degree in occupational health and safety or in a related scientific or technical field like engineering, chemistry, or biology. More and more positions are requiring a master degree in occupational health and safety, industrial hygiene or environmental health and safety. Coursework usually includes radiation science, hazardous material management and control, risk communications, and respiratory protection. Classes will often have practical application as well and will have students donning protective equipment (various kinds) and practicing working with hazardous materials. The course of study will vary with what field the student wants to study.

Licensing and Certifications

At this time, there is no licensing for occupational health and safety specialists in Texas or in the rest of the USA. There are, however, different certification programs in the USA depending on what the specialty is.

Certification is offered through several different organizations through examination. In order to qualify to take the exams, applicants must have the required degree in the correct field of study and work experience. Usually specialists must take continuing education courses throughout the years to keep their certifications.

Important Qualities

As with other jobs in health, occupational health and safety specialists should possess certain important qualities. Some of those traits are as follows:

- Ability to use technology
- Communication skills
- Detail oriented
- Decision-making skills
- Physical stamina
- Problem-solving skills[18]

Job Outlook

The employment of occupational health and safety specialists is projected to grow only four percent from 2014 to 2024 and that is slower than the average for all occupations. Specialists will be needed to work in a wide variety of industries to ensure that employers are complying with regulations and laws. In additions, as technology advances, specialists will be needed to create safe machinery as well as procedures for its safe use.[19] In addition, insurance costs and workers' compensation from high injury rates is a big concern for many employers and insurance companies. As the baby boomers age, they are not retiring as young as their parents and grandparents did. This leaves older workers and older workers have a larger proportion of insurance and workers' compensation claims. Candidates with certifications will probably enjoy more job opportunities so if one is considering this field, he or she should take that into consideration, also.

Reference

http://www.bls.gov/ooh/healthcare/occupational-health-and-safety-specialists.htm

Orthotics and Prosthetics

*Orthotics and prosthetics design and build medical supportive devices and measure and fit patients for them. These devices may include artificial limbs (arms, hands, legs, and feet), braces, and other medical or surgical devices.

Duties

- Evaluate and interview patients to determine their needs

- Take measurements or impressions of the part of a patient's body that will be fitted with a brace or artificial limb

- Design and fabricate orthopedic and prosthetic devices based on physicians' prescriptions

- Select materials to be used for the orthotic or prosthetic device

- Instruct patients in how to use and care for their devices

- Adjust, repair, or replace prosthetic and orthotic devices

- Document care in patients' records

- Orthotists and prosthetists may work in both orthotics and prosthetics, or they may choose to specialize in one area. Orthotists are specifically trained to work with medical supportive devices, such as spinal or knee braces or shoe inserts. Prosthetists are specifically trained to work with prostheses, such as artificial limbs, breasts and other body parts.

Some orthotists and prosthetists construct devices for their patients. Others supervise the construction of the orthotic or prosthetic devices by medical appliance technicians.[20]

Work Environment

In the USA in 2014, there were about 8,300 jobs for othotists and prosthetists. Medical equipment and supplies manufacturing employed about 31%, health and personal care retail stores employed about 21% and ambulatory healthcare services employed about 18% of othotists and prosthetists. The rest were employed by hospitals and the federal government (includes the Veterans Administration). When building assistive devices, there is always the risk of injury because of the use of power tools and other manufacturing equipment. Most orthotists and prosthetists use protective equipment such as goggles, gloves, and masks when working in hazardous environments and follow safety procedures.

How to Become an Orthotist or Prosthetist

*All orthotists and prosthetists must complete a master's degree in orthotics and prosthetics. These programs include courses in upper and lower extremity orthotics and prosthetics, spinal orthotics, and plastics and other materials used for fabrication. In addition, orthotics and prosthetics programs have a clinical component in which the student works under the direction of an orthotist or prosthetist.

Master's programs usually take 2 years to complete. Prospective students seeking a master's degree can have a bachelor's degree in any discipline if they have fulfilled prerequisite courses in science and math. Requirements vary by program.

In 2015, there were 13 orthotics and prosthetics programs accredited by the Commission on Accreditation of Allied Health Education Programs (CAAHEP)[21] and two of those programs are in Texas: one in Dallas and one is in Houston. To learn more about those programs go to the CAAHEP website at http://www.caahep.org/.

*Following graduation from a master's degree program, candidates must complete a residency that has been accredited by the National Commission on Orthotic and Prosthetic Education (NCOPE). Candidates typically complete a 1-year residency program in either orthotics or prosthetics. Individuals who want to become certified in both orthotics and prosthetics need to complete 1 year of residency training for each specialty or, less commonly, an 18-month residency in both orthotics and prosthetics.

Licenses and Certifications

Some states require orthotists and prosthetists to be licensed, Texas is one of those states. States that license orthotists and prosthetists often require certification in order for them to practice, although requirements vary by state. Many orthotists and prosthetists become certified regardless of state requirements, because certification demonstrates competence.

The American Board for Certification in Orthotics, Prosthetics and Pedorthics, and the Board of Certification and Accreditation offer certifications for orthotists and prosthetists. To earn certification, a candidate must complete a CAAHEP-accredited master's program, an NCOPE-accredited residency program, and pass a series of three exams.[22]

The Texas Board of Orthotics and Prosthetists can be found at http://www.dshs.state.tx.us/op . At the time of this writing, Orthotics and Prosthetics require licensing under the Texas Department of State Health Services but that is transitioning to licensing under the Texas Department of Licensing and Regulation. To qualify for a license in Texas, an applicant must be a Texas resident and successfully complete the academic requirements for the requested license, the clinical residency requirements for license and pass the examination specific to the requested license. An application must also complete an application form supplied by the board and pay the appropriate fee. For more information about licensing requirements see the

Texas Board of Orthotics and Prosthetics Licensing page at http://www.dshs.texas.gov/op/op_req.shtm.

Important Qualities

Orthotists and prosthetists must possess a certain set of important qualities. Some of those qualities include the following:

- Communication skills
- Detail oriented
- Leadership skills
- Patience
- Physical dexterity
- Physical stamina
- Problem-solving skills[23]

Job Outlook

*Employment of orthotists and prosthetists is projected to grow 23 percent from 2014 to 2024, much faster than the average for all occupations. However, because it is a small occupation, the fast growth will result in only about 1,900 new jobs over the 10-year period. The large aging baby-boom population will create a need for orthotists and prosthetists, because both diabetes and cardiovascular disease, which are two leading causes of limb loss, are more common among older people. In addition, older people will continue to need other devices designed and fitted by orthotists and prosthetists, such as braces and orthopedic footwear.

Advances in technology are allowing more people to survive traumatic events. Patients with traumatic injuries, such as some veterans, will continue to need orthotists and prosthetists to create devices that allow the patients to regain or improve mobility and functionality. Moreover, the number of individuals who have access to health insurance is expected to continue to increase because of federal health insurance reform. Patients who were previously uninsured or found treatment to be cost prohibitive may opt for new or replacement devices, such as braces or artificial limbs.

Job prospects should be best for orthotists and prosthetists with professional certification. Although it is not required in all states, certification shows a specific level of educational knowledge and training that employers may prefer.[24]

There are many different types of healthcare professions that do not involve direct hands-on patient care. Only some of these jobs are included here. For more information about other opportunities that may be available to you, visit the US Bureau of Labor Statistics website.

Endnotes

*Denotes the beginning of a multiple-item reference.

1. http://www.bls.gov/ooh/management/medical-and-health-services-managers.htm#tab-2

2. Ibid

3. http://www.bls.gov/ooh/management/medical-and-health-services-managers.htm#tab-3

4. http://www.bls.gov/ooh/management/medical-and-health-services-managers.htm#tab-4

5. Ibid

6. Ibid

7. Ibid

8. http://www.bls.gov/ooh/management/medical-and-health-services-managers.htm#tab-6

9. Ibid

10. http://www.bls.gov/ooh/healthcare/medical-records-and-health-information-technicians.htm#tab-2

11. Ibid

12. http://www.bls.gov/ooh/healthcare/medical-records-and-health-information-technicians.htm#tab-4

13. Ibid

14. http://www.bls.gov/ooh/healthcare/occupational-health-and-safety-specialists.htm#tab-2

15. Ibid

16. Ibid

17. http://www.bls.gov/ooh/healthcare/occupational-health-and-safety-specialists.htm#tab-3

18. http://www.bls.gov/ooh/healthcare/occupational-health-and-safety-specialists.htm#tab-4

19. Modified from http://www.bls.gov/ooh/healthcare/occupational-health-and-safety-specialists.htm#tab-4

20. http://www.bls.gov/ooh/healthcare/orthotists-and-prosthetists.htm#tab-2

21. http://www.bls.gov/ooh/healthcare/orthotists-and-prosthetists.htm#tab-4

22. Ibid

23. Ibid

24. http://www.bls.gov/ooh/healthcare/orthotists-and-prosthetists.htm#tab-6

Chapter 10

Trends in Health Professions

Allies Interactive / Shutterstock.com

Mobile Clinics For Diagnostic Tests and Treatment

As technology progresses and machines to make diagnoses become smaller and smaller, some governments and healthcare facilities are using mobile outreach clinics for diagnoses treatments. Often, they are specialty clinics who work with certain populations or perform certain tasks. Texas Children's Hospital in Houston has two mobile clinics that provide excellent medical services to children who may not have the means to receive health care. Their mobile clinics travel to low-income neighborhoods to provide free, comprehensive health care to children who normally receive none. Their mission statement is: "The mission of the Texas Children's Mobile Clinic Program is to provide underserved children in the Houston area with comprehensive health care and preventive education." Their staff is bilingual and includes pediatricians, nurse practitioners, a manager, nurses, medical assistants and a community health worker. They provide a wide range of services such as well-child visits, school physicals, illness examinations, immunizations, hearing and screening exams, and some laboratory tests. They also provide assistance for applying for health insurance and make referrals to medical and social services.

Another entity in Houston that has a mobile health clinic is the Houston Health Department. It has a HIV/STD and Viral Hepatitis Prevention Mobile Clinic. This clinic's priorities for the mobile clinic are based on actual STD cases, outreach screenings and other Houston Health Department initiatives. It has regularly scheduled stops and information about this clinic can be found at http://www.houstontx.gov/health/HIV-STD/mobile_clinic.html.

There are a plethora of mobile clinics in the USA, including Texas. All states have licensing requirements and the clinics are highly regulated. Some clinics only do mammography, and some do stroke screenings. One regional health center in Central Texas does heart catheterization in their clinic and use it for outreach in rural areas. Often mobile clinics are associated with academic institutions or nonprofit organizations. Mobile clinics are seen as a cost-efficient way to deliver care to people who would either have to drive long hours in order to receive care or for people who for several reasons, including economics or cultural barriers, do not have access to health care services. There is a professional organization for mobile clinics called the Mobile Health Clinics Association and its goal is to advocate on behalf of mobile healthcare, encourages the design and tools used in mobile clinics, and fosters communication among healthcare providers.

The following article is a National Clearinghouse on Families & Youth Report and can be found on the US Health and Human Services website. It gives a good example of what some of these clinics do.

*A Day in the Life of a Mobile Health Clinic

Harvard Square in Boston, Massachusetts, is a renowned tourist area, known around the world for its shopping, dining, entertainment venues, bookstores, architectural landmarks, and cultural destinations. It is also a place where a large number of runaway and homeless youth sleep every night—some suffering from medical illnesses, others just hungry and alone.

A mobile health clinic run by Bridge Over Troubled Waters, a FYSB grantee in Boston, Massachusetts, parks in front of Harvard Square every night for one hour, from 8:30 to 9:30 p.m.

The van runs from 6 p.m. to 10 p.m.—the hours that they can reach the most homeless teens—and stops at shelters, parks, and subway stops. The street outreach team accompanies the van, passing out sandwiches on Tuesdays along with "survival guides"—brochures that highlight food banks, transitional living programs, and shelters that serve homeless youth.

For some street youth, the majority of whom are uninsured and ineligible for Medicaid, this is the only health care that they will receive. Many young people on the streets do not have money for public transportation to get to a local hospital or clinic. The mobile health clinics meet the needs of runaway and homeless youth by bringing the services to them.

"We have an open access policy," says Dr. Rhonique Shields-Harris, medical director of the mobile health programs at the Children's Health Project in Washington, D.C. "You come in, we don't ask questions. We would rather they use us as a resource than go to the emergency room, where the wait time will be longer."

This policy appeals to street youth who are often wary of going to hospitals or clinics for fear of being turned in to police or social services.

"People are more trusting of the medical van," says Peter Ducharme who runs the medical van for Bridge Over Troubled Waters. He adds that many homeless youth have escaped abusive situations and are scared of being returned to their homes.

When street youth are looking for additional support, however, the mobile health clinic can refer them to drop-in, basic center, and transitional living programs. Mobile clinics address the needs of runaway and homeless youth, who have a high risk of getting infectious diseases from being out on the street.

Many youth from Covenant House—a FYSB grantee and runaway and homeless youth program located onsite with the Children's Health Project—come to the agency because they are referred by doctors with the mobile health clinic. For example, when a pregnancy test reveals that a young woman is expecting, a mobile health clinic will often refer her to a transitional living program.

In fact, Bridge Over Troubled Waters began in 1970 as a mobile health clinic and grew into a human service organization which includes a street outreach program, a transitional living program, and residential housing. Of the 4,000 youth the agency comes in contact with each year, 2,000 are seen on the medical van and 2,000 are serviced by onsite facilities. About 1,300 are referrals from street outreach workers.

"We run into a lot of people who will come to the van and ask questions, and it might not be an absolute emergency or a crisis, but we will get them answered at the van, rather than risk going to a hospital," says Ducharme. When youth go to the hospital, he says, the van program misses the opportunity to refer youth to additional services like drop-in programs.

Treating the Whole Person

It's a clear morning and two large blue vans—a mobile health clinic and a mobile dental clinic—pull away from the Children's Health Project on Mississippi Avenue in Southeast Washington, D.C.

The vans rumble along turning down streets in the Parkland neighborhood before arriving at the Atlantic Terrace Apartments, allow-income housing project where they will park for the day.

Inside the mobile clinic at the Children's Health Project, Dr. Terry Gray Brown sits in a swivel chair waiting for her next patient. She comes out from time to time, maneuvering her 8-month pregnant belly past her colleagues and patients in the narrow 2-foot hallway. She works in the mobile clinic 5 days a week, from 10 a.m. to 4 p.m. each day, in four low-income D.C. neighborhoods.

The medical team collaborates with the mobile dental unit, a clinical social worker, a family services associate, a patient liaison, and legal aid services, and provides help with taxi transportation with specialist appointments and in-home counseling.

"Not only do they have medical needs, but they have social needs that we try to fulfill because that impacts their health a great deal," says Brown. "We try to make sure the whole person is taken care of. Substance abuse, mental illness, all of that affects their medical needs."[1]

http://www.houstontx.gov/health/HIV-STD/mobile_clinic.html

Telemedicine

Telemedicine has been used for many years in clinical settings, maybe not the way it is used today, but it has been used. For example, since the radio was invented and its broadcast abilities improved in the 1920s, it was used to give medical advice to ship-based clinics. In the modern world, telemedicine is often used to transmit images and actual provider-patient interviews and exams. This is especially helpful in remote or rural areas. Alaska has been a leader in the development of telemedicine. Nurses, community health aides, EMTs, or paramedics can visit villages, perform certain exams while showing the physician at the other end of the computer or flat screen the same images they see. Physicians can interview patients and tell their aides what type of physical exams to do. If a child has an ear ache, the aide can perform otoscopy and the physician can actually see the eardrum just as if he or she were using the otoscope. For a couple of decades, physicians have controlled pacemakers via telephone. The person with the pacemaker calls a certain number and then puts the phone directly over where they pacemaker is. The computer on the other end of the phone detects certain signals in the pacemaker and can speed it up, slow it down, or tell the patient to come into the office for an in-depth examination. In some communities that do not have many specialists, patients can see their physicians remotely through telemedicine. For example, a 12 year old girl has recurring headaches and sees a pediatric neurologist in a town 75 miles away from her home. After the initial visit, the neurologist will send the specially trained nurse to perform certain exams at the same time the pediatric neurologist will watch everything from his or her office. The physician can then prescribe treatment and send a prescription to her pharmacy if needed. The neurologist can then examine several patients in that town or surrounding areas that same day. Often it is difficult for patients with chronic diseases or who are seriously ill to travel for long periods of time. One very small town in Texas in a very sparsely populated county had no medical services of any kind, including no ambulance services. They wrote a grant to purchase a highly equipped ambulance and nurse's clinic at the local school. There were only 60 students from kindergarten to high school in that entire county. With the funds, they also hired a nurse and a paramedic who shared duties at the school and on the ambulance. They also used telemedicine to have different clinical days for people who lived in the county to come to the school and consult a physician either for chronic or acute care.

Another example of telemedicine is "teledentistry" in which dental hygienists can perform exams and teeth cleaning and communicate via the Internet with a dentist. This is especially popular in areas without any dentists or dental services. Dermatology and psychology are other areas that use telemedicine often. Studies show that there are high rates of agreement between diagnoses made in physician offices and diagnoses made by telemedicine. As telemedicine evolves and technologies evolve, there will be more opportunities.

There are so many new applications for telemedicine that law makers are failing to keep up. Some states are now starting to look into regulations as are some federal law-makers since physician-patient interviews may cross state lines. There are already phone apps that people can use to directly consult with a physician who can then write a prescription for them if necessary. These are known as digital offices and for people who are extremely busy or who are terrified of physician offices, this is a good alternative. With the development of new fitness monitoring apparatus, there are many new implications in the use of this type of health monitoring. They can be used to monitor heartrates, sleep cycles, and amount of activity in which a patient may engage. Some of this information can be transmitted directly to your physician via email or a patient portal on the Internet. Many practices established patient portals for patients to use Patients can check their test results, schedule an appointment, send a message or email their doctor or nurse, or can look at their account and see what they owe for services rendered. You can find many good articles on telemedicine on the CDC website if you are interested in learning more.

At this time, new technology has provided new opportunities for patients and providers to make appointments more convenient and less stressful, especially for people in underserved areas with maldistribution of healthcare providers. Telemedicine, teledentistry, and digital offices are only three of the new applications of this new technology. It makes it exciting to be alive and makes one wonder what will be available in the future.

Endnote

*Denotes the beginning of a multiple-item reference.
  1. http://ncfy.acf.hhs.gov/features/street-outreach-programs-reach-out-youth-diverse-needs/day-life-mobile-health-clinic

CPSIA information can be obtained
at www.ICGtesting.com
Printed in the USA
LVOW02s0845290617

539625LV00006B/25/P